THE AUSTRALIAN

A collection of the finest, most dramatic, funniest yarns, ballads, sayings, legends, superstitions, anecdotes, and traditions of the Australian people.

Bill Wannan, a leading Australian folklorist, has gathered together the cream of his many years of study of what, in our history, has made Australians what they are.

From Press comments on earlier editions:

"Nothing could better it for bed-side reading." (*Australian Journal*)

"As fresh as a handful of gum leaves." (*The Age*)

. . the Great Lone Land of magnificent
distances and bright heat; the land of reliance
and never-give-in, and help-your-mate. . . .
Australia! My Country! Her very name is
music to me. God bless Australia! for the
sake of the great hearts in the heart of her!

HENRY LAWSON

THE AUSTRALIAN

Yarns Ballads Legends Traditions
of the Australian People

Gathered together by
BILL WANNAN

seal books

RIGBY LIMITED

Rigby Limited, Adelaide • Sydney • Melbourne • Brisbane • Perth

First edition September 1954
Second edition January 1955
Third edition September 1958
Second impression August 1959
Third impression February 1961
Fourth, revised, edition November 1963
Second impression April 1965
Published in Seal Books 1969
Reprinted 1971
Reprinted 1972
Copyright © by Bill Wannan
National Library of Australia Card Number & ISBN 0 85179 387 8

Printed in Hong Kong

In Memory of
JEFF
Little Son and Mate

FOREWORD

HERE, for the first time in book form, is a collection of Australian folklore—tales, sayings, customs and superstitions that have originated from amongst the Australian people. There is nothing here that is the creation of one man; this is the folklore of a people composed by the people themselves.

It is sometimes said that Australia is too young a country to have produced a folklore; that folk tales are the product of older countries where tales and sayings have gained the richness and sharp detail that emerges from constant repetition over centuries. It is true that the folklore of a young country does not feature knights who slay dragons or tales of battles where heroes clash, but their folk heroes are mighty men just the same.

The folklore of Australia has much in common with the folklore of America. In both countries the people's tales reflect a society cut loose from its roots. They emerged in a time of migration, of shifting populations, and they reflect the spirit of their day.

In Australia men pushed in from the coast in bullock drays, the tilted waggon. Families were scattered. Men met and swapped experiences over camp fires, in shearing sheds. Bullock waggons laden with wool crept over salt-bush plains. The bullockies ate together, camped together and boasted about their teams, their loads, their strength, their dogs. In lonely little halls bearded accordion players sent the settlers and their wives stamping over floors made slippery with candle grease. Men collected round the door to talk. They told tales to impress each other. In this young country a man was valued according to the number of post holes he could dig, the horses he could ride, the sheep he could shear. So, many of our folk tales had their origin in efforts to impress. The boasting story became the tall story and the tall story passed from man to man till it acquired a richness that established it as the creation of a people and not of an individual.

In mines, in cities where factories were beginning to pour their smoke over industrial suburbs, the English language of the emigrants and convicts began to be enriched by words born of conditions and experiences peculiar to Australia. Sayings created by city workers, by diggers of the first world war, by men of the last war, by coal miners, shearers, cooks—these became part of our tongue, our heritage.

Most of this book, I feel, reflects an Australia that is passing. The teller-of-tales thrived in the days when amusements were confined to an annual race meeting and an occasional dance. Now that he is disappearing his tales and sayings would be lost to us were it not for the enthusiast who collects and preserves them.

Mr. Wannan is such an enthusiast. In the compilation of this book he has rendered valuable service to Australia. Here is a unique record of Australian folklore gathered by a man who, over the years, has listened, questioned, then written down the result of his searching for those sayings and tales that reflect the spirit of the Australian people.

ALAN MARSHALL.

PREFACE

THIS book, so far as I am aware, is a new kind of anthology—new, that is, in this country—based largely on the materials of Australian folklore. Through this collection of yarns, ballads, local allusions, legends and popular anecdotes, I have indicated some aspects of the character and traditions of the Australian people, taking shape in the years between the establishment of the first convict settlement in 1788 and the emergence of a nation at the end of the first world war.

Although the book is intended for the general reader—a companion for the leisure hour—I hope it will be of use to the student of Australian history and to those writers, artists, and musicians among us who are concerned with the realities of their environment. Most of the factors that have made our people what they are to-day can be traced back to the period covered by this book. In these pages will be found not the detailed recital of historic events but the expression, in a variety of forms, of the attitude of ordinary men and women to the life around them and to the broad movements that were shaping their destinies and that they in turn were helping to mould.

Some of the material may at first sight appear irrelevant to the main theme—the striving of a people for democracy and nationhood. What can the yarns about bullockies, and the superstitions of bushmen contribute to this theme? The purpose of this book is to show the Australians of earlier generations "in the round"; as they saw themselves in their day-to-day occupations, in their leisure, in their social strivings. Their humour, their superstitious beliefs, the experiences that they have crystallised in a yarn or a saying, are of vital importance if the general picture is to have focus and clarity.

I know that many readers will be critical of what they may regard as indefensible omissions and shortcomings. This is inevitable when such a large canvas is attempted. Out of the vast amount of material collected over a score of years I had to make a choice of what I considered most representative within the limits of the space available. I had also to discard from this collection many items which, interesting and important as they are, could be regarded only as repetitions of material already selected.

My arrangement of the contents is designed to group the material according to folk-themes or motifs—popular heroes and hero-worship; yarn-spinning; superstitions; place-lore; phrases, sayings and local allusions; and finally, under the heading "Some Perspectives," a number of tales and references alluding to the major traditions of the Australian people.

What emerges from this book will be for each individual reader to assess. For me, the materials taken as a whole give a many-sided picture of a great and lovable people, strong in its determination to win a true democracy, quick to sense the humour in a situation however unpromising, firm in its belief in mateship and irreverent towards pompous, arrogant, unimaginative officialdom. Finest of all, perhaps, as the visiting American scholar, Mr. C. Hartley Grattan has noted, is its "aggressive insistence on the worth and unique importance of the common man."

BILL WANNAN.

ACKNOWLEDGMENTS

MY WARMEST thanks are due to the following, for permission to reprint copyrighted material:

Mrs. Mary Adamson for the lines, "The Toast of Honour," by her husband, the late Bartlett Adamson.

Messrs. Angus and Robertson Ltd., Sydney, for passages from the work of Henry Lawson and A. B. ("Banjo") Paterson and for "To Wagga-Wog-ah!" by Jack Moses, in his *Nine Miles from Gundagai*.

Mr. Sidney J. Baker and Messrs. Angus and Robertson Ltd., Sydney, for extracts from *The Australian Language*.

Dr. C. E. W. Bean for a passage on the Anzacs from *The Australian Imperial Force in France during the Allied Offensive, 1918*. Also to Dr. Bean and Messrs. Angus and Robertson for extracts from *On the Wool Track*.

Mr. Hugh Brady and Mr. Edwin Brady, and Messrs. Robertson and Mullens Ltd., Melbourne, for excerpts from *River Rovers* by the late E. J. Brady.

Messrs. Cassell and Company Ltd., Melbourne, for a passage from *The Sunlit Land* by Charles Barrett.

Mr. Warren Denning and The Australasian Publishing Company Pty. Ltd., Sydney, for the references to Fisher's Ghost from *The Road to Canberra*.

The Right Hon. H. V. Evatt and Messrs. Angus and Robertson Ltd., for the passage from *Australian Labour Leader*.

Dr. Charles Fenner and Georgian House Pty. Ltd., Melbourne, for material from *Gathered Moss*.

The late Miss Miles Franklin and Messrs. Angus and Robertson Ltd. for the extract from *Joseph Furphy: The Legend of a Man and his Book*.

Messrs. Georgian House Pty. Ltd. for a short anecdote from *Australian Son*, a biography of Ned Kelly, by Max Brown.

Mr. Edward Harrington and Messrs. Allan and Company Pty. Ltd., for "My Old Black Billy" from *The Kerrigan Boys and Other Australian Verses*.

The Herald and Weekly Times Ltd., Melbourne, and The Home Entertainment Library for passages from George E. Boxall's *History of the Australian Bushrangers*.

Mr. John Manifold and Messrs. Dennis Dobson Ltd., London, for "The Death of Ned Kelly," from *Selected Verse*.

Mrs. Bertha Lawson for two passages from *My Henry Lawson* (Frank Johnson, Sydney).

Mr. Vance Palmer and Melbourne University Press for the reference to Judge Higinbotham from *National Portraits*.

Messrs. Robertson and Mullens Ltd., Melbourne, for extracts from *A Shanty Entertainment* by E. S. Emerson, and two books by Fred J. Mills ("The Twinkler")—*Dinkum Oil* and *Square Dinkum*.

I have not been able to trace the authors or publishers of some of the material reprinted, and to these, as well as to any other individuals or firms whose rights may have been overlooked, I extend my sincere thanks and ask their forgiveness.

My thanks are due to many authors, anonymous and otherwise, to newspapers and to periodicals, quoted in the text, especially *The Bulletin*, Sydney, which has been, perhaps, the foremost recorder of Australian folklore since 1880; and *Salt*, Australian Army journal.

*

A deep debt of gratitude is due to the following, who have given me most valuable help and advice in the preparation of this book:

My father, the late William F. Wannan, scholar and teacher, and my mother, Ruby Wannan, who first taught me to know and love the ballads, yarns and democratic traditions of our people.

Mrs. Lyndall Hadow, of Perth (W.A.), who introduced me to the writings of her father, the late Julian Stuart, one of the finest chroniclers of Australia's early trade union history and folklore. I am indebted to Mrs. Hadow for permission to reprint from Julian Stuart's work, and also for much information and constant encouragement.

Mr. Alan Marshall, of Melbourne, folklorist and friend, whose tales and articles are a particularly rich mine for the student of Australian life and lore.

Mr. John Manifold, of Brisbane, whose researches into our heritage of folk-song have added considerably to our knowledge of this field.

Mr. Les Barnes, Mr. Ian Turner, Mr. Stephen Murray-Smith, Mr. Hume Dow, Mr. Lance Loughrey, Mr. Judah Waten, and a great many others who researched and delved into their libraries, files and personal experience in order to make this a much fuller and better book than it would otherwise have been.

The Chief Librarians and staffs of the Public Library of Victoria and the Mitchell Library, Sydney.

To my wife, a special indebtedness, because she has endured not a few inconveniences in order that I might have time to speak and write about the folklore of the Australian people.

●

This book has resulted from the work of many people. Concerning the books I have consulted, reference is made in most instances throughout the text. I would particularly acknowledge the help I have received from *Old Bush Songs*, "Banjo" Paterson's fine collection, the basis on which all our subsequent ballad anthologies must rest. Mr. Brian Fitzpatrick's *The Australian People, 1788-1945*, and his *The British Empire in Australia, 1834-1939*; Mr. Sidney J. Baker's *The Australian Language*; Mr. Geoffrey C. Ingleton's collection of old Australian broadsheets, documents, etc., *True Patriots All*; the great work of Dr. Percy Jones in the field of our folk-song; Mr. Frank Clune's *Wild Colonial Boys*; *Australian Bush Songs and Ballads*, edited by Will Lawson—these have been a major source of help and of inspiration.

B.W.

CONTENTS

Foreword by Alan Marshall   vi
Preface   viii
Acknowledgments   xi

AUSTRALIAN SALT
Popular Sayings, Jests, Rhymes and Anecdotes   1

PART ONE: HEROES AND REBELS

Comment   8

1. BUSHRANGERS
   The Wild Colonial Boy   13
   The Last Words of Fred Lowry   15
   Dunn, Gilbert, and Ben Hall   15
   Death of Johnny Gilbert   17
   Ballad of Ben Hall   17
   The Ballad of Jack Power   18
   Ned Kelly, Folk-Hero   19
   Kelly was Their Captain   20
   Ned Kelly and Judge Barry   21
   Number One Hero   21
   The Death of Ned Kelly   22

2. MEN OF FIFTY-FOUR
   Eureka—Seal of Mateship   23
   Brave Lalor   26
   The Diggers Gather at Eureka   26
   Mrs. Ralph's Retort   27
   Forward from Eureka   27
   Peter Lalor—A Man Among Men   28
   The Death of Peter Lalor—1889   28
   The Men of Fifty-four   28
   Remembrance of Eureka   28

3. THE ANZAC TRADITION
   The Man with the Donkey   30
   The Diggers   31
   Captain Throssell   32
   Albert Jacka   33

4. CHAMPIONS
   The Flying Pieman   34

Gordon's Leap   35
Sandy's Fight   36
Carbine's Cup Victory, 1890   37
Jacky Howe's Tally   37
The Death of Les Darcy   38
The Darcy-McGoorty Fight: Darcy the Winner   38
"Up There, Cazaly!"   39
Spofforth, "The Demon Bowler"   40
Phar Lap's Melbourne Cup   40
Phar Lap   41
Bert Hinkler, Airman   42

PART TWO: THE YARN-SPINNERS

Comment   45

1. SILENT AUSTRALIANS
   The Great Australian Joke   47
   The Magger   47
   Getting to the Bottom of It   48
   Silence of the Bush   48
   The Silent Station-Hand   49

2. CASUAL AUSTRALIANS
   A Lazy Match   50
   A Casual Bet   51
   Lazy Feat   52
   Fence-Leaner   52
   Easy Stages   52

3. BULLOCK DRIVERS
   How to Tell a New Chum   53
   The Old Bullock Dray   53
   The Phantom Bullocky   55
   Holy Dan   57
   Winning Terms   58

4. SHEARERS
   On the Road to Gundagai   60
   The Big-Gun Shearer   61
   Widgeegowera Joe   62
   Crooked Mick from the Speewah   62
   Another Fall of Rain   64
   "Comollyers"   65

5. STATION COOKS
   Crooked Mick's Pastry   67

Station Cooks   67
Old-Time Cooks   68

6. STOCKMEN
A Thousand Miles Away   69
The Overlander   70
The Eumerella Shore   71
White Logic   72
Too Dangerous   72

7. SWAGMEN
My Four Little Johnny-Cakes   73
The Ramble-eer   74
Henry Lawson's Ghost   74
Just Right   77
My Old Black Billy   77

8. SOLDIER YARNS
The Slouch Hat   79
Blowing Cold and Hot   80
Easy!   80
Borrowed Plumes   80
A Scrap of Paper   81

9. THE GREAT AUSTRALIAN ADJECTIVE
"_____"   83

10. BUSH LIARS AND TALL YARNS
Tim Smith Tells a Yarn   84
The Kick in It   86
Fence-Sitters   86
A Bunch of Tall Yarns   86
Sundry Mosquitoes   87

11. BUSH DIRECTIONS
Across the Street   89
Getting to Hogan's Pub   89
A Change of Air   90
Stone the Crows!   90
Black Logic   90

12. DAD AND DAVE
Early Rising   91
Running Late   91
Dave and Mabel   92
The Long View   92
Desperate Remedies   92
Dave Gets a "Talking-to"   92

xvii

13. BUSHMEN'S DOGS
    "My Best Sheep Dog" 93
    The Pumper's Dog 93
    Pat 94

14. IRISH-AUSTRALIAN
    The Prospector's Toast 95
    "Tommy" Bent's Panegyric 95
    Comfort 96
    Absenteeism 96

PART THREE: SUPERSTITIONS AND FALLACIES

Comment 98
Sir Henry Hayes and the Irish Soil 98
Craig's Dream 98
The Town That Lost 98
Bush Superstitions of New South Wales 99
Toads that Poison Fowls 100
The Birth of the Kangaroo 100
Snake Fallacies 101
Old-time Country Cures and Bush Remedies 101

PART FOUR: PLACE LORE

Comment 103

1. PLACE NAMES
   Fisher's Ghost Creek 106
   Old-Time Bendigo Gullies 108
   Big Jack 108
   Bread and Dripping Valley 108
   Some Victorian Place Names 109

2. LOCAL ALLUSIONS
   Rockhampton and the Three S's 110
   Mount Morgan and the Four G's 110
   Bourke—Where You Never Get Sick 110
   The Never-Never 110
   Old Jack Robertson on Victoria 111
   "Happily . . . Not a Victorian" 111
   Taking Sides 111
   Melbourne—Pro and Contra 111
   Popular Labels 112
   "The Place for a Village" 112
   The Beechworth Horseshoes 112
   The Man Who Rode the Bull Through Wagga 113

The Dog on the Tucker Box — 114
The Man from Snowy River — 115
Mark Twain on Maryborough (Vic.) — 118
Mark Twain on the Blue Mountains — 118
A Tale of Drought — 119
The *Gem's* Cabins — 119
Melba and the Bendigo Chimes — 119
Humour in Signs — 119

PART FIVE: AUSTRALIANISMS

Phrases, Terms and Local References

"The Botany Bay Dozen" — 121
The Currency Lads and Lasses — 122
"I am Sterling" — 122
Oakes' Oath — 123
The Shearers' Vote — 123
A Burketown Mosquito Net — 124
The Larrikin — 125
The Larrikin "Pushes" — 125
Portrait of the Larrikin — 125
Larrikin Language — 126
"Such is Life!" — 128
The Bushmen's Bible — 128
The Braddon Blot — 128
Buckley's Chance — 129
Tom Collins — 129
Furphy — 130
Jimmy Wood — 131
The Old Jimmy Woodser — 133
Wowsers — 133
Sundowners — 133
"Waltzing Matilda," Humping the Bluey, Whaling, Etc. — 133
Origin of the Bunyip — 135
Like a Baboon, an Emu, and a Man — 135
A Recent Bunyip — 136
Coinage—Australian Style — 136
Why "Drongo"? — 137
Dear Bill! — 137
"Digger" — 137
The Two-Up Game — 139

PART SIX: SOME PERSPECTIVES

Comment — 142

1. CONVICTS AND GOVERNORS

"The Schemers Above" 148
True Patriots All 149
Botany Bay 149
The Convicts' Oath of Mateship 150
A Reckless Magistrate 151
The Convict's Letter 151
"Tasmanian Justice" 151
Lieutenant Dawes and the Headhunters 152
The Flogging of Paddy Galvin 153
The Castle Hill Rebellion 154
Rum Rebellion 156
The Convicts' Rum Song 157
Crawlers—Keep Out! 157
Musquito on Hanging 157
Governor Arthur and the Proclamation—The "Black War" 158
The Female Factory 159
Botany Bay Courtship 160
Jim Jones 161
Bold Jack Donahoe 163

2. THE GOLD DIGGINGS

A Convict's Discovery 165
A Memorable Day 165
The Diggers 166
Gold Fever 166
The Roaring Fifties 167
Golden Cradles 167
Diggers' Jingle (circa 1854) 168
"Where's Your Licence?" 168
"Joe!" 169
Police on the Diggings 169
The Squattocracy 169
The Diggers' Demands 170
The Miners' Oath—1854 170
Mark Twain on Eureka 171
The Removal of Inspector Lobbs from Ballaarat to Melbourne 171
Passing of the Alluvial Gold Days 172
No. 2 Reef, Before Crushing 172
A Remarkable Escape 173

3. SQUATTERS AND SELECTORS

Colonial Curiosities: The Squatter 175

Portrait of a Squatter, 1857   175
The Squatter's Man   176
Give Every Poor Man a Home   177
The Free Selector   178
Description of a "Cocky"   179
The New England Cocky   179
The Sheep-Washer's Lament   179
A "Cocky's" Work   181
Jack Dow   181
"Hungry Tyson," Squatter   181
A Tale of Tyson   182
Kiley's Run   182
The Premier Who Went to Bourke   183

4. IMMIGRANTS
That'll Tell You About Emigration   185
Colonial Experience   186
Paddy Malone in Australia   187
Playing the New-Chum Jackeroo   188
Jimmy Sago, Jackeroo   189
The London Swell   190
The "Raw" New-Chums—1888   191
New-Chums Become "Dinkum Aussies"   191

5. EARLY TRADE UNIONISM
8-8-8   194
An Australian Paean—1876   195
Eight-Hours Day Rhyme   197
The New Unionism   197
A Tale of the Paroo   198
Judge Higinbotham and the Strike Fund   198
Jock McPhail   199
Strikers and New-Chums—1891   203
"Socialism is Being Mates"   204
The Sinking of the *Rodney*   204
Freedom on the Wallaby   206
The Wolf in Snake's Clothes   207
Spence's Station   209
The Stories that are Wanted   210
A Union Town   212
A Wise Steward and a Silent Worker   214
Billy Lane's Description of Mateship   215
Jack Dunn of Nevertire   216
They Were Men   216

"Our Last Man and Our Last Shilling" 216
Pollie 217
Bump Me into Parliament 217
The Twelve 218
The Release of the I.W.W. Men 219

6. REPUBLICANISM AND NATIONALISM

(i) REPUBLICANISM
Dr. J. Dunmore Lang, Republican 221
Against Republicanism 221
Republicanism and the Sydney *Bulletin* 222
A Republican Converted 222

(ii) AUSTRALIA AND ENGLAND
Australia versus England 223
"Australia for the Australians" 224
Australia Through English Eyes—
    1. "Bare, bold, prosaic" 224
    2. "Scentless and songless" 224
    3. "Weird melancholy" 225
    4. "No ancient churches, castles, ruins" 225

Australia Through Australian Eyes—
    1. "Oh! 'tis jolly" 225
    2. "Home" 225
    3. "The bush is never sad" 226
    4. "Worthy to be loved" 226
Postscript to Texas Jack 227
"Birthstains" 227

(iii) PRIDE OF NATIONHOOD
Australia in the Eighties 229
Fling out the Flag! 230
The Dream of Federation 230
The Nation is Born 231
The Toast of Honour 232

Editor's Note 233

AUSTRALIAN SALT

Popular Sayings, Jests, Rhymes and Anecdotes

Game! He's as game as Ned Kelly.

That scrub was so thick a dog couldn't bark in it.

Mean! He was so mean he wouldn't even let his dog drink from a mirage.

It was so wet that even the mirages overflowed!

I'm that unlucky that if it rained soup, everybody else would have a spoon and I'd be left with a fork.

> RANDOLPH BEDFORD, *Naught to Thirty-three.*

If it rained gravy everyone else would have a frying-pan—and I'd be left with a gridiron.

No more sense than a native bear, an' not half as good-lookin'.

> E. J. BRADY, *River Rovers.*

Know yer! I'd know yer skin if I saw it hanging on a bush.

> ibid.

> The squatters, too, are cricketers,
>   And very knowing ones,
> And you'll own they are good players,
>   For they're always taking runs.

> CHARLES THATCHER, *Thatcher's Colonial Minstrel* (1864).

Don't pray for rain—dam it!

> Attributed to an eminent Australian ecclesiastic.

> Question not, but live and labour
>   Till yon goal be won,

1

Helping every feeble neighbour,
  Seeking help from none;
Life is mostly froth and bubble,
  Two things stand like stone,
Kindness in another's trouble,
  Courage in your own.

ADAM LINDSAY GORDON, "Ye Wearie Wayfarer."

"What's the idea of that double layer of wire on your fly-door, Jack?"
"They're two different meshes, Joe. A coarse mesh with big holes and a fine mesh with little holes."
"Yes, but why?"
"Well—the big holes to keep out the big flies, and the little holes to keep out the little flies!"

"It was so cold where we were in Greece that the candle-light froze and we couldn't blow it out."
"That's nothing. Where we were, the words came out of our mouths in pieces of ice, and we had to fry them to see what we were talking about."

"German Charlie," an old-time shanty keeper, used to make this famous boast concerning the quality of his home-made liquor: "Der man that shall take two drinks of my rum, and then vill not vight his own fader, he is plutty gowardt."

RANDOLPH BEDFORD, *Naught to Thirty-three.*

Ye, who can revel upon wholesome tea
And good dry bread, how would ye like to be
Condemned day after day (and not complain)
To eat roast turkey, and to drink champagne?

VICTOR DALEY ("Creeve Roe"), "The Sweater."

A newly arrived migrant wanted to visit the outback, so he asked the first bushman he met how to get there.
"Outback is away out west, out in the never-never where the crows fly backwards; it's away out west o' sunset and right out back o' beyond; it's away out back o' Bourke in the great open spaces, where men are men and women are few and far between; it's right away out—well, it's away out back, yer can't miss it," was the reply.

2

"Y'oughter see the cockatoos at Speewah," said the old man.

"Cripes! They wus thick. There was so many of them that if they flew over when it was raining not a drop touched the ground for a mile around.

"When they landed to feed, one always kept nit so you couldn't get near enough to shoot them.

"They always landed on a big, dry, red-gum when you frightened them, so the boss covered that red-gum from top to bottom with bird lime.

"Next day when the cockatoos landed on it he ran down with his gun. Just as he was going to fire they took off and tore that tree up by the roots. The last the boss saw of that tree it was about a mile up, making south."

ALAN MARSHALL in *Australasian Post*, June 21, 1951.

Things are crook
In Tallarook,
But they're a bloody sight worse
In Bourke (or Wagga, or Rockhampton, as
the case may be).

Meaner than Hungry Tyson.*

"I once knew a bullocky by the name of Eighty-mile Mick. We used to call him Seventy-nine-mile Mick for short.

"His bullocks were so poor they had to stand in the one spot for half an hour before they could cast a shadow."

An old bagman was tramping across a station property, when the station owner appeared in his utility truck, travelling in the same direction.

"Like a lift?" the owner called out.

"No flamin' fear!" said the bagman. "You open yer own gates."

"A flash of lightning struck the ground outback once, and started a twenty-mile-an-hour grass fire.

"I was just about to make some tea, so I decided to hold me billy over the flames.

"Talk about stiff! I had to chase that fire for ten miles before me billy came to the boil. . . . And then I discovered I'd left me tea behind!"

*James Tyson, a millionaire pastoralist of the nineteenth century.

Mad! He's as mad as a gum-tree full of galahs!

As lonely as a bandicoot on a burnt ridge.

One morning on one of our many golden surfing beaches a
steamer with one funnel was passing, going south. Turning to
old Yorky, the beachcomber, I asked:
"What is that steamer out yonder?"
He replied quickly, without looking:
"That's the *Innamincka.*"
Next morning another steamer passed north. She had two funnels.
I asked Yorky what her name was.
"The *Innamincka,*" he replied.
"But," I said, "she has two funnels."
"Yes. They put the other funnel on her larse night. Diden they,
Robert?"
Robert, his mate, drawled out:
"Ya-as. They's no other boat but the *Innamincka* passes this way.
We oughter know."

JACK MOSES, *Nine Miles from Gundagai.*

A publican whose hostelry is opposite the National Gallery and
Museum, Melbourne, where Phar Lap's stuffed hide is on view,
used to announce his address as "opposite Phar Lap's stable."

A wounded soldier was being carried across no man's land on the
back of a perspiring comrade. Rifle and machine-gun fire was
heavy.
"'Ere," suddenly exclaimed the wounded soldier, "what about
turning round and walking backwards for a spell? You're getting the V.C., but I'm getting all the flamin' bullets."

> The brigadier, he gets turkey,
> The colonel has his duck;
> The officers have poultry—
> They always were in luck.
>
> The sergeants they get bread and cheese,
> And mop up all they can;
> But all the poor old privates get
> Is bread and apple jam.

Farmer (calling out across a paddock alive with rabbits, to two
bagmen going out through his gate): "Hey, you blokes! Shut
that blinkin' gate properly, will youse! D'yer want to let all me
flamin' rabbits out?"

4

He was so short that to mount his horse he had to stand on his head to get his foot in the stirrup.

Quoted by SIDNEY J. BAKER, *The Australian Language.*

There is a story about Old Bill, who drove sheep from Newmarket to the city abattoirs. He got there later and later each day, so the boss got tired of this and told him he'd have to smarten up a bit. He couldn't keep the slaughtermen waiting.

"Anyway, what makes you so late?" asked the boss.

"Well," said Old Bill, "it's like this. I can't wake me flamin' dogs!"

The boss's comment was that Old Bill was either the greatest dill or the greatest humorist of the century.

Droving songs are very pretty, but they call for little thanks
From the people of a country in possession of the banks.

HENRY LAWSON, "The City Bushman."

They tramp in mateship side by side—
The Protestant and Roman—
They call no biped lord or sir,
And touch their hat to no man!

HENRY LAWSON, "Shearers."

Stringybark will light your fire,
Greenhide will never fail yer,
Stringybark and greenhide
Are the mainstay of Australia.*

"I'm Ned Kelly, son of Red Kelly, and a better man never stood in two shoes!"

Ned Kelly on Police Inspector Brooke Smith, of Beechworth: "I would like to know who made this article who reminds me of a poodle dog half-clipped in lion fashion, called Brooke E. Smith, Superintendent of Police. He knows as much about commanding police as Captain Standish (the commissioner) does about mustering mosquitoes and boiling them down for their fat on the backblocks of the Lachlan."

* Bush jingle, based on "Stringy Bark and Green Hide", a song by the gold-fields minstrel, George Chanson, " . . . as sung by Mr. J. S. Brice at the Theatre Royal, Maitland, Lambing Flat, Forbes, etc." The words are given in full in Hugh Anderson's *Colonial Ballads.*

5

The late W. M. ("Billy") Hughes, well-known politician, on his indigestion: "If I had had a constitution I would have been dead long ago."

> Our Billy's talk is just like bottled stout,
> You draw the cork and only froth comes out.

From Brisbane *Truth*, 1916.

The old-time shearers' grace before meat:

> One word's as good as ten.
> Wire in. Amen.

During the last stand of the Kelly Gang at Glenrowan, the following conversation was overheard.
"Is that you, Ned?"
"Yes; is that you, Joe? Come here!"
"Come here be damned! What are you doing? Come here and load my rifle. I'm cooked."
"So am I—I think my leg's broken."
"Leg be damned! You've got the use of your arms."

Frank the Poet* introduces himself:
"My name is Frank Macnamara, a native of Cashell, County Tipperary, sworn to be a tyrant's foe, and while I've life, I'll crow."

"Moral persuasion is all humbug. There's nothing convinces like a lick i' the lug. . . ."

> THOMAS KENNEDY, one of the miners' leaders at Eureka.

Up in Darwin—where everything bites but the butterflies.

Joseph Furphy's description of his novel, *Such is Life*:

> "Temper, democratic; bias, offensively Australian."

The proper way to cook a cockatoo is to put the bird and an axehead into a billy. Boil them until the axehead is soft. The cockatoo is then ready to eat.

---

* Frank the Poet was the popular name of Frank Macnamara or Frank Goddard, a familiar figure in the eighteen twenties and thirties. Transported as far as is known for forgery, he composed many verses, including "The Seizure of the Cyprus Brig in Recherche Bay" and "A Poet's Tour of Hell", which were widely recited by his fellow-convicts.

PART ONE

HEROES AND REBELS

But then we've got our heroes, too . . .

HENRY LAWSON, "A Word to Texas Jack."

*Hero tales tell us more about a people than perhaps any
other tales. For as admirable or exceptional men, heroes
embody the qualities that we most admire or desire in
ourselves.*

B. A. BOTKIN, *A Treasury of American Folklore.*

COMMENT

EVERY nation in the making has its heroes—those figures standing out in the popular imagination because of certain marked qualities of leadership in the people's struggles or prowess in various fields of endeavour.

I have included in this part a number of representative hero tales or references from the many hundreds that have been handed down. While some of the names mentioned here have become household words—Ned Kelly, Peter Lalor, Albert Jacka, for instance—others will be less widely known to-day. Few people talk about Spofforth, "the demon bowler," or Larry Foley, or "the Flying Pieman." Each was an heroic figure in his time and every now and again a writer or researcher comes along to rescue him from oblivion.

The title of this part, "Heroes and Rebels," may be a little misleading. Some of the foremost of our heroes, like Lalor and Kelly, were both heroes and rebels—it was their very act of rebelling against the law and authority of their times that ultimately raised them to the status of heroes. Nevertheless, I have retained the title because it does indicate that a distinction is drawn between those who became popular and legendary figures of hero-worship and those lesser rebels, like the bushrangers Power and Lowry, whose notoriety was short-lived, but who did display (at least in the eyes of their contemporaries) certain heroic attributes.

There is, as there must be throughout the whole of this book, a grave list of omissions. I have included none of the explorers, though heroism of the highest order was to be found among them; nor are the names of Billy Lane, W. G. Spence and other leading trade unionists of the last century to be found in the section. My purpose, however, has not been so much to set down narratives of individual feats of heroism, of which there are countless thousands in our history, but rather to show the pattern of hero-worship as one motif of our folklore.

Carl Sandburg has said of Abraham Lincoln that he emerged from the American civil war as the hero of the people who fought under him; while for him the common people were his heroes. And so it is in all countries. The popular hero is, in the final analysis, the symbol of the finest qualities and aspirations of the people who gave him birth.

1. BUSHRANGERS

Bushranging in Australia can be divided into two fairly distinct periods or phases. The first bushrangers were convicts who escaped from their chains to the comparative, and often temporary, freedom of the wilds. Of these, Matthew Brady and Martin Cash in Van Diemen's Land, and William Westwood ("Jackey Jackey") and Bold Jack Donahoe in New South Wales, are best known. Their careers were, with few exceptions, short and tragic. A ballad about Jack Donahoe will be found in the section "Convicts and Governors."

The second and major period of bushranging dates from the early sixties of the last century, when alluvial gold had largely petered out and gold-diggers, unable to afford the expense of quartz mining, turned to the land for a livelihood. Under public pressure, the legislature of New South Wales introduced a Land Act in 1861, with the object of unlocking the lands to small farming. The squatters, holding the best lands as sheep runs, resented this intrusion on their preserves. They opposed the new "selectors," the small-scale farmers, with every weapon at their disposal. They employed "dummies" to buy up the blocks of land—the "selections"—as they were put up for sale. With enormous reserves of capital at their disposal, they were able in large measure to defeat the intentions of the Land Act, and to ensure that only the poorer, "stringybark" type of country went to the farmer of small means.

Besides their wealth, the squatters had behind them the power of the legislature, in which they were overwhelmingly represented. They fenced the small selectors in with a variety of repressive measures. The police force was of a generally poor calibre and showed little sympathy for the lot of the farmers.

Traditionally, then, the selectors as a class were opposed to the big landholders, and the troopers who policed their law. With few exceptions, the bushrangers of this period and up to the time of Ned Kelly's death in 1880 sprang from this class; and while their motives for turning to robbery under arms varied considerably, in each instance an underlying hatred of the squatters seems to have been involved. Jack Doolan, the legendary "Wild Colonial Boy," Ben Hall, "Darkie" Gardiner, Johnny Gilbert, Dunn, "Thunderbolt" and, later, Ned Kelly and his mates all became the people's hero-symbols of the fight against the squatters. The legends that surround them conform to a fairly general pattern. It was claimed for them that they did not rob the needy, that they were sworn enemies of the pastoralists, that they treated women and children with gallantry, that they fought fairly, and that they "died game."

2. THE MEN OF FIFTY-FOUR

In the dawn light of December 3, 1854, on the Eureka Lead at Ballarat, some three hundred gold-diggers, ill-armed and protected only by a barricade of logs and rubble, fought against Lieutenant-Governor Sir Charles Hotham's military and police in defence of their rights and liberties.

They had come together from many parts of the world—from Ireland, Canada, England, Germany, America, Scotland, Italy and other lands, as well as from the native Australian soil. Some had already fought in other battles for human freedom; all were determined that the iniquitous licence system (requiring a digger to pay a fee of thirty shillings each month whether he found gold or not), the arrogant policing of the gold-fields by the commissioners, and similar abuses, must cease. They went much further in their demands. Chartist influence was evident in their programme of democratic reforms—universal male suffrage; equal electoral districts; annual parliaments; payment of members; no property qualifications for members; secret ballot. There were those among them who sought to create a Republic of Victoria.

A month earlier they had set up a Ballarat Reform League. It was the forum for the many viewpoints of the diggers. They discussed their wrongs in an orderly fashion, despite the provocation of the gold commissioners. Out of the discussions they welded their firm demands. With passionate sincerity they made their oath of loyalty to their cause, pledging themselves to fight and, if need be, to die, that their liberties should be widened and their dignity as people upheld.

The battle of Eureka was short-lived and bloody. The police, some of them the worst dregs of the Tasmanian convict system, killed and wounded indiscriminately. Upwards of thirty diggers died in battle.

But the victory was with the miners. Their courageous stand hastened the introduction of the political reforms they sought, as well as the alleviation of some of their immediate distresses. The long struggle for Australian democracy and for Australian nation-hood was immeasurably assisted by the men of Eureka.

The Eureka Stockade became the heart and fire of the Australian tradition. It became the people's symbol of unity, of mateship, of selfless devotion to the fight for freedom. It has given inspiration to Australians in their struggles for a richer, fuller life.

3. THE ANZAC TRADITION

The Anzac tradition was not born in the first world war, although the word "Anzac" dates from that period.

The Australian soldiers who stormed Gallipoli and served with equal distinction on the other battlefronts were inheritors of a legacy of manhood bequeathed to them by former generations of bushmen, drovers, miners, shearers, selectors and industrial workers. Their courage, their comradeship, their laughter and lack of affectation, their irreverence towards undeserved authority, were all traits of their fathers and forefathers. Dr. C. E. W. Bean has stressed the team spirit, the very real need for mateship, existing among the Australian soldiers. As you read through this book you will know why.

E. S. Sorenson, in his fine book *Life in the Australian Back-blocks*, has summed up the essentials of the "digger" spirit of the Anzacs in the following passage, written several years before the outbreak of war in 1914.

> Like all high-spirited animals, the bushman frets under restraint, and of authority he has a hatred that is liable at any moment to blaze into fierce rebellion. If he is ordered or commanded instead of asked respectfully to do things by his employer, the position becomes intolerable. Though he may not have a second shirt to his back at the time, he is likely to inform the boss to do it himself, or sarcastically inquire, "Are you talking to me or to the dog?" Neither can he tolerate the word "master." As I heard one say to the squatter: "You are my employer, not my master. If you think otherwise, take your coat off and prove it." For this reason he makes an unsatisfactory sailor. He won't go sailoring. In war he combines all the essentials of a fine soldier, a superb fighter, but he must be led by a fighter—and a shrewd, solid-thinking man, not by a gilded Johnny. Used to thinking and acting for himself in all manner of emergencies, and to doing things according to his own ideas and inclinations, he is not inclined to obey unquestioningly the command of one in

11

authority, but will judge for himself and argue the point if the step appears unnecessary or unwise.

4. CHAMPIONS

This section needs no introduction beyond the expression of regret that so many good tales had to be omitted. As the scope of this book does not extend beyond the early nineteen twenties, many of the great names in Australian sport will not be found here. I have included the ballad on Phar Lap because the name of this horse is usually linked with that of Carbine and no book of Australiana would be acceptable which did not refer to these champions. The inclusion of the ballad on the death of the late Bert Hinkler is justified, I feel, on the grounds that much of his life and work come within the chronological period of this book. It is not intended, of course, to set his achievement above that of the late Sir Charles Kingsford-Smith, whose name in a later period, as "Smithy," became a household word and whose "old bus"—the *Southern Cross*—became a legend among aircraft.

THE WILD COLONIAL BOY

John Meredith, an authority on Australian popular balladry, has put forward cogent arguments for the now generally-held view that "The Wild Colonial Boy" derives from an older song about "Bold Jack" Donahoe, the notorious outlaw of the eighteen-twenties. (See under "Convicts and Governors".) In the course of several decades, Meredith suggests, the oral transmission of a Donahoe ballad led to many changes in the names and detailed activities originally mentioned, although the sentiment and social attitude remained constant. Jack Donahoe becomes, in course of time, Jack Doolan or Dowling or Donovan. And McQuade becomes McWoe, McVoe, Mac-Evoy, or Maccoboy.

Despite long and industrious research by historians and others, the fact remains that no records have so far been found of any bushranger of the eighteen-sixties operating under the name of Jack Doolan, Dowling or Donovan, who "stuck up the Beechworth mail coach, and robbed Judge MacEvoy."

John Meredith's excellent monograph on Jack Donahoe, The Wild Colonial Boy *(1960), which covers the main facts of the bushranger's career, contains the words and music of several Donahoe songs.*

There was a wild Colonial boy, Jack Doolan was his name,
Of poor but honest parents he was born in Castlemaine;
He was his father's only hope, his mother's only joy,
The pride of both his parents was the wild Colonial boy.

Chorus:

Come, all my hearties, we'll roam the mountains high,
Together we will plunder, together we will die;
We'll wander over valleys, and gallop over plains,
And we'll scorn to live in slavery, bound down with iron chains.

He was scarcely sixteen years of age when he left his father's home,
And through Australia's sunny clime a bushranger did roam;
He robbed those wealthy squatters, their stock he did destroy,
And a terror to Australia was the wild Colonial boy.

In sixty-one this daring youth began his wild career;
With a heart that knew no danger, no foeman did he fear;
He stuck up the Beechworth mail coach, and robbed Judge MacEvoy,
Who trembled, and gave up his gold to the wild Colonial boy.

He bade the judge "Good morning," and told him to beware,
That he'd never rob a hearty chap that acted on the square,
And never to rob a mother of her son and only joy,
Or else you may turn outlaw, like the wild Colonial boy.

One day as he was riding the mountain side along,
A-listening to the little birds, their pleasant laughing song,
Three mounted troopers came in view—Kelly, Davis, and FitzRoy,
And thought that they would capture him—the wild Colonial boy.

"Surrender now, Jack Doolan, you see there's three to one.
Surrender now, Jack Doolan, you daring highwayman."
He drew a pistol from his belt, and spun the little toy,
"I'll fight, but not surrender," said the wild Colonial boy.

He fired at Trooper Kelly, and brought him to the ground,
And in return from Davis, received a mortal wound.
All shattered through the jaws he lay still firing at FitzRoy
And that's the way they captured him—the wild Colonial boy.

                                                            Traditional.

14

THE LAST WORDS OF FRED LOWRY

Fred Lowry, a native of the Goulburn district, turned to bushranging, and his short career ended in 1863 after a duel with the police at the Limerick Races Hotel, Cook's Vale Creek. He was then twenty-seven years of age.

Suddenly Lowry threw the door open, and the sergeant almost fell into the room. The bushranger shouted: "Come on, you —— I'll fight you fair," and fired. The police returned the fire. Stephenson, who was inside the room, took steady aim and pulled the trigger. The robber fell, saying "I'm done for! Where's the priest?" . . . Lowry was made as comfortable as circumstances permitted while a messenger was sent off to the nearest town for a doctor. For more than an hour Detective Camphin sat by Lowry's side reading prayers from a Catholic prayer-book which Mrs. Vardy lent him. The robber gradually grew weaker and died. His last words were, "Tell 'em I died game."

GEORGE E. BOXALL, *History of the Australian Bush-*
rangers.

DUNN, GILBERT, AND BEN HALL

Come! all ye lads of loyalty,
    And listen to my tale;
A story of bushranging days,
    I will to you unveil,
'Tis of those gallant heroes,
    God bless them one and all,
And we'll sit and sing: "God save the Queen,
    Dunn, Gilbert, and Ben Hall."

To see the mounted troopers
    Scouring the bush,
Like diggers in the olden times,
    Hasting to a rush;
But those bushranging heroes
    They do deceive them all,
There's one thousand pounds, alive or dead,
    For Dunn, Gilbert, or Ben Hall.

As Ben was riding out one day,
    His trade being rather slack,
By private information

The troops got on his track,
Saying, "Hall, you are my prisoner,
    Surrender unto me,"
And Ben bolted from his saddle
    And climbed up in a tree.

With rage and disappointment
    The troopers cursed and swore;
They moped and poked about the bush,
    And tracked him o'er and o'er;
They kept the watch till daylight,
    And no Ben could be found;
At length they saw his cabbage-tree
    A-lying on the ground.

Then away goes eight or ten of them,
    Like so many yelping curs,
To capture bold Morgan,*
    In his shining boots and spurs;
But the horses, they knocked up at last,
    He cannot captured be;
They turned back from a fruitless chase,
    And Morgan still is free.

The troopers now, in latter days,
    They're only paper men,
Not like the mounted heroes
    We had in thirty-nine;
But a man that's carrying on the road
    Is taken from his dray,
With a pair of bracelets on his wrists,
    He's captured—led away.

So now my song is ended,
    I think I will resign,
We'll toast those gallant heroes
    In a glass of sparkling wine;
We'll give them three times three, my boys,
    We'll toast them one and all,
And we'll sit and sing "Long live the Queen,
    Dunn, Gilbert, and Ben Hall."

                                    Traditional.

* Daniel Morgan, a bushranger, contemporary of Ben Hall, although not
one of Hall's gang. He was fatally shot at Peechelba station in Victoria in 1865.

DEATH OF JOHNNY GILBERT

There's never a stone at the sleeper's head,
  There's never a fence beside,
And the wandering stock on the grave may tread
  Unnoticed and undenied;
But the smallest child on the watershed
  Can tell you how Gilbert died.

A. B. ("BANJO") PATERSON, "How Gilbert Died."

BALLAD OF BEN HALL

Come all Australia's sons to me,
  A hero has been slain,
Butchered by cowards in his sleep
  Upon the Lachlan plain.
Ah, do not stay your seemly grief
  But let the tear drops fall,
Australian hearts will always mourn
  The fate of old Ben Hall.

He never robbed a needy man,
  The records sure will show
How staunch and loyal to his mates,
  How manly to his foe.
No brand of Cain e'er stamped his brow,
  No widow's curse can fall:
Only the robber rich men feared
  The coming of Ben Hall.

For ever since the good old days
  Of Turpin and Duval,
The people's friends were outlaws,
  And so was bold Ben Hall.
Yet savagely they murdered him,
  Those coward blue-coat imps
Who only found his hiding place
  From sneaking peelers' pimps.

Yes, savagely they murdered him;
  Oh, let your tear drops fall,
For all Australia mourns to-day
  Her bravest son, Ben Hall.

No more he'll mount his gallant steed
  To roam the ranges high;
Poor widow's friend in poverty,
  Our bold Ben Hall, good-bye!

Traditional.

THE BALLAD OF JACK POWER

Air: "Erin-go-Bragh."

'Twas the eighth day of August
  In the year sixty-nine,
On a lovely spring morning,
  The weather being fine,
When a bolter from Pentridge,
  Jack Power by name,
An aspirant for the gallows,
  To Beechworth he came.

Well armed, well mounted,
  The traps for his foes,
To the scrub for concealment
  The highwayman goes.
From Beechworth to the Buckland
  And on the highway
Run Cobb and Co.'s coaches
  By night and by day.

Early one morning
  The outlaw approached
Towards Bowman's forest
  And bail'd up the coach.
And he bail'd up two draymen,
  A new saddle stole
And a horse, a coachwheeler—
  It's true, by my soul!

He met with a trooper
  Near the small town of Yea—
"Good morning, Sir Trooper,
  My orders obey.
Hand here that revolver
  Or, if you refuse,
You may fight or deliver,
  Pray, which do you choose?"

The trooper surrender'd
　　His horse and his arms,
Then hastened to Yea town
　　To give the alarm.
"Farewell," shouts the rover,
　　"This revolver's my shield;
To the traps or the gallows
　　I never will yield!"

We may sing of young Gilbert,
　　Dan Morgan, Ben Hall,
But the bold reckless robber
　　Surpasses them all.
The pluck that was in him
　　Is beyond all belief—
A daring highwayman,
　　A professional thief!*

NED KELLY, FOLK-HERO

... Though the historical Kelly may lie in a felon's grave, Kelly, the folk-hero, goes marching on and is likely to, as long as the Australian story lasts.

This idolisation of Kelly infuriates some people, who see in him nothing but a cattle-thief who murdered three policemen. But, after all, it is not what Kelly was, but what people think he was, that matters, and there is no doubt that the popular hero-worship of Kelly is due not to his criminal acts but to the fact he is seen as the personification of qualities which most Australians especially admire—courage and resourcefulness; a certain mordant humour; loyalty to his mates; and a concern for the less fortunate members of the community.

As well try to put down Kelly as Robin Hood or Stenka Razin —the hero of the Cossacks—it can't be done.

C. T. in the Melbourne *Herald*, December 24, 1948.

* From the Melbourne *Argus*, August 19, 1950. Quoted by Mr. Clive Turnbull, together with this note: "You may remember that a few months ago we had quite a correspondence about the old song, 'The Wild Colonial Boy'. Miss Elsie Heath of Grasmere, Sheep Hills, whose father was one of the pioneers of the Wimmera when it was thrown open for selection, writes that she has vivid recollections of the song as her father sang it to the children sitting round the fire on cold wintry nights — it varies slightly from the versions already published. Better still, Miss Heath tells me that her mother, not long ago, found in her own mother's work-box a copy of the song, 'Bushranger Jack Power'. It is written on blue-lined foolscap, still readable though worn, in a fine hand and, Miss Heath suggests, is probably eighty years old."

KELLY WAS THEIR CAPTAIN

Come all you wild colonial boys, and attention to me pay,
For in my song I will unfold the truth without delay;
'Twas of a famous outlawed band, that roamed this country
round;
Ned Kelly was their captain and no better could be found.

But the Governor of Victoria was an enemy of this man,
And a warrant he likewise put out to take his brother Dan.
But alas, one day some troopers came, young Dan to apprehend,
And he like a tiger stood at bay, his mother to defend.

Five hundred pounds reward was made for Ned, where'er was
found,
And from place to place was hunted as if he was a hound.
Now driven to desperation to the bush brave Ned did take,
Young Dan, Steve Hart and brave Joe Byrne, all for his mother's
sake.

And although they deemed them outlaws, brave men they proved
to be,
And vengeance ranked in every breast for Kelly's misery.
They burnt his mother's vine-clad hut, which caused his heart to
yearn,
And angered his companions, Dan, Steve Hart and brave Joe
Byrne.

One day as Ned and his comrades in ambush were concealed,
They spied three mounted troopers and their presence did reveal.
They called to them, "Surrender!" These words to them he said—
"Resist a man amongst you and I'll surely shoot you dead!"

Now Kennedy, Scanlon and Lonergan, in death were lying low,
When Ned amongst them recognised his old and vitr'ous foe;
Then thoughts came of his mother with a baby at her breast,
And it filled Ned's heart with anger and the country knows the
rest.

It was at the Wombat Ranges where Ned Kelly made his haunt,
And all those Victorian troopers at that name would truly daunt;
For months they lay in ambush until finally were betrayed
By traitor Aaron Sherritt, and his life the treachery paid.

It was at the Glenrowan station where the conflict raged severe,
Where more than fifty policemen at the scene then did appear.
No credit to their bravery, no credit to their name,
Ned Kelly terrified them all and put their blood to shame.

Contemporary ballad. Collected by BILL SHAWCROSS, Lithgow (N.S.W.) Published in *Songs from the Kelly Country*, Edited by JOHN MEREDITH (Bush Music Club of New South Wales).

NED KELLY AND JUDGE BARRY

"We find the accused guilty of murder in the first degree." As the foreman of the jury spoke the dread words, a pent-up gasp swept through the court and was swiftly hushed. The man in the dock displayed no emotion except for a momentary tightening of the lips.

The judge, his movements made awkward by a carbuncle on his neck, fumblingly donned the black cap and turned to the prisoner. Was the verdict pronounced by the jury the one which the accused expected? The man replied that under the circumstances he could expect no other.

Had the accused anything to say before the sentence was passed? There was no reply. The judge then pronounced the sentence: That the prisoner be hanged by the neck until he was dead, and added the formal, "May the Lord have mercy on your soul."

The people in the gallery looked at the unyielding man whose life was soon to end. They saw his lips move, and moved forward to catch his softly-spoken words.

"I will go further than that and say that when I go to the Great Beyond, I will see you there. . ."

Thus defiantly and with a challenge on his lips, Ned Kelly accepted death. Early in the morning of November 12, 1880, he was hanged.

And on November 23, eleven days later, Sir Redmond Barry, the judge who sentenced him, died from pneumonia whilst being treated for a carbuncle on his neck.*

"The Storyteller" in the Castlemaine *Mail*.

NUMBER ONE HERO

All sorts of Australians, or people in the Australian story, such as Captain Cook or Governor Macquarie, may be more eminent, more worthy, more significant; but, in the popular myth, Ned

---

* The facts of Ned Kelly's trial are given in *Australian Son* by Max Brown.

Kelly remains No. 1 Australian; and whether you like it or not, it is improbable that anything can be done about it.

CLIVE TURNBULL in the Melbourne *Argus,* October 15, 1949.

THE DEATH OF NED KELLY

Ned Kelly fought the rich men in country and in town,
Ned Kelly fought the troopers until they ran him down;
He thought that he had fooled them, for he was hard to find,
But he rode into Glenrowan with the troopers close behind.

"Come out of that, Ned Kelly," the head zarucker calls,
"Come out and leave your shelter, or we'll shoot it full of holes."
"If you take *me*," says Kelly, "that's not the speech to use;
I've lived to spite your order, I'll die the way I choose!"

"Come out of that, Ned Kelly, you done a lawless thing:
You robbed and fought the squatters, Ned Kelly, you must swing."
"If those who rob," says Kelly, "are all condemned to die,
You had better hang the squatters; they've stolen more than I."

"You'd best come out, Ned Kelly, you done the government wrong,
For you held up the coaches that bring the gold along."
"Go tell your boss," says Kelly, "who lets the rich go free,
That your bloody rich men's government will never govern me."

"You talk all right, Ned Kelly, your tongue is slick, I own;
But I have men to help me and you are all alone."
They burned the roof above him, they fired the walls about,
And head to foot in armour Ned Kelly stumbled out.

Although his guns were empty he took them by surprise;
He wore an iron breastplate and armour on his thighs.
Although his guns were empty he made them turn and flee,
But one came in behind him and shot him in the knee.

And so they took Ned Kelly and hanged him in the jail,
For he fought single-handed although in iron mail.
And no man single-handed can hope to break the bars;
It's a thousand like Ned Kelly who'll hoist the Flag of Stars.

JOHN MANIFOLD: *Selected Verse*, London, 1948.

EUREKA—SEAL OF MATESHIP

On Sunday, 3rd December, 1854, 100 mounted men (30 soldiers and 70 police), and 176 men on foot (152 soldiers and 24 police) assembled at the Government Camp, Ballarat, at 0230 hrs. At 0300 hrs. Captain J. W. Thomas, captain commanding troops, Ballarat, accompanied by three civil officials, left the camp with his force.

In excellent order and in perfect silence, the force arrived in about half an hour in front of an entrenchment on the Eureka diggings, and about 300 yards from it. It was the celebrated Eureka Stockade. Under cover of a rise of the ground, detachments of the 12th and 40th regiments extended in skirmishing order, each having its proper support.

Part of the mounted force of military and police moved towards the left of the position to threaten its flank and rear; the remainder of the mounted force and the foot police were kept in reserve. Over the Stockade, "all higgledy-piggledy slabs of wood," floated a strange flag, a blue flag with five white or silver stars—the flag of the Republic of Victoria.

Raffaello, the historian of Eureka, wrote the rest of the tale in song:

> Blood-hounds were soon let loose, with grog imbued,
> And murder stained that Sunday! Sunday morning;
> The Southern Cross in diggers' gore imbrued,
> Was torn away, and left the diggers mourning!

As a military operation the assault on the Stockade was negligible. The defenders, in some cases armed with nothing better than crude pikes, were outnumbered and overwhelmed. The Southern Cross was torn down. Some, at least, of the police lost their heads, bayoneting and burning indiscriminately when the field was already theirs.

An uncertain number of men, 15 or so perhaps, were left dead on the field and it is likely that as many more died later. Peter Lalor, the leader in the crisis, was severely wounded and smuggled away by friends. His arm was amputated. He lived to become Speaker of the Victorian Legislative Assembly and to refuse a knighthood.

Eureka was the climax of a long series of clashes between the floating populations of the goldfields and the authority represented by the colonial government. Fifty years ago it was lightly dismissed, in some quarters, as a petty riot—a clash between "Tipperary boys" (many of the men of the Stockade were Irish) and constituted authority.

To-day its importance is everywhere recognised; but often the issue is over-simplified as a clash between democrats and the colonial autocrats which resulted in the establishment in Victoria of the democratic forms of government. It is not as simple as that. Many men had a hand in Eureka, and many currents of thought met there.

Let us look back on the scene. Victoria (the District of Port Phillip), a placid pastoral province given over to great sheep-runs, was suddenly plunged into chaos by the discoveries of gold in the early fifties, which, following hard upon those of California, brought a torrent of adventurers from all quarters of the globe.

All in Melbourne itself who could do so rushed off to the diggings. Seamen deserted their ships, and day after day came more and more until the bay was a forest of masts, while through the once lonely bush a steady stream of fortune-hunters wore down the highways to the fields.

The squatters hated the newcomers, trespassers on their own dubiously acquired empires. The land was locked up, administration in chaos. Of the superintendent, La Trobe, an astute American observer remarked, "The governor had lived, moved, and had his being so long among the squatters as superintendent of a sheep country numbering some 50,000 souls, it was impossible for him to enlarge his views of administration so as to comprise the 250,000 immigrants which the riggings had brought into the country. The times had changed; other metal was wanted."

The Home authorities, however, supplied as new metal an honourable and well-meaning but stiff-necked and entirely unsuitable naval martinet, Sir Charles Hotham, who had distinguished himself in a minor affray in South America.

The men who came to the diggings were as various in outlook as in nationality—aristocrats and yeomen, artisans and clerks, European exiles, Irish patriots, English Chartists, American adventurers, varying in politics from extreme conservatism to open preaching of rebellion. In a very rough fashion they may perhaps be divided into three groups:

The majority, of no passionate political convictions but inclining to conservatism and angered, not by the political forms of the colony, but by being personally "pushed around" and the offensive methods adopted for collecting an inequitable licence fee; and likewise angered by revelations of official graft on the fields;

The Chartists, and their equivalents from other countries, who wanted democratic forms, most of which are now commonplaces; and

A minority of rebels and revolutionaries who wanted to sever the British connection and to set up the five-star Republic of Victoria.

In the first group was Lalor who took no part at all in the early political agitations. In the third group were many Americans, American republicanism then being an article of export.

Corruption of officials, maladministration, an unjust licence fee and the harrying of the miners by troopers caused all these forces to coalesce. But, when the showdown came, many of the plotters faded out of the scene and it was the plain men, with a plain man, Lalor, at their head, who bore the brunt and prepared to die true to their oath of comradeship.

Lalor's subsequent acts and utterances proved him anything but a revolutionary, but only a misunderstanding of the whole situation would present him as one. Lalor rose to his greatest height as the embodiment of the mateship of the fields. He was a brave man and, when his hour struck, he nobly responded. But, beyond that, he was, as his political career showed, in some ways even a reactionary. . . .

The vision of the Republic of Victoria faded; and even to claim that Eureka was itself responsible for the constitutional reforms thereafter enacted would be to ignore processes which were already in train before the Stockade. Its significance is not to be found only on the plane of politics; it lies deeper.

Let us go back to the scene on Bakery Hill, where Lalor

stands on a stump, holding with the left hand the muzzle of his rifle, while eighty feet above floats the Southern Cross. Lalor calls on the five hundred armed diggers to take the oath of loyalty. Then kneeling down, his head bared, his right hand pointing to the standard, he says in firm and measured tones:

"We swear by the Southern Cross to stand truly by each other and fight to defend our rights and liberties."

Five hundred hands stretch toward the flag and there is "an universal well-rounded Amen" . . .

Here is the heart of the matter—the oath of comradeship, the passionate determination on liberty. The spirit of Australia became articulate that day, the spirit of the Australia of the common man. Eureka is both the seal of mateship and and the death-knell of tyranny. Its message is in all our later history. Wherever men of good will swear to stand truly by each other and fight to defend their rights and liberties its tattered banner flaunts again.

CLIVE TURNBULL in *Salt*, December 3, 1945.

BRAVE LALOR

When Ballaarat unfurled the "Southern Cross,"
   Of joy a shout ascended to the heavens;
The bearer was Toronto's Captain Ross;
   And frightened into fits red-taped ravens.

Chorus:

For brave Lalor—
   Was found "all there,"
   With dauntless dare:
His men inspiring:
   To wolf or bear,
Defiance bidding,
   He made them swear—
Be faithful to the Standard, for victory or death. (*Bis.*)

CARBONI RAFFAELLO, *The Eureka Stockade*.

THE DIGGERS GATHER AT EUREKA

But now another match is lit that soon must fire the charge,
A digger murdered in the camp; his murderer at large!
"Roll up! Roll up!" the poignant cry awakes the evening air,
And angry faces surge like waves around the speakers there.

"What are our sins that we should be an outlawed class?" they say,
"Shall we stand by while mates are seized and dragged like lags
    away?
Shall insult be on insult heaped? Shall we let these things go?"
And with a roar of voices comes the diggers' answer—"No!"
The day has vanished from the scene, but not the air of night
Can cool the blood that, ebbing back, leaves brows in anger white.
Lo, from the roof of Bentley's inn the flames are leaping high;
They write "Revenge!" in letters red across the smoke-dimmed sky.
"To arms! To arms!" the cry is out; "To arms and play your part;
For every pike upon a pole will find a tyrant's heart!"
Now Lalor comes to take the lead, the spirit does not lag,
And down the rough, wild diggers kneel beneath the Diggers'
    Flag;
Then, rising to their feet, they swear, while rugged hearts beat
    high,
To stand beside their leaders and to conquer or to die!
Around Eureka's stockade now the shades of night close fast,
Three hundred sleep beside their arms, and thirty sleep their last.

        HENRY LAWSON, "Eureka" (A Fragment).

MRS. RALPH'S RETORT

Of the veterans (of the Eureka Stockade—Ed.) whose stories
were printed, that by George Ferman—one of the "four jolly
diggers"—is corroborative: "While the disturbances of '54 were in
progress, the wife of James Ralph went to the camp, and one of
the commissioners came out of his tent and held a revolver at
her head. 'You coward!' exclaimed the woman; 'that's all you're
good for, is to frighten women and children; you're afraid to
tackle men like my husband.'"

        ROBERT ROSS, *Eureka, Freedom's Fight of '54.*

FORWARD FROM EUREKA

But not in vain those diggers died. Their comrades may rejoice,
For o'er the voice of tyranny is heard the people's voice;
It says: "Reform your rotten law, the diggers' wrongs make right,
Or else with them, our brothers now, we'll gather to the fight."

    .   .   .   .   .

'Twas of such stuff the men were made who saw our nation born,
And such as Lalor were the men who led the vanguard on;
And like such men may we be found, with leaders such as they
In the roll-up of Australians on our darkest, grandest day!

        HENRY LAWSON, "Eureka" (A Fragment).

D

PETER LALOR—A MAN AMONG MEN

> No form more grand, no kind heart bigger,
> Than those that graced the noble digger;
> Honour his name for truth and valour—
> A man among men—*Peter Lalor*.

> ARTHUR WILSON ("Dalry"): *Mining Lays, Tales and*
> *Folklore.*

THE DEATH OF PETER LALOR—1889

Roll up, Eureka's heroes, on that Grand Old Rush afar,
For Lalor's gone to join you in the big camp where you are;
Roll up and give him welcome such as only diggers can,
For well he battled for the rights of miner and of man.

> HENRY LAWSON, "Eureka" (A Fragment).

THE MEN OF FIFTY-FOUR

And sometimes they'd get talking, low and mysterious like, about "Th' Eureka Stockade"; and if we didn't understand and asked questions, "what was the Eureka Stockade?" or "what did they do it for?" father'd say: "Now run away, sonny and don't bother; me and Mr. So-and-so want to talk." Father had the mark of a hole on his leg, which he said he got through a gun accident when a boy, and a scar on his side, that we saw when he was in swimming with us; he said he got that in an accident in a quartz-crushing machine. Mr. So-and-so had a big scar on the side of his forehead that was caused by a pick accidentally slipping out of a loop in the rope, and falling down a shaft where he was working. But how was it they talked low, and their eyes brightened up, and they didn't look at each other, but away over the sunset, and had to get up and walk about, and take a stroll in the cool of the evening when they talked about Eureka?

> HENRY LAWSON, "An Old Mate of Your Father's."

REMEMBRANCE OF EUREKA

> *The poem from which these lines are taken, tells of old Dad,*
> *"just a bent cripple now," and of the memories of this fine*
> *old battler "who fought and lost and still fought on."*

> Again Eureka's voices ring
> From blazing bivouacs of night;

Again the rifle bullets sing
  Across the palisaded height;
Again we hear the bugle call,
  And, where Raffaello's ardour led,
We watch one fight, and fighting fall
  Where Lalor fought and Lalor bled.

      E. S. EMERSON, "Gum Leaves on the Fire."

3. THE ANZAC TRADITION

THE MAN WITH THE DONKEY

In the gardens surrounding Melbourne's Shrine of Remembrance there is a bronze statuary group commemorating the gallant exploits of one of the many brave Australians who fought at Gallipoli. His story has become one of the hero-tales of the people.

The spirit of Anzac is epitomised in the story of the man with the donkey. He enlisted as Private Simpson and John Simpson Kirkpatrick was his name, but to the men on that bloodstained battlefield he was "Murph. and his donkey."

On the night of April 25 at Gallipoli Landing he obtained a donkey and each day and most of the nights he worked continuously between the firing line and the beach with the donkey, carrying wounded men to safety. Through the deadly sniping and most furious shrapnel he emerged unscathed.

On May 19 he went up the valley past the water post where he generally had his breakfast, but this day it was not ready. "Never mind," he called, "I'll have a good feed when I come back." But he never came back.

Scores of men he had carried down the valley, and many lives he had saved but at the cost of his own.

Riverine Herald, April 26, 1949.

THE DIGGERS

Yet at heart even the oldest Australian soldier was incorrigibly civilian. However thoroughly he accepted the rigid army methods as conditions temporarily necessary, he never became reconciled to continuous obedience to orders, existence by rule, and lack of privacy. His individualism had been so strongly implanted as to stand out after years of subordination. Even on the Western Front he had exercised his vote in the Australian elections and in the referendums as to conscription, and it was largely through his own act in these ballots that the Australian people had rejected conscription and that, to the end, the A.I.F. consisted entirely of volunteers. He was subject to no death penalty for disobedience or failure to face the enemy.

His outlook contrasted sharply with that of most English soldiers of that time, whose discipline was largely founded on the social division of their nation into upper, middle and lower classes. English officers were mainly drawn from the two former, and their troops accepted the principle that the general business of the great world was the affair of their superiors alone rather than of themselves; if action outside routine was called for, they looked to their officers to tell them what to do and how to do it. In Australia the distinction into social classes was so resented that it was difficult to get born Australians to serve as officers' batmen and grooms, who by the English tradition were servants. . . Those Australians who did so serve regarded themselves as their officers' guardians or helpers; they would look after the boss in those matters in which he was deemed incapable of looking after himself. . .

From early childhood the average Australian had regarded himself and everyone around him as masters of their own lives. . . He was accustomed to make decisions; and was always ready to run risks for an object in which he was interested—whether the saving of a mate, the securing of a souvenir or an unlicensed trip to Paris (or, after the war, to Cologne). He was less affected than most men by risk of punishment, but was bound to his fellows, and to the Old Country and the Allies, by a tense bond of democratic loyalty —a man must "stand by his mates" at all costs; and as he knew only one social horizon, that of race, most of his officers came within that category. He was the easiest man in the world to interest and lead, but was intolerant of incompetent or uninteresting leaders. . .

Except for a few demoniac spirits, one immersion in a great battle more than satisfied the eagerness that had led many to enlist, and left in almost all minds an often sub-conscious but never-absent dread. Most Australians yearned for return to their country with an intensity of longing of which they had not believed themselves capable, but which was remarked by most other soldiers who met them; so much so, that their word-pictures of their dry, sunlit, war-free land freely sketched by them to their British friends amid the smoke and vin rouge of the estaminets, or to their girl admirers on English leave, not infrequently determined their hearers to seek homes there after the war.

C. E. W. BEAN, *The Australian Imperial Force in France during the Allied Offensive, 1918.*

CAPTAIN THROSSELL

A memorial to Capt. Hugo Throssell, V.C., whose valorous deeds epitomised the spirit of Anzac, was unveiled at Greenmount (West Australia) in February 1954.

The first West Australian to gain a Victoria Cross in World War I, he was renowned for his qualities of leadership, which were supremely displayed at Gallipoli's Hill 60 on August 29 and 30, 1915.

Then a lieutenant, he and his men were detailed to capture and hold a vital position at the foot of the hill.

After a desperate sprint of ninety yards to the Turk-held trench, Throssell and his men captured the position.

Lieut. Throssell with four other ranks, was on the right flank, which was the most exposed part of the trench. While building a sandbag barricade they defended it with bomb and rifle fire against repeated charges by the Turks. During the fight Throssell was severely wounded.

"To be in such a fight was worth ten years of a man's life, and to win it was worth as many again," one of his men, Sgt. Macmillan, wrote in the London *Daily Mail*, of October 27, 1915. "Every man was at his top, but I shall always think we owed our victory to one man: Throssell, V.C.

"The fighting spirit that I always knew was in Throssell showed out as clear as sunlight. He stood there in the hottest part of the fight, a leader of men. His head was thrown back in the sort of exultation that you always imagine in the fights of olden days when it was honest man-to-man. His voice rang out cheerfully, 'Stick it out boys! Get 'em good!' And not a man of us would have yielded a yard for the sure salvation of his immortal soul."

Capt. Throssell was a son of George Throssell, who was Premier of W.A. in 1901.

When war broke out he was farming with his brother at Cowcowing.

On his return, he married Katharine Susannah Prichard, the well-known West Australian authoress. They settled at Greenmount just opposite the site of the memorial at the junction of the old York Road and the Great Eastern highway.

Capt. Throssell died in 1933 but his valiant spirit and example still live in the minds and hearts of those who knew him.

West Australian, February 20, 1954.

ALBERT JACKA

For most conspicuous bravery on the night of the 19th-20th May, 1915, at Courtney's Post, Gallipoli Peninsula. Lance-Corporal Jacka, while holding a portion of our trench with four other men, was heavily attacked. When all except himself were killed or wounded, the trench was rushed and occupied by seven Turks. Lance-Corporal Jacka at once most gallantly attacked them single-handed, and killed the whole party, five by rifle fire and two with the bayonet.

ALBERT JACKA's Victoria Cross citation in the *Official London Gazette,* July 24, 1915.

4. CHAMPIONS

THE FLYING PIEMAN

Some years ago, when a Sydney journalist, with an ear for our folklore, described a well-known contemporary as "the flying pieman of Australian politics," the reference must have been lost on many people.

He was referring to William King, who came to New South Wales from England in 1829. King first got a job as a schoolmaster at Sutton Forest, but later drifted to Sydney, where he became a barman. Tiring of this, he turned his hand to piemaking.

King sold his tasty wares in the streets of Sydney and gradually built up a great reputation as a pieman. His tall figure, clad in beribboned top hat, knee-breeches and stockings, and white shirt with Byron collar, marked him out as one of the city's "characters."

During the 1840's William King performed a series of athletic feats which must surely entitle him to a place among Australia's greatest athletes.

On September 28, 1847, he started off round the Maitland racecourse to prove that he could walk 192 miles non-stop in 48 hours. Although he had failed in a previous attempt, he managed it easily on this occasion, his time being 46 hours 30 minutes.

Two months later, at the back of the Fitzroy pub in Maitland, he had no difficulty in walking a thousand quarter-miles in a thousand quarter-hours.

At the same locality in December, 1847, the Flying Pieman

undertook in the time of one hour 30 seconds to run a mile, walk a mile, wheel a barrow half a mile, draw a gig with a lady in it for half a mile, walk a half-mile backwards, pick up 50 stones, and perform 50 leaps. He allowed himself 5¼ minutes' rest, and won the contest with 45 seconds to spare.

At Dungog (N.S.W.) next January, King turned on some spectacular performances, one of which was to carry a live goat weighing 80lb. a mile and a half in 12 minutes!

We next hear of him at Singleton (N.S.W.) performing amazing feats; and in October, 1848, while on a trip to Queensland, he walked from Brisbane to Ipswich carrying a pole weighing 100lb., and beat the mail coach by one hour.

Such a man was William King, worthy to be remembered for his athletic prowess.

His nickname seems to have a secure place among Australian expressions. "Indeed," wrote famous Sydney bookseller James R. Tyrrell recently, in *Old Books, Old Friends, Old Sydney*, "I find his accurately descriptive title, the Flying Pieman, in quite frequent current use for anyone who is always in a hurry."

Australasian Post, June 7, 1956.

GORDON'S LEAP

The Gordon Leap was reckoned an impossibility. When poet Adam Lindsay Gordon first performed it, it was said it could never be done again. Gordon, a morose man, and a remittance man, didn't care whether he lived or died. He wanted only to be remembered as a superb horseman, which he was. He had a mount which could jump anything—the fork of a tree or a high wire. His favourite sport was to lead a field at follow-the-leader and leave them behind. One day his companions kept up with him all day, and they were pretty vocal about their success. Gordon said, "Well, damn well follow me now," and put his horse at a high guard fence.

Beyond the fence, as they well knew, was a narrow ledge at the top of a 350-foot drop to jagged rocks bordering Mt. Gambier's Blue Lake. Gordon's horse took the fence, turned in mid-air, and landed steady on his feet parallel to the fence in the only way in which he could have saved his life and that of his rider. Gordon's companions cut a panel out of the fence and let the poet-horseman return.

The impression was that Gordon had tried to kill himself, as indeed he later did, but that the horse had foiled him. Lance

35

Skuthorpe repeated the performance, for a bet, on a horse named Wallace which he chose from a team of seven. His motive was to prove that the Australian was a better horseman than the Englishman any day and to cut away the arguments of those who took the other view and quoted Gordon's Leap. There are still parts of Australia where the night-long argument about the camp-fire will turn on the respective merits of these two horsemen.

From *People*, August 30, 1950.

SANDY'S FIGHT

Air:"The Wearing of the Green."

Oh! Paddy dear, and did you hear,
   The news that's going round,
How Sandy Ross has lost his fight
   On the George's River ground?

"Begorrah!" Larry Foley said,
   As he saw his man close by,
"I'm here to fight for Ireland's sake,
   And for her sake I'll die."

"Here's at you then, here's at you!"
   Bold Sandy Ross did say,
"I'm here to fight for old King Bill,
   Upon this glorious day."

His orange scarf around his waist,
   Was plainly to be seen,
As Foley stepped into the ring
   A-wearing of the green.

For three long hours they fought, till Ross's
   Seconds came between,
And skied the towel reluctantly,
   In favour of the green.

The devil hears with keen regret,
   The news that's going round,
Poor Sandy Ross has lost the fight,
   On the George's River ground.*

* Larry Foley was a well-known prize-fighter of the last century, who died in 1917. This great fight against Sandy Ross, which first brought him into prominence, took place in 1871 — one hundred and forty rounds in all! Actually, the bard allowed his prejudice to get the better of him, as the fight ended in a draw. Foley later beat Ross at Port Hacking, New South Wales.

CARBINE'S CUP VICTORY, 1890

One writer said of Carbine's win that he raced to a victory which was, as mortal things go, immortal.

Under the heaviest weight a winner had ever carried, through the biggest field which had ever started (both records still stand) he made himself a turf idol.

It was also reported that on that far-off November day in 1890 Carbine threw the spectators into a riot of excitement and jubilation.

"Many people became hysterical in their delight; women shrieked and even wept; and quite decorous old gentlemen in frock coats and 'toppers' abandoned their head-gear and shook hands with everybody within reach."

Such horses as Carbine built the tradition which surrounds the Melbourne Cup, plus, of course, the many capable reporters who have since recorded the glorious turf deeds of the great winners.

Some writers immortalised the successes of the winners of the Cup in verse.

I can well remember reading (and memorising in my youth—between lessons) two of about twenty verses on Carbine's win:

> Fly, Carbine, fly faster and save a disaster;
>   Ride, Ramage, ride, ride man, ride all you know how;
> There may be a slip yet between Cup and lip met,
>   Ride hard, ride, your hand's on the Cup even now.

> A length he is leading, what riding and breeding!
>   Two lengths and a half clear he flees past the post
> Half deafened in thunder. Great Carbine! Great wonder,
>   The horse of the world, not a word of a boast.

"Cardigan" in the Melbourne *Herald*,

November 4, 1952.

JACKY HOWE'S TALLY

On October 10, 1892, Jacky Howe shore 321 weaners at Alice Downs, in the Blackall district of Central Queensland. Howe, number one among blade shearers, by this feat established a record which has yet to be broken by any blade shearer. However, on October 22, 1947, Daniel Cooper Jnr., of South Perth, W.A., shore 325 in eight hours with the machines at Glenara, a property in the Langkoop district of Victoria, owned by Mr. C. G. Stewart. He established a new world record, eclipsing

Jacky Howe's 321 with the blades, and his father's (Dan Cooper) 316 with the machines.

Dan Cooper had shorn his 316 in 7 hours 40 minutes at Bundooran, in Queensland, in 1910. He thus broke Jimmy ("Happy") Powers record of 315, which were shorn in 7 hours 20 minutes at Barenya, in Queensland, in 1895.

ALAN MARSHALL, in *Australasian Post,* December 20, 1951.

THE DEATH OF LES DARCY

He arrived in America on an oil tanker, his goal the world's middleweight championship. Instead, he found frustration, injustice and finally death. Branded a slacker by the Governor of New York, and unable to box in America, his spirit began to fade; and on the 24th May, 1917, he awoke from a short sleep at the Gartly-Ramsey Hospital, Memphis, opened his eyes and beckoned to his friend, Mick Hawkins. He gasped for words and found none.

America at last discovered Les Darcy. Otto Floto, of the *Denver Post* wrote:

"James Leslie Darcy is no more. When the curfew tolled its knell at Memphis, the shell of clay which had housed a champion released its tenant, and Les Darcy, the greatest pugilistic idol Australia had ever known passed to his niche down the dust-laden aisle of the lofty-arched Unknown.

"Punishment and physical torture were as nothing to Darcy. He took all that came to him with the ever-present smile. His body was perfect—his heart immune to cowardice, but even the strongest cannot endure the tongue of criticism. So it was with Les Darcy. His physical self could not repel the onslaughts—the charge that he ran away when his country called him. They wound their tentacles around the heart of this strong young man and it shrunk until it was no longer able to beat true and strongly—and he fell victim to a malady that would have caused him no serious concern had he been himself.

"He died of a broken heart and because his fellow men had forgotten that six feet of earth makes us all of one size."

DEL WILLIAMS, "A Youth Named Darcy."

THE DARCY-McGOORTY FIGHT: DARCY THE WINNER

It's of a young hero now well-known to fame,
That I write these few verses, Les Darcy is his name;
He was born in Maitland, as all of you know,
Where good men were born in days long ago.

He is quick and he's active, with limbs strong and loose,
He has beaten the best men that the Yanks could produce,
Being a prophet by nature, I prognosticate
That he'll beat heavy-weighters at no distant date.

McGoorty's an honest and straightforward youth,
When he uttered the following he expressed the real truth—
"I never felt better in my life, I must say,
As when I entered the Stadium that night for the fray."

In days that's gone by we've had champions galore,
But never a fighter like this blacksmith before.
The people of Maitland idolise him today
Far more than Frank Slavin, that's a big thing to say.

Success to Dave Smith who helped him along,
And smilingly cheered him at the sound of the gong.
May both of these heroes soon gain great renown,
May Dame Fortune's Daughter on them never frown.

If Darcy meets Gibbons, Ahearn or Brown,
Each of these fighters must surely go down,
And if ever he's challenged outside New South Wales,
May he gather fresh laurels and weather all gales.

Broadsheet by P. F. Collins (Sydney)

"UP THERE, CAZALY!"

Probably no sportsman in the glittering history of Australian sport has so completely captured the popular imagination as the dashing, high-marking Cazaly.

Aussie Rules* followers in four States will always remember him as "Up There, Cazaly!"—a cry that his spectacular brand of football put into a hundred thousand throats on playing fields from Albury to Hobart, and from Hobart to Perth!

All along the battle zones of the Middle East, from Alexandria to Tobruk, "Up There, Cazaly!" was the battle-yell that accompanied Victorian battalions into action.

On the streets of Cairo, and also in England, the familiar "Up There, Cazaly!" was the greeting by which ex-Aussie Rules players claimed each other.

---

* "Aussie Rules": Football, played according to Australian rules, mainly in the southern States.

New Zealanders hearing their Australian comrades using the cry reckoned that Cazaly must surely be the Phar Lap of Aussie Rules—something like their own George Nepia or Morrie Brownlee of All Black fame.

They were correct. Cazaly was to his game all that those famous N.Z.-ers were to Rugby.

And, in one very important aspect he even outshone them. His actual playing life extended into just twice as many years.

WARD McNALLY in *Sports Novels*, February, 1952.

SPOFFORTH, "THE DEMON BOWLER"

A feat, probably without equal in the history of cricket was performed by Spofforth, the Australian bowler, in a match against eighteen of Burnley, including five professionals. The Australians made 148 in their first innings and the Burnley eighteen were disposed of for 43.

Spofforth, in this innings, bowled 14 overs of which 11 were maidens. In three overs 10 runs were made off his bowling but at the cost of 12 wickets. The "Demon" has never done anything like this hitherto and there is no similar record in the English chronicle of the king of sports.

From the East Charlton *Tribune*, August 4, 1880.

PHAR LAP'S MELBOURNE CUP

I'll never forget Phar Lap's Cup. He started the hottest favourite on record to make a one-horse race of the 1930 Melbourne Cup.

In the saddling paddock his massive chestnut frame dwarfed other horses in the race and, if looks counted, he was a racecourse certainty. One look at bookmakers' odds confirmed my thoughts.

Phar Lap made the race a one-horse race from start to finish, despite his heavy weight. For the bookmakers it was "Black Tuesday."

Phar Lap had completed one of the most popular Caulfield-Melbourne Cup doubles in the history of the events; Amounis, a raging hot favourite with Billy Cook in the saddle, having won the Caulfield event.

I arrived in Melbourne that year just in time to read that an attempt had been made to shoot Phar Lap as he exercised along a peaceful street near the Caulfield racecourse the Saturday morning before the race.

A car had driven along the road close to where Phar Lap was

walking, slowed down, and two shots had been fired at the chestnut. They missed and burrowed into a paling fence near where the horse was exercising.

Phar Lap was rushed from his stables in Caulfield to a secret hide-out at Geelong—forty miles from Melbourne. He was not seen until he arrived at Flemington the day of the race under strong police escort.

It rained heavily the night before that Cup and Flemington was saturated. It always seems to rain in Melbourne for the Cup. Many doubted whether even the mighty Phar Lap could lump his 9.12 around the slush for two miles.

Jim Pike, his jockey, soon dispelled any fears about Phar Lap's ability. He was one person who knew of what the champion was capable and the manner he rode the chestnut that day showed his confidence in the horse. Pike had Phar Lap third or fourth on the rails the first time around. Other horses seemed to take two strides to his one. Pike restrained Phar Lap, but at the back of the course Pike gave Phar Lap his head and he bounded to the front with ease.

Turning into the straight, Tregilla, the horse best backed to down the champion, emerged from a wall of horses and made a challenge. For a moment he appeared to have Phar Lap's measure but Pike took one quick glance, shook the reins and Phar Lap left Tregilla and the field standing.

Pike eased Phar Lap down at the post to win by three lengths.

Phar Lap was the greatest racehorse I've seen—even better than "Old Jack"—Carbine.

GREG. KEIGHERY in *Sporting Life*, November, 1951.

PHAR LAP

(To the memory of Phar Lap, the world's greatest horse)

> He was a mighty horse indeed,
>   Alas! he's passed away,
> But the world will remember him
>   Until the latest day.
> Robert the Divil was a steed
>   Whose name will ever shine.
> Another name will live in fame—
>   The famous Carbine.
>
> They forced Phar Lap to do too much,
>   That much we know quite well,

What caused his death when in his prime
   The future may yet tell.
He closed his eyes in Yankee-land
   Of every evil thing.
And there Les Darcy passed away,
   A champion of the ring.

His speed was wonderful, no doubt,
   His staying power was great,
It's very sad that he should meet
   With such a tragic fate.
He was the marvel of the age,
   The swiftest beast on earth;
New Zealand loved his Lightning name—
   The land that gave him birth.

Australia too was proud of him,
   This land of sun and shine,
For Telford and his partner
   He was a rich gold mine.
Pike tells us that he knew his work,
   His temper was perfect:
In fact, some say he was possessed
   Of Human Intellect.

Five hundred years may come and go
   Before another's bred
To equal that swift noble steed
   Now numbered with the dead.
But if a man did poison him
   May his flesh and blood decline,
May his grave be made on a mountain-side
   Where the sun will never shine.

                    Broadsheet by P. F. COLLINS (Sydney).

BERT HINKLER, AIRMAN

Farewell to you Bert Hinkler,
   Your days on earth are o'er,
You were an airman of the best
   But you will fly no more;
At Bundaberg, your native place,
   Your friends are sad to-day,
Would to God that you stayed at home
   Instead of going away.

You've crossed the world in the air
    And gained yourself renown,
Your name became a household word
    In country and in town;
You were a fearless man indeed,
    No better could be found,
Your spirit now flies in the air,
    Your body's on the ground.

Kingsford Smith and Lindbergh
    Are wonderful we know,
You were the best of them all,
    Alas you're lying low;
Yes, you're dead, good-bye to you,
    Until the end of time,
The world will write your good name
    In language most sublime.

Although you were but a young man,
    The world knew you well,
And in a thousand years from now
    Your great deeds men will tell.
And now adue [sic] brave man to you,
    Far o'er the ocean swell,
We will not see your face again,
    Ten thousand times farewell.*

A broadsheet by P. F. COLLINS (Sydney).

* Hinkler was killed when his Puss Moth crashed in Italy, 1933.

PART TWO

THE YARN-SPINNERS

The children of gentle condition, whose evenings are made sweet with books and music, with theatres and the social intercourse of the cities, cannot appreciate the bush significance of the word "yarn." A yarn in the remote outback is the equivalent for a hundred enjoyments of the town. Where there are no pianos, no violins, not, mayhap, even an accordion, a banjo, or a concertina, under the bark roofs, under the hot iron roofs, under the roofs of thatch and canvas, under the open stars, when the day's labour or the day's march is done, they will sit and "yarn."

This makes the stranger doubly welcome. He has come from other places; he has new tales to tell. He in turn can be told old local lies and incidents that have staled in the ears of local audiences. He can be made the victim of ancient jests.

E. J. Brady, *River Rovers.*

They've spun the yarns of hut and camp, the tales of play and work,
The wondrous tales that gild the road from Normanton to Bourke.

W. H. Ogilvie, "From the Gulf".

COMMENT

THESE yarns and ballads are arranged according to popular theme and are intended to give as broad a picture as space permits of the subjects that have urged the Australian to laughter over the past sixty or seventy years.

In each instance the jest or anecdote has arisen out of local experience and in that sense is distinctly Australian. But humour has long since acquired the habit of crossing all national boundaries and many of these stories will be recognised as of ancient vintage, though the bottles are new.

The "Silent Australian" yarns had their origin in the last century when men were often forced by circumstances—lack of work, and the necessity to look for jobs on stations scattered over a wide area of country—to spend much time tramping the outback roads. They usually travelled in pairs as mates, and though the Australian is ordinarily fond of conversation, the itinerant bushman often became reserved and even taciturn. A "magger" or voluble person was rarely a welcome companion in such circumstances.

Another type of bushman, the hatter, usually a fossicking miner living alone, gave rise to a similar type of yarn. The hatter's specialty was talking to himself or to his dog. He did not welcome other company.

I have grouped together a number of allusions to "Casual Australians". Banjo Paterson and others have referred to the outback country as "the Land of Lots-o'-Time", and the legend grew up, largely nurtured in the cities, that the bushman and the itinerant worker were lazy individuals. It has long been the practice in some quarters to equate unemployment with laziness and the fact that the man with a swag was frequently out of work in the off seasons led to the assumption, by the well-fed city dweller, that all swagmen were lazy and sheered away from work.

The casualness of the Australian has been the target of many jokes. In this connection the comment by E. S. Sorenson in *Life in the Australian Backblocks* is apposite:

> . . . he is constant and persevering, but he is not a hustler. He tells you that the world was not made in a day, or "there are plenty more days" and will set to work to dig away a

mountain with the utmost serenity. But he will do a big day's work, and can hustle to some account when it is necessary.

Early in the history of Australia bullock drivers acquired a reputation for the vividness of their language, especially when their teams got bogged. The majority of yarns about them hinge in one way or another on this point. A bush parson was often introduced as a foil for the bullocky's swearing propensities.

For a superb picture of the old-time bullock drivers and the authentic colour of their conversation you cannot do better than read Joseph Furphy's *Such is Life*.

I have included only one reference to "The Great Australian Adjective," feeling that the heart of the matter is more than adequately demonstrated in Goodge's rhyme. However, the student of swearing should also read C. J. Dennis's "Australaise".

Those who wish to further their acquaintance with "Bush Liars" should meet the king of them all—Bob, in Furphy's *The Buln Buln and the Brolga*, an artist if ever there was one.

The "Dad and Dave" yarns are included only because they are in such currency to-day that the student of folklore cannot ignore them. They are examples of the "city slicker's" hoary jests at the expense of the mythical moronic farmer. The original Dad and Dave were members of a typical selector's family of the last century—courageous, hard-working folk with the dignity that came naturally to those pioneers of the outback. "Steele Rudd" (Arthur Hoey Davis) has portrayed them lovingly and faithfully in his famous book *On Our Selection.*

On the subject of bushmen's dogs read also Henry Lawson's very funny yarn, "The Loaded Dog," and Edward Dyson's "A Domestic Difference."

THE GREAT AUSTRALIAN JOKE

Two swagmen who had been mates for a long time were tramping out west in the wheat country. There were good young crops on either side of them.

Harry took his pipe from his mouth and pointed to one of the paddocks. "Nice crop of wheat," he grunted.

Five hours later, when they were seated by their campfire, Bill broke the silence. "Wasn't wheat. 'Twas oats." Then he rolled up in his blanket and went to sleep. The sun was well up when he woke next morning. Harry and his swag were gone. Bill found a roughly scribbled note under a stone at the foot of the nearest tree. "Too much b—— argument in this here camp," it said.

THE MAGGER

The old yarn about those bush mates, travelling, who parted for ever because one of them said there was too much sugar in the tea, and the other said there was too much conversation in the camp, is better than gospel truth. You can live mates with a murderer, but you can't live mates with a magger.

THOMAS DODD in the *Australian Worker*, March 21, 1928.

GETTING TO THE BOTTOM OF IT

Farmer: So there's one of them city blokes down on the river. What's he getting? Rabbits?
His Son: No!
Farmer: Is he getting fish?
Son: No!
Farmer: Well, what *is* he getting?
Son: Drowned!

SILENCE OF THE BUSH

Next night we were camped cosily in a clump of myall. It was 100 miles from civilisation. A dry myall log glowed on the fire (what "boshter" fuel those dry myalls make bushmen!) and having dined heartily on tinned dog and tinned jam, and a pot of tinned tea, we sat back enjoying the pipe as we gazed into the cloudless starry sky with the big full moon humping her bluey over the top of a distant patch of scrub. It was a silent, fragrant, bush night. Suddenly a "squeak, squeak, squeak" sounded on the plain. "Wheels!" exclaimed the driver, "but it ain't no cart!" Presently a dark object loomed up out west a bit. "Cripes, a wheelbarrer!" remarked the driver. In a few moments a long wheelbarrow propelled by the sorriest-looking individual who ever borrowed a meal for life moved into the fire zone. He had more whiskers, more dirt, and more holes in his clothing than any hunted criminal native. "Where'd you come from?" inquired the mailman in astonishment. "Up 'ere," he replied jerking a finger westward. "Where's up 'ere?" "Oh, jest up 'ere," he answered again. "And where are yer goin'?" "Oh, down there," he said jerking a finger eastward. And that was all we could get out of him. He ate solidly of our fare for an hour, then taking a dirty swag from his wheelbarrow, he spread it near the fire, wrapped himself up, and went to sleep. In the morning when we awoke our guest had lit the fire, boiled the billy, and was shoving huge chunks of our tinned dog into a cavern which opened frequently amid his multitudinous whiskers. He never vouchsafed a word, but simply ate on till his hunger was appeased, and then rolling up his swag he placed it

48

on the wheelbarrow; after which he picked up the handles, looked at us, and said, "So long."

FRED J. MILLS ("The Twinkler"): Square Dinkum.

THE SILENT STATION-HAND

The nights had grown colder, the mornings crisp and sharp. I lingered over the breakfast fires, and spent the forenoons in an overcoat, with my toes to the cylinder of the engine. An out-station at the Ana Branch was the first place of habitation to present itself. I went ashore and conversed with an unimaginative station-hand while he skinned and cut up a sheep. The conversation was mainly on my side.

"Good morning," I began pleasantly.

The man favoured me with a reluctant nod.

"How far is it to Morna?"

"Dunno," said the man, "never bin there."

He went on with his work, plying a very sharp knife with great dexterity.

"Can I buy a loaf of bread here?"

"Nawl!"

"Haven't you got any bread?"

"Naw; ain't baked."

More knife play.

"Can I get any bread at Morna?"

"Dunno!"

Slish-slash of knife over the hanging carcase.

"Know if I can get any bread anywhere?"

"Naw."

"Dry country, this?"

Several scientific cuts, which relieved the skin.

"Dry country!" I repeated.

"Dunno. Yairs."

"Say," I cried, determined to drag him out somehow, "did you read yesterday's papers?"

"Nawl! Don't get 'em."

"Then you didn't hear the news?"

"Naw. What's that?"

Knife still working rapidly.

"James the Second is dead."

"Naw. What of?"

"Barcoo rot!" I announced, and left him cutting up his sheep.

E. J. BRADY, River Rovers.

2. Casual Australians

A LAZY MATCH

The typical Cornstalk is naturally indolent and easy going, but capable of great exertions when roused. He is born in a delightful country, and is philosophic enough to enjoy it. He is satisfied with himself and the world in general. He believes the Lord made Australia at his leisure, and that the Cornstalk is the chosen people. Should any question this fact the Cornstalk arouses. No one must question his country's supremacy; no one must question his own prowess. If they do he will convince them otherwise. When he takes a thing up he must be ahead. The Cornstalk must be first in anything he handles, or he leaves it severely alone. That is the typical Cornstalk—slow, easy, indolent in the ordinary way, proud of his country and himself, and capable of holding his own in anything in which he is interested.

The job is to interest him in matters of import.

It was a country genius who, while the Cornstalks were distinguishing themselves in all departments of athletic sport, hit upon a novel idea, whereby one more bright link could be added to the victor's chain, i.e., by holding a "lazy match" open to representatives of all nations. England, Ireland, Scotland and Australia had worthy representatives, but the European nations sent forth no one anxious for the palm of laziness. The plan adopted was to have the contestants cover sixty yards in sixty minutes and pick up an apple at the limit mark, and the one who performed this feat in the laziest manner was to be declared the winner, a sovereign being awarded him for his pains.

In the presence of a concourse of people the contest punctually was begun, the Scotsman being given first trial. His circumlocutory mode of progression, at the rate of a yard a minute, would bring tears of envy to the face of a tortoise or a civil servant. It would be somewhat difficult to cover the ground in a lazier manner was the general verdict.

The Englishman next appeared and, at the signal, he walked calmly towards the apple and lay down, to quietly turn and pick it up on the sixtieth second. The public looked surprised. He had had a rest of some fifty-nine minutes while the Scotsman had slowly laboured through the whole hour. This could not be beaten by much.

The Irishman at the signal lay down at the starting point, and at the sixtieth minute made one bold rush and picked the apple on time. There was loud applause at this performance, as he had rested some seconds longer than the Englishman.

The Australian came to the mark, looked at the apple sixty yards away and asked: "I have to pick that apple up in sixty minutes, and get a sovereign if I do it in a lazier manner than the others?"

"Yes," he was told.

"Oh! let them have the sovereign," said he, "I can't be bothered."

"You refuse to travel the distance?" asked the umpire.

"Too much bother," said the Cornstalk.

The crowd hooted and yelled when they found the Cornstalk would not move, but above the din was heard the umpire's words: "Well, if the Cornstalk is too lazy to even pick up the apple he must get the award."

When the crowd found that his unfathomable laziness had gained him the victory their groans and hooting turned to ringing cheers and shouts of approbation.

> "Whaks Li Kell" (DANIEL HEALEY), *The Cornstalk, his Habits and Habitat* (1893).

A CASUAL BET

The horses were jogging along comfortably, and the mail driver was pitching me a yarn about one Bill Hogan, when suddenly a rifle shot rang out and a bullet whistled between the foot of space which separated our heads. I went clean through my spectacles. The driver, I regret to record, whispered "'Ell!" Immediately two station hands, one carrying a rifle, burst from a clump of mallees a quarter of a mile away, and came running up to us. "Hey, cobbers!" yelled he with the gun. "Did you hear a bullet whistle?" "Yes, you ijets," replied the driver, "it came clean between us." "Ah, then I've won my wager. I bet Jim 'ere a pound o' tobacker I could put a bullet between yer without touchin' either!" "Good Lord," I exclaimed, "s'posing the bullet had gone through my head?" "Oh well, I'd 'ave lost me bet!" was the casual reply.

FRED J. MILLS, *Square Dinkum*.

LAZY FEAT

Passer-by (seeing a tiger snake moving perilously close to the feet of a resting sundowner) : Hey there, mate, mind out! There's a snake near your foot.

Weary Sundowner (continuing to lie at rest) : Which foot, mate?

FENCE-LEANER

Hiker (to weary-looking character leaning against a paling fence) : Excuse me, but could you direct me to Dead Dingo Road?

The weary one yawns.

Hiker (anxiously): I'll give you a shilling for your trouble.

The weary one: All right. Well, you follow this track up to Sheehan's pub. Sheehan'll tell you where to go from there. It's not far.

Hiker: Thanks very much. By the way, here's your shilling.

Weary one: Okay. Shove it in me hip pocket, will yer.

EASY STAGES

So, toward undreamt-of destinies
He slouches down the centuries.

ARTHUR ADAMS, "The Australian."

3. BULLOCK DRIVERS

HOW TO TELL A NEW CHUM

I know the new chum instantly,
    I've seen him pull up short and stare,
And then quite horror-stricken be
    When ribald bullock-drivers swear;
And shocked by curses loud and deep,
    With Strawberry he's sympathised,
And at each stroke I've seen him weep—
    Poor new chum he ain't colonised.

CHARLES THATCHER, *Thatcher's Colonial Minstrel.*

THE OLD BULLOCK DRAY

Oh, the shearing is all over,
    And the wool is coming down,
And I mean to get a wife, boys,
    When I go up to town;
Everything that has two legs
    Represents itself in view,

From the little paddy-melon
 To the bucking kangaroo.

Chorus:

So it's roll up your blankets,
 And let's make a push;
I'll take you up the country
 And show you the bush;
I'll be bound you won't get
 Such a chance another day,
So come and take possession
 Of my old bullock dray.

Now I've saved up a good cheque,
 I mean to buy a team,
And when I get a wife, boys,
 I'll be all serene;
For, calling at the depot,
 They say there's no delay
To get an off-sider
 For the old bullock dray.

Oh, we'll live like fighting cocks;
 For good living, I'm your man.
We'll have leather jacks, johnny cakes,
 And fritters in the pan;
Or, if you'd like some fish,
 I'll catch you some soon,
For we'll bob for barramundies
 Round the banks of a lagoon.

Oh, yes, of beef and damper
 I take care we have enough,
And we'll boil in the bucket
 Such a whopper of a duff;
And our friends will dance
 To the honour of the day,
To the music of the bells,
 Around the old bullock dray.

Oh, we'll have plenty girls,
 We must mind that.

There'll be flash little Maggie
    And buckjumping Pat;
There'll be Stringybark Joe,
    And Greenhide Mike.
Yes, my Colonials, just
    As many as you like.

Now we'll stop all immigration,
    We won't need it any more;
We'll be having young natives,
    Twins by the score;
And I wonder what the devil
    Jack Robertson would say
If he saw us promenading
    Round the old bullock dray.

Oh, it's time I had an answer,
    If there's one to be had,
I wouldn't treat that steer
    In the body half as bad;
But he takes as much notice
    Of me, upon my soul,
As that old blue stag
    Off-side in the pole.

Oh, to tell a lot of lies,
    You know it is a sin.
But I'll go up the country
    And marry a black gin.
Oh, "Baal gammon white feller,"
    This is what she'll say,
"Budgery you
    And your old bullock dray."*

Traditional.

THE PHANTOM BULLOCKY

I was boss on Thurloona at the time.

The chap who wanted a job was of the all-round run of bushmen, and as I needed a bullock-driver I gave him a try-out. I told
him that the team he would have to handle was one of eight-yoke,
with the wildest cattle in Australia in it, and showed him the

* Paddy-melon: A small wallaby. Jack Robertson: See under "Squatters and
Selectors". Budgery you: Good fellow, you.

graves of fourteen men killed at one time and another by the oxen.

"I'll try 'em," he said.

I asked him if he had the language. He said that often when he had been bogged in the timber his conversation had set the stringy-bark trees on fire—not the big ones, but the saplings.

I told him he might suit, and asked him to give me an example of himself starting a team.

"You take eight panels of the fence of the yard," I said. "Imagine that's your team, and get 'em going." The eight panels of the yard were new timber, big posts, each with four strands of galvanised wire run through and tied to a four-foot stringybark. He said it would do him.

I handed him a whip—the same the fourteen dead bullockies had used in turn. The handle was six feet, the lash eighteen feet of plaited greenhide, and there was two feet of silk cracker. He bent the handle over his knee in two or three places, to test it for flaws, then ran the lash slowly through his hand as if feeling it for a loose strand.

Then he started the team. He walked along and tapped each post with the butt of the handle, as a hint to the bullocks to tighten the chains. Then he gave a cheer, the whip kept cracking, and presently a little blue flame ran along the top wire of the fence. He kept on exhorting the bullocks and cheering loudly. The flame danced along the wire, and the whip cracking sounded like the Day of Judgment.

When the outfit fairly started, he cheered like ten thousand, and, to my amazement, the fourteen graves opened, and the fourteen killed bullockies jumped out, each carrying a whip. They walked right up to the new man. When he saw them he gave another and louder cheer, and the fourteen phantoms hailed him as the King of the Bullockies. All together the fifteen whips fell on the top wire, and the flame ran up and down as if it were alive.

Then the posts began to walk forward, step by step, straining on the wires. Then the drivers gave a louder cheer than ever, talked faster and louder, and the team strained in the yokes until the four-foot stringybark tree came out of the ground and fell in behind. The driver that I had hired cheered wildly, and kept on going up the hill with the tree. The others gave him a cheer as he disappeared, and all rushed back and jumped into their graves.

He went round the foot of the hill and came back. "I think I could drive your team," he said to me. I said, "You can have the job. You're the best man with a fence that I ever saw."

Then he laughed, gave another cheer, and jumped up in the air. He never came down again.*

HOLY DAN

It was in the Queensland drought,
    And over hill and dell,
No grass—the water far apart,
    All dry and hot as hell;
The wretched bullock teams drew up
    Beside a waterhole—
They'd struggled on through dust and drought,
    For days to reach this goal.

And though the water rendered forth
    A rank, unholy stench,
The bullocks and the bullockies
    Drank deep, their thirst to quench.

Two of the drivers cursed and swore
    As only drivers can;
The other one, named Daniel,
    Best known as Holy Dan,
Admonished them and said it was
    The Lord's all-wise decree,
And if they'd only watch and wait
    A change they'd quickly see.

'Twas strange that of Dan's bullocks
    Not one had gone aloft,
But this, he said, was due to prayer
    And supplication oft.
At last one died, but Dan was calm,
    He hardly seemed to care,
He knelt beside the bullock's corpse
    And offered up a prayer.

"One bullock Thou hast taken, Lord,
    And so it seemeth best;
Thy will be done, but see my need
    And spare to me the rest!"

* This is a variant of Lance Skuthorpe's masterly bush yarn, "The Champion Bullock-Driver" (included in *Twenty Great Australian Stories*, compiled by J. L. Waten and V. G. O'Connor, Melbourne, 1946). The present version differs in only a few respects from Skuthorpe's. I have given it here largely as a matter of interest to those who are familiar with "The Champion Bullock-Driver", but also because it is an excellent example of how folklore develops.

A month went by. Dan's bullocks now
    Were dying every day,
But still on each occasion would
    The faithful fellow pray,
"Another Thou hast taken, Lord,
    And so it seemeth best;
Thy will be done, but see my need
    And spare to me the rest!"

And still they camped beside the hole,
    And still it never rained,
And still Dan's bullocks died and died
    Till only one remained.
Then Dan broke down—good Holy Dan—
    The man who never swore.
He knelt beside the latest corpse,
    And here's the prayer he bore:

"That's nineteen Thou hast taken, Lord,
    And now you'll plainly see
You'd better take the bloody lot,
    One's no damn good to me."

The other riders laughed so much
    They shook the sky around,
The lightning flashed, the thunder roared,
    And Holy Dan was drowned.

Traditional.

WINNING TERMS

According to an Australian statistician, the average bullock
driver takes the palm for persuasive and eloquent swearing, which
reminds me that there once was an occasion when one bullocky,
at least, found his vocabulary quite unequal to the occasion.

He was walking beside his team on a Gippsland road, when they
suddenly sheered off the corduroy, and the next moment the outfit
was bogged to the axle. He began his usual efforts to get the bullocks to pull out, belabouring them, and using the choicest of
repertoire. But this time it was all a failure.

Then a horse and buggy appeared, and its occupants were two
parsons. They drew up beside the bullocky. "My dear man," said
one, "what on earth is the use of swearing like that? You'll never
pull them out that way." The bullocky spat disdainfully. "Try to

get 'em out without it, that's all," he said, and began again with added fury. The clerical gentleman got down from the buggy, stepped through the mud, and said, "Let me try," and the fun began.

Walking alongside the team, he stroked each bullock in turn, and talked to it, and the sweating beasts rolled wild eyes at the unusual proceedings. Then the parson seized the great whip from the staring bullocky, swung it aloft, and in a stentorian voice, he shouted: "Get up, you rectangular hypotenuses! Come on, you horned parallelograms! Get up!!!"

The team quivered from stem to stern; the bullocks strained at their yokes, and then the wagon moved out of the morass, and the next minute was on firm ground. The bullocky was speechless, but as the reverend gentleman prepared to mount again into the buggy, he went over to him, and in an awed voice said, "Mister! What's it worth to teach a bloke a few of them specials of yours? I've never heard the like of them in all my born days!"

"Observer" in the Bendigo *Advertiser*,
December 27, 1949.

F

4. SHEARERS

ON THE ROAD TO GUNDAGAI

Oh, we started down from Roto when the sheds had all cut out.
We'd whips and whips of rhino as we meant to push about,
So we humped our blues serenely and made for Sydney town,
With a three-spot cheque between us as wanted knocking down.

Chorus:
But we camped at Lazy Harry's, on the road to Gundagai.
The road to Gundagai! Not five miles from Gundagai!
Yes, we camped at Lazy Harry's, on the road to Gundagai.

Well, we struck the Murrumbidgee near the Yanco in a week,
And passed through old Narrandera, and crossed the Burnet
　　Creek,
And we never stopped at Wagga, for we'd Sydney in our eye,
But we camped at Lazy Harry's, on the road to Gungadai.

Oh, I've seen a lot of girls, my boys, and drunk a lot of beer,
And I've met with some of both, chaps, as has left me mighty
　　queer;
But for beer to knock you sideways, and for girls to make you sigh,
You must camp at Lazy Harry's, on the road to Gundagai.

Well, we chucked our blooming swags off, and we walked into
    the bar,
And we called for rum-an'-raspb'ry and a shilling-each cigar.
But the girl that served the pizen, she winked at Bill and I—
And we camped at Lazy Harry's, not five miles from Gundagai.

In a week the spree was over, and the cheque was all knocked
    down,
So we shouldered our "Matildas," and we turned our backs on
    town,
And the girls they stood a nobbler and we sadly said "Good-bye,"
And we tramped from Lazy Harry's, not five miles from Gundagai.

                                                    Traditional.

THE BIG-GUN SHEARER

Now, some shearing I have done, and some prizes I have won,
    Through my knuckling down so close on the skin;
But I'd rather "tommyhock" every day and shear a flock,
    For that's the only way to make some tin!

Chorus:

I am just about to cut out for the Darling:
    To turn a hundred out I know the plan;
Give me sufficient cash, and you'll see me make a splash,
    For I'm Tomahawking Fred, the ladies' man!

Put me on a shearing floor, and it's there I'm game to bet,
    That I'd give to any ringer ten sheep start;
When on the whipping side, away from them I slide,
    Just like a bullet or a dart.

Of me you might have read, for I'm Tomahawking Fred
    My shearing laurels known both near and far;
I'm the Don of River-ine, 'midst the shearers cut a shine;
    And the tar-boys say I never call for tar.

Wire in and go ahead, for I'm Tomahawking Fred;
    In a shearing shed, my lads, I cut a shine.
What of Roberts and Jack Gunn—shearing laurels they have won,
    But my tally's never under ninety-nine.*

                                                    Traditional.

* S. J. Baker, in *The Australian Language*, defines "to tomahawk" as "to
shear roughly and gash a sheep." A ringer is one who "rings the board," that
is, proves "the most expert shearer in the shed."

WIDGEEGOWERA JOE

Air: "Castle Gardens."

I'm only a back-blocks shearer, as easily can be seen,
I've shore in almost every shed on the plains of Riverine;
I've shore in most of the famous sheds, I've seen big tallies done,
But somehow or other, I don't know why, I never became a gun.

Chorus:

Hurrah, my boys, my shears are set, I feel both fit and well,
To-morrow you'll find me at my pen when the gaffer rings the
    bell;
With Hayden's patent thumb-guards fixed, and both my blades
    pulled back,
To-morrow I go with my sardine blow for a century or the sack.

I've opened up the windpipe straight, I've opened behind the ear;
I've practised every possible style in which a man can shear.
I've studied all the cuts and drives of the famous men I've met,
But I've never succeeded in plastering up them three little figures
    yet.

As the boss walked down the board this morning, I saw him stare
    at me,
For I'd mastered Moran's great shoulder cut, as he could plainly
    see;
But I've another surprise for him, that'll give his nerves a shock,
To-morrow he'll find that I have mastered Pierce's rangtang block.

And if I succeed as I expect to do, then I intend to shear
At the Wagga demonstration, which is held there every year;
And there I'll lower the colours, the colours of Mitchell and Co.,
Instead of Deeming, you will hear of Widgeegowera Joe.*

                    Traditional; collected by Sydney Folklore Society.

CROOKED MICK FROM THE SPEEWAH

Tom Mann, in his memoirs, mentions that when in Queensland
about twenty years ago, he was told of a shearer who had shorn

---

* "I never became a gun": A big-gun shearer was one with an outstanding
tally of sheep shorn in a day's work. Moran and Pierce were such "big-gun"
shearers. Deeming, referred to in the last line, was the notorious murderer.
    Since the first edition of this book was published, the Sydney Bush Music
Club under the able guidance of Mr. John Meredith, has done notable work
in the collection and publication of Australian folk songs. Mr. Ron Edwards and
Mr. Hugh Anderson, both of Melbourne, have also done much to enlarge the
horizons in this field.

340 in a day. He admits a doubt about it, and his incredulity is justifiable, for neither then nor since has Jacky Howe's tally of 321 (with the blades—Ed.) been beaten. Probably the figures quoted belonged to Crooked Mick, a mythical personage, whose mighty deeds have been recounted in sheds, mostly for the benefit of new chums.

I first heard of him on the Barcoo in 1889. We were shearing at Northampton Downs, and the musterers brought in a rosy-cheeked young English Johnny who, in riding from Jericho, the nearest railway station to Blackall, where he was going to edit the new paper, had got lost and found himself at the station, where we were busily engaged disrobing about 150,000 jumbucks.

He was treated with the hospitality of the sheds, which is traditional, and after tea we gathered in the hut—dining-room and sleeping accommodation all in one those days—and proceeded to entertain him.

Whistling Dick played "The British Grenadiers" on his tin whistle; Bungeye Blake sang "Little Dog Ben"; Piebald Moore and Cabbagetree Capstick told a common lie or two, but when Dusty Bob got the flute I sat up in my bunk and listened, for I knew him to be the most fluent liar that ever crossed the Darling.

His anecdotes about Crooked Mick began and ended nowhere, and made C.M. appear a superman—with feet so big that he had to go outside to turn round.

It took a large-sized bullock's hide to make him a pair of moccasins.

He was a heavy smoker. It took one "loppy" (rouseabout) all his time cutting tobacco and filling his pipe.

He worked at such a clip that his shears ran hot, and sometimes he had half a dozen pairs in the water pot to cool.

He had his fads, and would not shear in sheds that faced north. When at his top it took three pressers to handle the wool from his blades, and they had to work overtime to keep the bins clear.

He ate two sheep each meal—that is, if they were small merinos—but only one and half when the ration sheep were Leicester crossbred wethers.

His main tally was generally cut on the breakfast run. Anyone who tried to follow him usually spent the balance of the day in the hut.

Between sheds he did fencing. When cutting brigalow posts he used an axe in each hand to save time, and when digging post holes a crowbar in one hand and a shovel in the other.*

JULIAN STUART.

(From a cutting, probably from *The Australian Worker*, Sydney, supplied by Mrs. Lyndall Hadow.)

ANOTHER FALL OF RAIN

Air: "Little Low Log Cabin in the Lane."

The weather had been sultry for a fortnight's time or more,
    And the shearers had been driving might and main,
For some had got the century who'd ne'er got it before,
    And now all hands were wishing for the rain.

Chorus:

For the boss is getting rusty, and the ringer's caving in,
    For his bandaged wrist is aching with the pain,
And the second man, I fear, will make it hot for him,
    Unless we have another fall of rain.

A few had taken quarters, and were coiling in their bunks
    When we shore the six-tooth wethers from the plain.
And if the sheep get harder, then a few more men will funk,
    Unless we get another fall of rain.

But the sky is clouding over, and the thunder's muttering loud,
    And the clouds are driving eastward o'er the plain,
And I see the lightning flashing from the edge of yon black cloud,
    And I hear the gentle patter of the rain.

So lads, put on your stoppers, and let us to the hut,
    Where we'll gather round and have a friendly game,
While some are playing music and some play ante up,
    And some are gazing outwards at the rain.

But now the rain is over; let the pressers spin the screw,
    Let the teamsters back the waggons in again,
And we'll block the classer's table by the way we'll put them
        through,
    For everything is merry since the rain.

* There are endless stories about Crooked Mick of the Speewah—not the Speewa on the River Murray, near Swan Hill, but a legendary region of mighty people and fantastic deeds "beyond the furthest outback". The stories are reminiscent of those told about America's Paul Bunyan. Mr. Alan Marshall, noted Australian story-teller, has gathered many of them in his wanderings, and they have appeared in various journals and newspapers.

And the boss he won't be rusty when his sheep they all are shorn,
  And the ringer's wrist won't ache much with the pain
Of pocketing his cheque for fifty pounds or more,
  And the second man will press him hard again.*

Traditional.

"COMOLLYERS"

About fifty years ago I first heard a "comollyer."† Dusty Bob
sang one in a Paroo hut as soon as the shearers' cook's offsider had
cleared the supper table.

Bob's ditty had unlimited verses and began:

Come all you overlanders and listen to my song,
You blokes what robs the hen roosts every time you pass along.

He would as soon have a fight as a feed any day. A favourite
trick, when lighting his pipe, was to sing out, "Gather round,
you Victorians! The Queenslander's going to strike a match."

A "comollyer" of which I remember only the chorus had a
great vogue:

There's justice in Queensland I cannot understand,
There's justice in Queensland, this free and happy land;
The rich man and the poor man tell their different tales,
But the rich man always seems to get the balance of the scales.

"The Wild Colonial Boy" was popular, but its length was
tiresome; it had 157 verses!

The refrain of one which I often heard in the robust basso
of Shearblade Martin was:

Oh, boys, oh! Have you heard the news?
  Jimmy the Pig is back again
After doing a cruise.
  He's been to the Melbourne races
While we starved on the bend,
  And having won a thousand quid
He's on the river again.

* "The strain of shearing": Banjo Paterson, in *Old Bush Songs*, points
out that shearing "is very severe on the wrists and the ringer or fastest shearer
is very apt to go in the wrists, especially at the beginning of a season. Hence
the desire of the shearers for a fall of rain after a long stretch of hot weather."

† "Comollyer": So named by bushmen to describe old-time ballads beginning
"Come all you . . ."

A correspondent sends me a few verses from "Dalgangal" (he says it contained over a hundred):

Dalgangal loaded his dray with wool,
As much as the flaming bulls could pull,
And tried to cross a creek that was full
   At four o'clock in the morning.

Dalgangal was cutting brigalow posts
In the scrub where the summer fairly roasts,
And he swore the camp was full of ghosts
   At four o'clock in the morning.

Dalgangal raved and threw down his axe,
And fast through the haunted scrub made tracks,
And went and lived with the Paroo blacks
   At four o'clock in the morning.

Dalgangal lived with them forty years,
And once again in the saddle appears,
Droving wild Coomooboolooroo steers
   At four o'clock in the morning.

Dalgangal next day was feeling sick,
And went on the booze with Crooked Mick,
And both got run in for being "shick"
   At four o'clock in the morning.

Dalgangal swagged it many a mile,
But camped at Comalong Creek awhile,
And got chawed up by a crocodile
   At four o'clock in the morning.

Another long-distance "comollyer" was "Goorianawa," telling of the tribulations endured by the shearers at the station of that name. Sung in the train, it lasted all the way from Bourke to Sydney.

The outlaw of the lot was "Little Dog Ben," too rough even for Barcoo audiences, yet I heard it given (late) at a vice-regal banquet at Mount Morgan, W.A., when Sir Gerald Smith was governor.

JULIAN STUART in the *Australian Worker*, June 29, 1927.

5. STATION COOKS

CROOKED MICK'S PASTRY

"Crooked Mick of the Speewah," a mythical make-believe much in evidence in the western sheds forty or fifty years ago.

Mick's name was generally brought to light for the purpose of putting the kibosh on anyone who was emulating Ananias or Munchausen, or Tom Pepper.

A stranger who was looking for cooking boasted in the traveller's hut one night that he could make thirteen kinds of pastry out of a pannikin of flour, and was put to the pack by an old chap in the top bunk, who said that when Crooked Mick was cooking at Lignum Downs he made twenty-three sorts of pastry at each meal, and it was so light that when the wind blew it off the table it floated about in the air. Then there was one quiet man in the hut for the rest of the night.

JULIAN STUART in the *Australian Worker*, October 31, 1928.

STATION COOKS

Why is it that station cooks develop mannerisms or strange quirks of mind that set them apart from their fellow-men? The most unusual specimen I ever met was in the Hay (N.S.W.) district. When my mate and I went to bite him for a handout his sullen face and contemptuous expression warned us to expect the worst, and his first words confirmed our suspicions.

"Dunno what youse blokes expect to get here," he growled. "I got nothin' at all to give yer." While he was speaking he grabbed our sugar bag and threw a cooked leg of mutton, a loaf of bread and a large brownie into it.

"I tell yer I got nothin' for you," he went on, hurling tins of jam and assorted foodstuffs into the bag. "It's all I can do to feed me own hungry mob of blankards here without providin' tucker for every deadbeat on the track."

As we staggered off with the bulging bag we wondered what sort of a handout we'd have clicked for if the peevish babbler chanced to have a fair supply of tucker in stock.*

"Valencia Creek" in the Sydney *Bulletin*.

OLD-TIME COOKS

"The Blue Stew Cook," a Darling identity, specialised in stew. He had a large, three-legged pot into which mutton and vegetables were thrown each day. This regular addition to the stew meant that the pot always remained full. It simmered away above the fire from week to week, always retaining its volume, though a score of men were patiently eating it.

It was only natural that they began, finally, to look at the three-legged pot with some distaste. It was said that pieces of meat and vegetables lying round the bottom of the pot had been resting there for a month or more, despite the frequent stirrings to which the cook subjected the stew.

Finally, a dyspeptic shearer, determined to have the pot completely emptied for once, tossed a couple of knobs of Reckitt's Blue into it as he passed.

Just before the next meal the cook gave the stew its customary stir, started visibly, then recovered and yelled to the men as he ladled out the stew on to the waiting plates: "Blue stew to-day, boys."

. . . There was no refrigeration on the stations. The meat was kept in hessian safes or excavated pantries, often inadequate protection against flies.

"Hey! the meat's blown," was a common complaint.

"They're dead, they won't hurt you," was the usual rejoinder from the cook.

ALAN MARSHALL in *Australasian Post*, February 18, 1954.

* The term "babbler" is an abbreviation of "babbling brook", which, in turn, is rhyming slang for cook.

6. STOCKMEN

A THOUSAND MILES AWAY

Air: "Ten Thousand Miles Away."

Hurrah for the Roma railway! Hurrah for Cobb and Co.,
And oh! for a good fat horse or two to carry me Westward Ho—
To carry me Westward Ho! my boys, that's where the cattle stray
On the far Barcoo, where they eat nardoo, a thousand miles away.

Chorus:
Then give your horses rein across the open plain,
    We'll ship our meat both sound and sweet, not care what some
       folks say;
And frozen we'll send home the cattle that now roam
    On the far Barcoo and the Flinders too, a thousand miles
    away.

Knee-deep in grass we've got to pass—for the truth I'm bound
    to tell—
Where in three weeks the cattle get as fat as they can swell—
As fat as they can swell, my boys; a thousand pounds they weigh,
On the far Barcoo, where they eat nardoo, a thousand miles
    away.

No Yankee hide e'er grew outside such beef as we can freeze;
No Yankee pastures make such steers as we send o'er the seas—
As we send o'er the seas, my boys, a thousand pounds they weigh—
From the far Barcoo, where they eat nardoo, a thousand miles
    away.*

Traditional.

THE OVERLANDER

There's a trade you all know well,
    It's bringing cattle over;
On every track to the Gulf and back
    They know the Queensland drover.

Chorus:

Pass the billy round, my boys,
    Don't let the pint pots stand there,
For to-night we'll drink the health
    Of every Overlander.

Oh, I'm a bushman bold,
    Since youth I've been a rover;
On every track to the Gully and back
    They know McVeigh the drover.

I come from northern plains
    Where grass and girls is scanty,
Where the creeks run dry or ten feet high,
    And it's either drought or plenty.

A girl in Sydney town
    Said, "Please don't leave me lonely";
I said, "I'm sad, but my old prad
    Has room for one man only."

I never stole a shirt
    As all my mates can say,
Unless I passed a town
    Upon a washing day.

* "Nardoo": an indigenous plant, the spore-cases of which are used, mainly
by the Aborigines of northern Australia, to produce a kind of flour.

Those little brats of kids,
  My God, they get my dander,
Singing, "Ma, bring in the clothes,
  Here comes an Overlander!"

And now we're jogging back;
  This old nag she's a doer;
We'll pick up a job with a crawling mob
  Somewhere on the Maranoa.

Traditional.

THE EUMERELLA SHORE

A Cattle Duffers' Song

There's a happy little valley on the Eumerella shore,
  Where I've lingered many happy hours away,
On my little free selection I have acres by the score,
  Where I unyoke the bullocks from the dray.

Chorus:

To my bullocks then I say
No matter where you stray,
  You will never be impounded any more;
For you're running, running, running on the duffer's piece of
    land,
  Free selected on the Eumerella shore.

When the moon has climbed the mountains and the stars are
    shining bright,
  Then we saddle up our horses and away,
And we steal the squatters' cattle in the darkness of the night,
  And we brand 'em at the dawning of the day.

Chorus:

Oh, my little poddy calf,
At the squatter you may laugh,
  For he'll never be your owner any more;
For you're running, running, running on the duffer's piece of
    land
  Free selected on the Eumerella shore.

If we find a mob of horses when the paddock rails are down,
  Although before, they're never known to stray,

Oh, quickly will we drive them to some distant inland town,
    And sell them into slav'ry far away.

Chorus:

To Jack Robertson we'll say
You've been leading us astray,
    And we'll never go a-farming any more;
For it's easier duffing cattle on the little piece of land
    Free selected on the Eumerella shore.*

Traditional.

WHITE LOGIC

Watty Marshall, who thrashed an Aborigine for branding a goanna, said, "Damn cruel."

"What for?" said the Aborigine. "What for you brandem bullock?"

"That's not cruel," said Watty. "You can sell bullocks."

RANDOLPH BEDFORD, *Naught to Thirty-three.*

TOO DANGEROUS

Flood water had cut the cattle off from any food and they were marooned on a small piece of high ground a mile away. The only way to save the cattle from starvation was to get a boatload of fodder to them, and this was rather a risky job, because the flood waters were flowing rather fast.

"What about you taking a boatload of hay out to the cows, Jacky?" the boss asked the Aboriginal handyman.

"Better you send a white man," Jacky replied. "They're still plentiful, but fellers like me are getting too plurry scarce."

* "Jack Robertson": John, later Sir John, Robertson, Premier of New South Wales, who introduced the Land Act of 1861, intended to assist small farming, but actually helped to consolidate the position of the big landholders. Robertson was sometimes known as "Dingo Jack". "Duffing" was the equivalent of the American "rustling", or thieving of cattle, horses, etc.

7. SWAGMEN

MY FOUR LITTLE JOHNNY-CAKES

Hurrah for the Lachlan, boys, and join me in a cheer;
That's the place to go to make a cheque every year.
With a toadskin in my pocket, that I borrowed from a friend,
Oh, isn't it nice and cosy to be camping in the bend!

Chorus:

With my four little johnny-cakes all nicely cooked,
A nice little codfish just off the hook;
My little round flour-bag sitting on a stump,
My little tea-and-sugar bag a-looking nice and plump.

I have a loaf of bread and some murphies that I shook,
Perhaps a loaf of brownie that I snaffled off the cook,
A nice leg of mutton, just a bit cut off the end,
Oh, isn't it nice and jolly to be whaling in the bend!

I have a little book and some papers for to read,
Plenty of matches and a good supply of weed;
I envy not the squatter, as at my fire I sit,
With a paper in my hand and my old clay a-lit.

73

And when the shearing-time comes round, I'm in my glory then;
I saddle up my moke and then secure a pen;
I canter thro' the valley, and gallop o'er the plain;
I shoot a turkey or stick a pig, and off to camp again.*

Traditional.

THE RAMBLE-EER

The earth rolls on through empty space, its journey's never done;
It's entered for a starry race throughout the kingdom come;
And, as I am a bit of earth, I follow it because—
And to prove I am a rolling stone and never gather moss.

Chorus:

For I am a ramble-eer, a rollicking ramble-eer,
I'm a roving rake of poverty, and a son of a gun for beer.

I've done a bit of fossicking for tucker and for gold;
I've been a menial rouseabout and a rollicking shearer bold;
I've "shanked" across the Old Man Plain, after busting up a
   cheque,
And "whipped the cat" once more again, though I haven't met it
   yet.

I've done a bit of droving of cattle and of sheep
And I've done a bit of moving with "Matilda" for a mate;
Of fencing I have done my share, wool-scouring on the green,
Axeman, navvy. Old Nick can bear me out in what I haven't been.

I've worked the treadmill thresher, the scythe and reaping-hook,
Been wood-and-water fetcher for Mary Jane the cook;
I've done a few "cronk" things too, when I have struck a town,
There's few things I wouldn't do—but I never did "lambing
   down."†

Traditional.

HENRY LAWSON'S GHOST

   J. Le Gay Brereton in *Knocking Round,* tells an amusing story
of something which happened when he and Harry (Henry Lawson

---

* Toadskin: a five-pound note. Murphies: potatoes. Whaling: leading an
idle, carefree existence on the banks of a river. Hence, Murrumbidgee whaler,
Murray whaler, etc. (See under "Australianisms"). Weed: tobacco, particularly
the ready-rubbed or flake cut varieties.

† "Whip the cat": to cry over spilt milk; "Matilda": a swag; "cronk":
worthless, ill; "lambing down": the practice, in outback grog shanties, of
encouraging excessive spending on liquor; a "lamber-down" was a shanty-
keeper.

—Ed.) were on the wallaby together. They camped in a haunted cottage at Gerringong. And sure enough a ghost came—but not the one they expected. The story runs:

Harry took the billy and fetched water from the swamp which lies between the beach and the camp while I lit a fire in the fireplace of the haunted house.

"Why not the big house?" my mate asked, slinging the billy on the wire hook which was suspended from an iron bar in the chimney.

"This is cleaner," I explained.

"Smaller and less room for dirt," he amended unrolling his swag in a corner near the fire, "I wonder why they say this place is haunted."

"Dunno. I reckon somebody put a notice up for a joke. There's a new notice now to say: 'Prepare to die when the ghost tramps on the front verandah.' "

"There's the ghost now," Harry said. "Have you got the tobacco?"

There was a shuffling step outside, as somebody made his way carefully among the ruins of the verandah. The door was thrust open and in stepped a traveller. . . . He advanced and lowered his swag. In accordance with etiquette, he asked:

"Any room, mates?" And I answered, "Lots!"

The ends of his moustache lifted and wrinkles rayed from the outer corners of his eyes, as he asked, "Ever read them stories called *While the Billy Boils?*"

We had.

"Pretty good, ain't they?"

We thought they were.

"Read *When the World Was Wide?*"

We passed favourable judgment on the volume of poems.

"Well, I wrote them poems; my name's Henry Lawson."

He looked for admiration and got it. When I considered that Lawson's portrait had been published throughout Australia, I was charmed by the audacity of the little impostor.

"I can prove it. You know Lawson's style—my style. Something about it a chap can't mistake."

"Oh, there is a strong individuality."

"Well, run your eye over that."

He took a couple of dirty sheets of paper from his pocket and handed them to me. I unfolded them and read these lines, written in a neat round hand.

Billy's Swag

It was just before the diggers made a rush for Lie-an'-Rot,
That a swaggie that was gone on Jimmy Nowlett's girl got shot,
He was drinkin' in the shanty where she useter serve the grog
When Jimmy got the needle and told him he must shog;
But the gleam of Mary Carey's single eye was like a star
Above a mighty tempest, as they jumped about the bar.

They bit each other's noses as along the floor they rolled;
(Oh, there's nothing in the present like the gory days of old.)
They plugged each other's peepers an' they gripped each other's
  hair,
An' Mary laughed and sooled 'em; but her dad began to swear,
For over every inch of floor an' wall they whirled an' crashed,
Till every bit of glass about the bloomin' place was smashed.

In the corner by the counter was a sorter canvas bag,
Where Carey kept his cartridges with bits of oily rag;
An' the lovers tumbled over, an' the back of Billy's head
Went bangin' on the canvas, an' next minute he was dead;
He'd bumped agin' a cartridge, an' it freed him from his pain,
For it went off like a blast an' lodged a bullet in his brain.

We buried him in secret an' a bit o' mulga scrub,
An' fought about his blankets at the back o' Carey's pub;
But I often think about him when I open up his swag
Or pull my tea and sugar from his swellin' tucker-bag—
Of course he doesn't want 'em now, he's got his bed and board,
An' rum-an'-nectar, maybe, at the shanty of the Lord.

I was astounded. The hand was the hand of Lawson, or a very
close imitation of his style. . . . "They are pretty lines," I said,
"pretty and pathetic."

He waved the paper aside when I held it toward him.

"If you think it's a good pome," he remarked diffidently, "you'd
better keep it. Sometimes when you're on your uppers in the city
you can publish it. You ought to be able to get a couple of quid
for it, if you tell 'em who wrote it. I don't think it's quite as good
as some of the pieces in the book, myself."

I thanked him for his gift and stowed the paper away in my
swag. Conversation drifted to other topics. . . .

"I always heard Lawson was a bit hard of hearing," Harry said,
"but you seem to hear all right."

"Well, in Sydney, you know, a man has to protect himself agin' these interviewers. If you sham stone deaf, it helps to keep 'em off."

Nothing daunted him. He was the most superb liar I have ever met.

BERTHA LAWSON, *My Henry Lawson*.

JUST RIGHT

Swagman (calling out from the door of the country pub): "How did you like the bottle of port wine I gave you for Christmas, Jacky?"

Aborigine: "It was just right, boss."

Swagman: "What do you mean . . . it was just right?"

Aborigine: "If it had been any better you wouldn't have given it to me, and if it had been any worse I couldn't have drunk it, so it was just right!"

MY OLD BLACK BILLY

I have humped my bluey in all the States
With my old black billy, the best of mates,
For years I have camped, and toiled, and tramped
    On roads that are rough and hilly,
With my plain and sensible,
Indispensable,
    Old black billy.

Chorus:

My old black billy, my old black billy,
Whether the wind is warm or chilly
I always find when the shadows fall
My old black billy, the best mate of all.

I have carried my swag on the parched Paroo
Where water is scarce and the houses few,
On many a track, in the great outback
    Where the heat would drive you silly
I've carried my sensible,
Indispensable,
    Old black billy.

When the days of tramping at last are o'er
And I drop my swag at the Golden Door,

Saint Peter will stare when he sees me there.
Then he'll say "Poor Wandering Willie,
Come in with your sensible,
Indispensable,
  Old black billy."

EDWARD HARRINGTON, *The Swagless Swaggie and Other Ballads.*

8. Soldier Yarns

THE SLOUCH HAT

Lord Gort arrived at the Somme battlefront one day to carry out a tour of inspection. He was accompanied by his A.D.C. and a small retinue.

At that time the Somme front was an ocean of mud and Lord Gort had to negotiate a long line of duckboards. Presently he spied a slouch hat lying in the mud. He asked his A.D.C. to retrieve it.

Over went the A.D.C. and after a bit of straining he had succeeded in raising the hat a few inches when an Aussie voice came from underneath. "Go easy, mate! I've still got the flamin' strap under me chin!"

Hearing this, Lord Gort and his companions hurried to rescue the Digger. After about ten minutes of straining and pulling the voice spoke again: "Ah-h! It's no b—— good. I've still got me flamin' feet in the stirrups!"

Australasian Post, April 26, 1956.

BLOWING COLD AND HOT

It was at a military hospital in England, and the convalescents were sitting in the garden chatting. The topic was cold weather. The American had the floor.

"Wal, I reckon it was a bit cold in those French trenches this winter. . . . But shucks! it was a heat wave compared with some of the cold snaps we get in Amurica. Why, look yere, children; I remember one day over'n New York it got so darned cold, kinder suddent like, that everybody's whiskers froze, and the people had ter shave themselves with dynamite. Of course the explosions shook up ther old city a trifle, but, by George Washington, some whiskers got shifted! Another day a cold jerk put in without notice, and freezed up all the whisky. The bartenders had to go about with axes chippin' nobblers off the whisky blocks. Some cold, I reckon!"

An Australian scratched his right ear with a crutch, and put in:

"Dunno much about cold in Australia, but I ken talk heat a bit. It does warm up over there. Now, once I was humpin' me bluey in ther bush. A heat wave came up. You could see it comin' in ther distance by ther kangeroos 'oppin' about with their tails on fire. I picked up a bit of old fencin' wire and lit me pipe with it. That was a sure sign too. In a few minutes that wave struck me, dealt with me, and then passed on, leavin' me with only me pocket knife and a quart pot to go on with. Of course I was new to the bush, or I couldn't have felt it so much. I met another bloke soon after. He was eatin' a baked goanna he'd picked up. I sez, 'Warm, mate, eh?' He sez, 'Oh, it's been jest nice to-day. Reckon it'll be fairly 'ot to-morrow.'"

FRED J. MILLS, *Square Dinkum*.

EASY!

Digger (to irate sergeant) : I *am* standing to attention, Sergeant. It's my uniform that's at ease.

BORROWED PLUMES

The Digger of the first world war, who pulled many British legs with his tall stories of kangaroo farms, walking-stick farms, bunyip farms and treacle mines, had a strong competitor in the Light Horseman, with his plausible story that the plume in his hat was a kangaroo feather. People who swallowed that story were fair game for the ensuing embellishments.

R. K. PEACOCK in *Salt*, April 20, 1942.

A SCRAP OF PAPER

Probably the best-known Army tale of World War II is the one usually known as "The Piece of Paper." One version of it was written by Sgt. F. Oliver-Seakins, of Queensland, for *Salt*, the journal of the Australian troops.

Sandy was a popular figure in his unit, always cheerful and high-spirited. But once, when he got back from leave, he told his mates he'd met a "beaut. sheila" and was anxious to get out of the Army to marry her. As many others were similarly placed, little notice was taken of Sandy when he "got down in the dumps" occasionally.

One evening he was out with two friends taking a stroll when he saw a piece of paper on the ground ahead of him. He ran forward, picked it up, scrutinised it carefully, and threw it away again, sadly shaking his head. His mates asked him whether he'd expected to find a fiver, but he only said, "It isn't what I'm looking for."

As time went on Sandy became the talk of the section. Every time he saw a piece of paper he picked it up and looked at it carefully; but he always shook his head and threw it away, saying sadly, "That's not what I'm looking for."

It began to be rumoured that Sandy was "troppo." The orderly sergeant thought he might need a break from his usual routine, so he placed him on pioneer fatigue. But one of Sandy's new jobs was to empty the orderly room wastepaper baskets.

His "disease" now really manifested itself. He closely studied each piece of paper in every basket he emptied. And, as usual, the paper wasn't what he was looking for.

Everyone was now thoroughly worried about Sandy.

The climax came when the section was on parade for an inspection by some visiting brass. The Colonel was highly pleased with his tour and was just about to compliment the Major when Sandy stepped forward three paces, picked up a piece of paper that had floated down to the ground in front of him, looked at it sadly, and then returned smartly to his place in the ranks.

Later, Sandy was paraded before the Major, who, nonplussed

at his behaviour, told the orderly sergeant to take him to the Medical Officer.

In the M.O.'s tent Sandy's first action was to pick up a couple of sheets of paper from the table and examine them, putting them back with a shake of his head. The M.O. couldn't get much out of Sandy. All he would say was that he hadn't found what he was looking for.

"Acute neurosis," was the M.O.'s verdict. He recommended that Sandy be sent down to have his case examined by a medical board. This was arranged and Sandy went south.

In due course the board considered his case. Obviously acute neurosis. It was agreed that Sandy should be discharged medically unfit.

As the officer at the G.D.D. handed Sandy his discharge certificate, he remarked with a grin, for he'd heard all about Sandy's case, "Hang on to THAT bit of paper, won't you!"

"By cripes I will!" said Sandy, laughing as he folded up the form and put it safely away in his pocket. "That's the bit of paper I've been looking for!"

Australasian Post, April 26, 1956.

9. THE GREAT AUSTRALIAN ADJECTIVE

"———"

The sunburnt ——— stockman stood
And, in a dismal ——— mood,
  Apostrophised his ——— cuddy;
"The ——— nag's no ——— good,
He couldn't earn his ——— food
  A regular ——— brumby,

              ———!"

He jumped across the ——— horse
And cantered off, of ——— course!
  The roads were bad and ——— muddy;
Said he: "Well, spare me ——— days
The ——— Government's ——— ways
  Are screamin' ——— funny,

              ———!"

He rode up hill, down ——— dale,
The wind it blew a ——— gale,
  The creek was high and ——— floody.
Said he: "The ——— horse must swim,
The same for ——— me and him,
  It's something ——— sickenin',

              ———!"

He plunged into the ——— creek,
The ——— horse was ——— weak,
  The stockman's face a ——— study!
And though the ——— horse was drowned
The ——— rider reached the ground
  Ejaculating: ———!

              ———!"

W. T. GOODGE, *The Bulletin Reciter* Enlarged Edition,
1940.

10. Bush Liars and Tall Yarns

TIM SMITH TELLS A YARN

Tim had been everywhere, seen everything, and killed snakes. Not just ordinary snakes, but reptiles that a man might start at the tail-end at noon, and ride till sunset and not reach the business end of. Once, in Queensland, one of these fabulous snakes embedded its fangs in Tim's cheek. The victim extracted a fang and sent it to the museum in Sydney. We could go and see it when we went back. Anyone could see it. They kept it on view in a glass case. Tim gave the exact measurement of the case, and the name of the man who made it. He was great on details, and never contradicted himself.

The Southern Cross in a shamefaced way burned on his right hand, the Milky Way covered itself with an apologetic mist, and still that mild, bearded man lied on.

"Onct," said Tim Smith, regarding the evening star with apparent reverence, "I was overseer on a cattle station in Monaro. It was owned by an English syndicate, and they went in for stud bulls. It kem a very cold winter, the coldest winter they ever had on Monaro, an' the manager—he was a young feller from t'other side o' Gippsland—he wrote in his report to head orfis 'ow at the last muster we 'ad 500 head of bulls, and how, owin' to the extreme cold, them bulls were all gone back into the mountains, an' he didn't think we'd save 'arf 'em by the time winter was over. Well, the English syndicate got a chill, because them bulls was worth something, each one of 'em worth more'n a 'undred anyhow, an' they wires back: 'Rug bulls at once.'

"When the manager got that telegram he *was* wild. ' 'Ow in 'ell,' sez he, 'am I goin' to rug five hundred mad Monaro bulls!' So he wires back—to put 'em off like: 'Cannot follow instructions; no rugs.'

"But the syndicate 'ad made up their mind them valuable animals 'ad to be saved at any cost, so they wires again: 'Sending rugs, insist on you following instructions.'

"Well, the young cove had a stiddy job, an' he didn't want to lose it. In about a week two twenty 'orse team loads o' bull rugs kem to hand, an' the manager called the hands together, an' sez: 'Boys, get all them bulls in an' we'll rug 'em, if it leads to a war between England an' Australia, an' takes till the day o' Giniril Jedgment to do it. I'll foller instructions,' he sez, 'if it lands the directors in gaol.'

"So we out after them bulls, an' we brought 'em in, every cow's son of 'em—but it took a week. One half-caste cove broke his neck over the job, an' my mate, 'Arry Moffat, got gored in the thigh, an' was crippled for nigh on twelve months. We took 'em one by one, an' got the rugs on 'em somehow, an' when they was all finished, the manager sings out:

" 'Take down the scarlet sliprails, an' let the blankers go!'

"Go!" said Tim Smith, standing up, and waving his patriarchal beard in the beautiful starlight. "Go! There was never anything on earth went like 'em. Some o' the rugs was red and some was blue, an' the whole bush for miles an' miles was just flying streaks o' red bull an' blue bull. An' beller! The bellerin' o' them bulls was enough to turn a man's hair white. Nobody ever 'eard anything like it. You could 'ear 'em for miles an' miles, tearin', an' rippin' an' roarin', an' goin' like mad back for the mountains.

"Well, would *you* believe *me*," concluded Tim, "that when we kem to muster that stock in the spring, we could only find 150 out of the mob, an' only one o' them 'ad kept the rug on 'im, an' 'e was as quiet as a sheep, an' let us ride up to 'im an' 'e put down 'is 'ead, an' sorta asked in a kinder shamefaced way to 'ave it took off, an' that's the gospel truth."

The narrator sucked at his pipe.

Presently the red-faced man asked in a quiet voice:

"What kem o' the rest o' them bulls, Tim?"

" 'Ow do I know?" said Tim Smith. "I reckon it's time to get to bunk."

E. J. BRADY, River Rovers.

THE KICK IN IT

Local farm-hand, to visitors: "See that joker over there, leaning against the bar? Well, he's the biggest liar between Albury and Mildura. He skites to everyone that he can drop-kick a bag of spuds across the River Murray."

Visitor: "He must be a liar!"

Local farm-hand: "Fair dinkum! I'm a flamin' good kick, and it takes me all my time to *punt* one over!"

FENCE-SITTERS

"I've put up fences all over the Commonwealth," old Dan told us, "but the only time I reely enjoyed the job was when me an' a mate was shovin' up half a mile of post-an'-rail down near the bottom end of the South Aus. border. Talk about good sinkin'! Marshy ground it was, with some sort of suction in it; just had to stand your post up, stick your foot in the bottom mortice hole, and give a shove downwards, an' your post was up. Matter er fact, she was just a bit *too* easy. When we brought the boss down to pass the job the mornin' after we finished, blast me if the flamin' fence ain't disappeared completely. A mob of starlin's had camped on it durin' the night an' pushed the whole damn line down to ground level!"

"Ellenvale" in the Sydney Bulletin.

A BUNCH OF TALL YARNS

Coming down in the north train to Adelaide was a carriage-load of smoke, whiskers, and good humour—a typical party of pleasure-seekers from away back. They were holding a sort of competition to find who came from the farthest out. A hatful of half-crowns had been subscribed, the lot, except the hat, to go to the winner. "Wal," said one, "I reckon I come from somewhere well up the map. I come from where the heat waves start. Some mornin's you ken git yer eyebrows singed off on one side of a certain fence up there and lose a leg with frostbite on the other side. Fact." "That's purty good," replied another citizen, as he lit his pipe with an old tandsticker match. "But I can beat that. I hail from where the rain begins. There ain't no rain no further up than where I sprung from. Some days there, rain starts

86

to come down, and there's a bushfire ragin' jest beside it; so that if yer stay in the rain yer git drowned, and if you git out of it yer git burnt." "And 'ow'd you manage to survive?" asked somebody thinking he had the old chap. "Wal, yer see," answered the old sinner, "if I was in the flood I floated about with a whisky cork in me mouth; if I was in the fire I wore me asbestos suit; see!" Well, the yarns got taller and taller, and were beginning to bulge the roof off the carriage, until it came to the last man, a real old stager in a slouch hat that covered him like a small tent, and with a face like a mallee root. "Yes," he remarked. "Yer've all done pretty well, pretty well, but I ken wallop yer. I come from farther out than any of yer. Why, there ain't no flies where I come from (gasps!) but that ain't all. Where I sprung from they —now this is a fact—where I come from the people don't know beer!" He got the half-crowns.

Fred J. Mills, Square Dinkum.

SUNDRY MOSQUITOES

There seems to be a good deal of jealousy in the various districts of South Australia in regard to the size of the mosquitoes they produce. A group of country men were discussing the question in King William Street, Adelaide, one Tuesday evening. "Yas," said a burly northerner, "I ain't seen no skeeters to equal them we 'ave up above. Now, look 'ere; there's an old stagnant dam on my farm, and at night yer ken hear the skeeters splashin' about in the water like birds. In fact, a new 'and I got last week shot a couple of 'em just afore dark one night, thinkin' they was ducks." "That's nothing," observed a thin, sunburnt little man with a squint; "over round Lake Wangary, on the west coast, yer can 'ear 'em goin' to roost on the fences at night. They make the wires twang like banjos; straight iron." "Wal," said a lanky individual, whose chief adornments were bell-bottomed trousers and an enormous tent of a hat, "yer wanter go along the Murray for them insects. On that strip of wetness yer git 'em big and good. 'Tain't nothin' jest 'fore sundown to see a moskeeto dive into the Murray and come up and fly away with a 20-lb. cod. They never miss 'em!" The last man now chipped in—a stout, dark person in a cork fly net. "Sorry to 'ear yer've got sech small miskeeters in your districts—very sorry, indeed. Now, if yer want real sizeable miskeeters jest go across to Yorke Peninsula. They seem to fatten up wonderful on Cornishmen. I was campin' over there in a tent last week, and about midnight I was woke up by a hummin' noise, like a motor car doin' a record, and next minute a small miskeeter settled on me chest. "Ere,' I yelled to me mate, 'give us a 'and; there's a miskeeter dropped on me.' 'Well, knock 'im off,' 'e sez. "Ow ken I,' sez I, 'when 'e's got both me 'ands pinned down!' " The meeting adjourned.

ibid.

11. Bush Directions

ACROSS THE STREET

Traveller: "Is there a garage anywhere near here, mate? I've done my fan-belt."

Bush publican: "Yer might get one at Wallace's service station across the street."

Traveller: "I can't see any service station. There's nothing but saltbush."

Publican: "I forgot to mention—the streets are thirty miles wide out here. And if you have no luck at the service station, you might try my next-door neighbour. He's only forty miles along the street."

GETTING TO HOGAN'S PUB

Traveller: "Could you direct me to Hogan's pub, mate?"

Local farmer: "Go as fur as the Methodist church over there be them pine trees. Turn to the right down towards Dingo Gully until you come to the school, then turn left and follow the track as fur as Alby Ryan's shack. That'll bring you on to the main road. Turn left along the road and keep on goin' for another three mile."

Traveller: "That's clear enough. Where does that bring me to?"

Local farmer: "Right back here."

Traveller (perplexed): "But what in the name of Larry do I come back here for?"

Local farmer: "So as I kin give you the rest of the directions. If I tried to tell 'em all at once, you'd only git real confused."

A CHANGE OF AIR

On the wallaby in western N.S.W., a sundowner came upon the crumbling remains of a hut in a desolate location. Tacked to the door was a still legible notice:

"Twenty miles from a neighbour, 40 miles from a post-office, 50 miles from a railway, 50 miles from a pub, 10 miles from wood and water, 1,000 miles from a city. Whoever finds this homestead can have it. The missus wants to see life. She has left for the city. So have I."

LEON STONE in the Melbourne *Argus*, September 3, 1949.

STONE THE CROWS!

Truck driver to outback farmer: "How far is it to Wagga, mate —as the crow flies?"

Farmer: "Blowed if I know, sport. The flamin' crows never leave here!"

BLACK LOGIC

Swagman: "How far is it to the next water-hole, Jacky?"
Aborigine: "How you knowem my name Jacky?"
Swagman (winking at his mate): "I guessem."
Aborigine: "Well guessem where plurry water-hole am!"

12. DAD AND DAVE

EARLY RISING

In darkest Muddleup, the Australian standard week is still un-known. Crack o' dawn is the local alarm clock, and the evening star is the beacon which calls a halt to the day's toil. His first day on the farm seemed more like a week to Claude, the English immigrant, and as he staggered home from the top paddock, he said to the boss:

"By jove, ye know, the sun beat us in to-night!"

"Yairs," answered old Bill, crisply, "but we'll beat it out in the morning."

RUNNING LATE

New dairy hand (awakened out of deep sleep): "Yes, I'm the new hand. What's the idea waking me up like this?"

Dave: "Cripes, it's twenty past three. You're runnin' late. Better step on it."

Ten minutes later the new hand is dressed and out in the yard.

Dave: "Now keep well back against the hedge with that lamp, mate. You don't want to let the old man see you startin' work so flamin' late!"

DAVE AND MABEL

Mabel: "Isn't it a beautiful moonlight night, Dave?"

Dave: "Yairs, Mabel. Cripes, a bloke's a silly coot not to be out after possums on a night like this."

THE LONG VIEW

Dave was paying a visit to the Waybacks, who had just had the telephone installed. The phone rang and Dave went to answer it. Presently he returned to the Waybacks and said, "Cripes, them telephone blokes are silly coots. They just rang up to say it's a long distance from Sydney!"

DESPERATE REMEDIES

Mum: "Dave's gone and broke his leg, Dad!"

Dad: "D'yer think we ought to shoot 'im?"

DAVE GETS A "TALKING-TO"

Dave, dissatisfied with life on the farm, was leaving home to enlist in the permanent army.

Mum, with thoughts of her 35-year-old son exposed to the pitfalls of the big city and the iniquities of the army, told Dad he'd better give the boy a "talking-to."

Out behind the dairy Dad coughed out his lecture:

"Be careful of that there liquor, Dave."

"Aw, I never touch it, Dad."

Dad proceeded with a tirade against gambling, but Dave protested he'd never wagered a penny in his life.

"Well," said Dad, "about women, now. They're a real trap for young fellers and you can land in a lot of trouble over them."

"Cripes, Dad," said Dave, "that's one thing I never do—go out with women!"

Dad went back to Mum looking rather dubious and thoughtful.

"Did you tell him?" asked Mum.

"Yairs," said Dad, "but yer needn't worry, Mum. I don't think the army'll have him. The boy's a half-wit!"

13. BUSHMEN'S DOGS

"MY BEST SHEEP DOG"

The recent floods in the north-west corner washed down a lot of characters. Our correspondent who spent an idyllic week around that part of the New South Wales border was amazed at the blooming of what was always imagined to be desert.

One day there would be a plain of saltbush and red sand, the next a sheet of water as far as the eye could see.

One morning, arising from a heavy sleep, he walked to the balcony and was confronted with what seemed like a muddy ocean at his feet. More astounding was a sheep dog's tail which protruded above the water like a periscope on a submarine. It moved, firstly about a hundred yards to the right and stopped. Then suddenly it moved about fifty yards to the left. An old character was watching from the corner of the balcony. Said our correspondent: "What's the matter with the dog? Is he drowning?"

The old man turned up his lip in a derisive sneer. "Nothing of the kind," he said slowly. "That's my best sheep dog. I told him to bring a mob of sheep in and come hell or high water, he's bringin' 'em in."

From *Holiday and Travel*, April, 1949.

THE PUMPER'S DOG

Outback in Queensland, there's an old pumper, who has only

a dog and a mouth organ for company. They say he can't play the mouth organ because the dog doesn't like it.

PAT

Another bird of passage was a most lovable old man, an Oxford scholar. With a beautiful voice and courtly manner, for some reason best known to himself he never settled, drifting on and on. He was poor, made no bones about it. His idea of Nirvana was a soft job with a high salary.

He had a beautiful collie which he called Pat. The two adored each other. Two lonely souls adrift in an alien sphere, they kept close together, the dog sprawled at the man's feet always, the man continually glancing about to make sure that Pat was there.

He liked to keep Pat close to him when travelling, and for that reason tramped everywhere. Once, having been offered a job which he fancied, he was about to board a train, and had bought two tickets—one for himself, one for Pat.

To his indignation, the guard refused to let the dog go in the carriage with him. Pat must travel as other dogs did—in the box provided. He cancelled the trip and sent word to his new employer that he was walking.

"Good gad, man, d'you expect my dog to travel in that?" he barked.

E. M. ENGLAND in the Melbourne *Sun*, May 8, 1948.

14. IRISH-AUSTRALIAN

THE PROSPECTOR'S TOAST

"I give you the toast of the prospectors. The prospector goes out into the music of the silent bush, with his pick in one hand, his water bag in the other hand, and his life in the other. He goes into the bush, where the hand of man has never set foot, and let me tell you, he don't come back again until he have left his bones to be picked clean by the crows and dingoes."

RANDOLPH BEDFORD, *Naught to Thirty-three.*

"TOMMY" BENT'S PANEGYRIC

When Bent died his panegyric was uttered by Paddy Reynolds, mine host of the Cathedral Hotel, Melbourne.

"Say what you like about Sir Thomas Bent, but he was a man. He mightn't have much honesty if there was big money to be got, and he liked his gin and tonic strong an' fraquint, an' a rovin' eye for wimmen, but outside them matters he was as pure as the drivellin' snow."*

ibid.

---

* Sir Thomas Bent, Premier of Victoria (1904-1909).

COMFORT

Passer-by: "That drain pipe's a bit hard for a pillow, isn't it?"
Swagman: "It's all right. I've stuffed it full of straw."

ABSENTEEISM

I still regard as an excellent example of the bull the words of an Irish-Australian who started an address to his employees on absenteeism with "Looking about me I see a number of faces that are not here; what I have to say applies particularly to those who are absent, and I hope they will listen attentively and make a note of every word."

From the *Bulletin,* November 11, 1949.

PART THREE

SUPERSTITIONS AND FALLACIES

Young Australians were once taught that Australian trees cast no shade—that the edges of the leaves were presented to the sun to avoid the heat of the cruel luminary; that Australian flowers had no scent, and Australian birds no song; that the stones of Australian cherries grew on the outside of the fruit, that the bees had no sting, and that the dogs did not bark. In those days a gentleman with a military title improved upon the then popular list of contradictions by asserting that in Australia the compass points to the south, the valleys are cold, the mountain-tops warm, the eagles are white, and so on.

E. J. BANFIELD, *Confessions of a Beachcomber.*

COMMENT

MOST of the superstitions current at one time or another in Australia have derived from overseas and are familiar in a number of countries. Black cats, horseshoes, ladders—such objects of superstitious belief need no elaboration here.

Those I have included are with one or two exceptions (superstitions about the opal, for instance) peculiarly Australian.

Dr. Charles Fenner in his informative and entertaining books, *Gathered Moss, Mostly Australian* and *Bunyips and Billabongs* has devoted some space to this fascinating subject, and I recommend them to the reader for this and for many other reasons.

SIR HENRY HAYES AND THE IRISH SOIL

There is a singular story current respecting him (Sir Henry Hayes), which is implicitly believed by the more ignorant part of the old colonists, to the effect that finding his place at Vaucluse much infested with snakes, and firmly believing that these reptiles could not exist on Irish soil, he sent home for several casks of that article, which he scattered over the place. His faith in his native land and its patron was amply rewarded, for, says the story, a snake has never been seen at Vaucluse from that time to this.

DAVID BLAIR, *History of Australasia.*

CRAIG'S DREAM

Superstitions, dreams, omens and hoodoos have a big part in the pattern of the Melbourne Cup. Some of the stories, retold many times, have become legends associated with the great race.

Probably the best-known story is set in 1870 when, it is claimed, Ballarat hotelkeeper Walter Craig dreamed some weeks before the race that his horse Nimblefoot had won the Melbourne Cup.

He was troubled by the fact that Nimblefoot's rider carried black armbands. Nimblefoot won the Cup, but Craig did not see the race. He had died a few days earlier.

THE TOWN THAT LOST

In 1891 came the Cup which, according to local reports, broke a Gippsland township. Someone dreamed that a bullock won the

Cup! The nearest the citizens could get to it was a horse called Oxide. They put their shirts on it. Oxide ran fifth to Malvolio after being well placed all the way.

J. A. FEELY in the Melbourne *Sun*, November 3, 1947.

BUSH SUPERSTITIONS OF NEW SOUTH WALES

Nobody tarries long in the north-western regions of N.S.W. without hearing tales of the Darling pea and the gem of White Cliffs (the opal—Ed.), arising mostly from the queer superstitions that cling to each, and especially to the flower.

The Darling pea is one of the most beautiful of wild flowers, but, despite its attractiveness, it is regarded as a pest by stock-owners on account of the maddening effect it is said to have on horses that eat it. . . .

"Darling pea" is a common colloquialism outback for madness. I heard it a thousand times before I saw the plant. It was applied to any eccentric person, especially one who was considered a "bit barmy." Even a foolish act or statement sometimes provoked the damaging remark, "He's got the Darling pea."

The superstitious left the flower alone, for there was a saying that anyone who picked it would not leave the Darling river for seven years. Instances were told by old residents of people who had gone there with no intention of staying; they had scoffed at the superstition and picked the flower, and through one circumstance or another they were anchored there for the allotted period.

One was a visitor from Sydney, who picked the flower at a bush picnic. On the way back to town he was injured by a fall from his horse, and went to hospital. Then he fell in love with a nurse, whom he subsequently married. Her father, a stock agent, then took him into partnership. Business was booming, and it was just seven years after the picnic when he returned to Sydney.

At times bunches of the flowers decorated the camps of the whalers, who had no wish to leave the river. One said of the nutritious Darling lily, whose bulbs make excellent flour or arrowroot, that it sustained those who were kept there by the Darling pea.

The superstition connected with opal, the belief that it is unlucky, is world-wide, and seems to have arisen from a simple and natural peculiarity of that mineral.

Opal is affected by extremes of temperature, so that when worn for a length of time in a hot atmosphere, and then taken into a cold atmosphere, it is liable to drop out of its gold setting through contraction. It was considered an unlucky stone because it was "always getting lost" through dropping out. According to an old digger, "that's all there's to it."

The belief that it brought bad luck to the wearer originated through a misunderstanding of that fact. But I have known many men in the western regions who would not wear opal, even though they delved for it at White Cliffs and Lightning Ridge (which got its name from another superstition—that thunderbolts dropped there during storms), and hoped to get enough to make a fortune; and they would quote instances of dead men being found by the track who were wearing opal.

"Haven't more dead men been found wearing trousers than opal?" one of the superstitious gougers was asked by a cynical listener.

"Yes, I suppose so," he replied.

"Then it must be the trousers that's unlucky," said the other. "Better leave yours off next time you set out on a journey."

E. S. SORENSON in the *Australian Worker*, January 11, 1928.

TOADS THAT POISON FOWLS

Belief that cane toads poison fowls in North Queensland is a fallacy. Many on the Atherton Tableland allowed fowls and ducks to gorge themselves with toads, but it was found they suffered no after-effects, excepting sometimes a duck which choked on a large one. Hens kept to the small fry. The toads did a lot of damage by dying in wells and dams, thus polluting the water, but it was noticeable that when they made their appearance in a locality the snakes seemed to disappear. Old hands reckon the toads emit a peculiar odour, repulsive to snakes.

THE BIRTH OF THE KANGAROO

There is a never-ending argument about this. The folk of the outback, but not all of them, believe that the kangaroo is "born on the teat." The teats are in the pouch. One can usually "get a bite" from the men of the back country by stating that kangaroos are born just like any other mammal. They will say: "On the teat for mine, every time." But they are quite wrong, and their belief that the young kangaroo comes out through the nipple of the mother's teat is anatomically ridiculous.

CHARLES FENNER, *Gathered Moss*.

SNAKE FALLACIES

Of the many fallacies about snakes, still current in parts of Australia, the most widespread is that these reptiles frequently eat their young. They do this, according to popular belief, to protect the young from impending danger.

There are farmers who will state emphatically that snakes can milk cows. Vernon Wheatley tries to find an explanation for the origin of this fallacy. "A farmer apparently found a snake beside a dry cow. Three and three equal seven; therefore the snake milked the cow. To do so, the snake would have to hold on with its fangs. No cow would permit this indignity. Anyway, if the snake was poisonous the cow would die."

Many bushmen believe that the death adder—often misnamed the deaf adder—injects poison into its victim through its tail.

Another erroneous belief is that snakes will not cross a rope. In my youth in Gippsland I remember bush workers circling their tents with a length of rope at night to ensure a sleep undisturbed by the reptiles.

A fabulous snake which still persists in spite of science, is the "hoop snake." This creature, still "seen" in some country places, forms itself into an upright circle by taking tail in mouth, and thus disguised, bowls itself along like a child's hoop.

The Editor.

OLD-TIME COUNTRY CURES AND BUSH REMEDIES

Venice Turps was used as a poultice for "drawing boils, etc." It was said of Venice Turps that it would pull rusty nails out of mulga planks.

For rheumatism, one widely known cure was to wind ten strands of copper wire round the wrist like a bangle. Another cure was to carry a potato round in the pocket. As it gradually withered it was supposed to "suck the acid out."

Goanna Oil was a popular remedy for many complaints. It was thought to be very penetrating, and many bushmen believed that is even seeped through the glass of the bottle containing it.

"Me blood's crook" was how country folk frequently diagnosed their minor ailments. For "crook blood" a tablespoonful of treacle and sulphur was often taken. Another cure was boiled nettle-juice; another, home-made beer, the stronger the better.

For backaches and chills, a red flannel belt was worn.

Vinegar was a universal remedy. A vinegar compress cured

headaches, and a teaspoon of vinegar put acid into you—if you needed acid. It was also used as a gargle for sore throats.

Garlic in the shoes was said to stop coughs, and a cut-up onion, bound to the soles of the feet would reduce a fever.

Apart from Venice Turps, various poultices were recommended for inflammations, etc. Some of the more popular poultices were made from bread soaked in hot water, potatoes, cow dung, bran or pollard and soap.

For festered fingers, the bushman often resorted to breaking a hole in a raw egg, pushing the finger into the yolk, and then bandaging egg and finger together.

For persistent sore throats, a dirty sock, wrapped round the neck, was believed to work wonders.

Cobwebs were supposed to stop bleeding if applied to an open wound. Cuts were bound with brown paper, after a liberal application of Friar's Balsam.

The cure for cramps was to tie black wool around each leg, or pieces of camphor behind each knee.

Brandy and salt was supposed to have the power of restoring the hair, though sheep dip was held by some in the outback to be much better.

The old-time bushman's medicine chest invariably contained these four items:

Perry's Painkiller (said to be better than Worcestershire sauce for curing a hangover), Holloway's Pills, Holloway's Ointment and Friar's Balsam.

ALAN MARSHALL, Unpublished notebooks; by kind
permission.

PART FOUR

PLACE LORE

COMMENT

FOLLOWING one of his many expeditions out from Sydney Cove,
Governor Phillip wrote: "We had a fine view of the mountains
inland, the northernmost of which I named Caermarthen Hills
and the southernmost Lansdowne Hills. A mountain between I
called Richmond Hill. . . ."

The uninspired lead given by Phillip in the naming of places
was faithfully followed by officialdom in succeeding generations,
with the result that the map of Australia is liberally scattered
with reminders of the British Isles—Newcastle, Windsor, Malvern,
Liverpool, St. Kilda, and so on *ad infinitum*.

Even when a little originality was applied to place-naming, the
result was not always impressive. Dr. Harris, an ex-naval surgeon
who came out in 1790, happened to be present at a court martial
"when a charge was read referring to the 12th ultimo. It should
have read the 12th inst. He was the only man present who understood the distinction, and was so pleased about it he called his
home 'Ultimo Place'."* Ultimo still lingers on as the name of a
Sydney suburb.

* A. E. Martin: *One Thousand and More Place Names in New South Wales.*

Dr. John Dunmore Lang, revolting against this repetitive dreariness and lack of imagination, put his thoughts into verse in 1824:

'Twas said of Greece two thousand years ago,
    That every stone i' the land had got a name.
Of New South Wales too, men will soon say so;
    But every stone there seems to get the same.
"Macquarie" for a name is all the go:
    The old Scotch Governor was fond of fame,
Macquarie Street, Place, Port, Fort, Town, Lake, River:
    "Lachlan Macquarie, Esquire, Governor" for ever!

I like the native names, as Parramatta,
    And Illawarra, and Wooloomooloo;
Nandowra, Woogarora, Bulkamatta,
    Tomah, Toongabbie, Mittagong, Meroo;
Buckobble, Cumleroy, and Coolangatta,
    The Warragumby, Bargo, Burradoo;
Cookbundoon, Carrabaiga, Wingecarribee,
    The Wollondilly, Yurumbon, Bungarribee.

I hate your Goulburn Downs and Goulburn Plains,
    And Goulburn River and the Goulburn Range,
And Mount Goulburn and Goulburn Vale! One's brains
    Are turned with Goulburns! Vile scorbutic mange
For immortality! Had I the reins
    Of government a fortnight, I would change
These Downing Street appellatives, and give
    The country names that should deserve to live.

Yes! let some badge of liberty appear
    On every mountain and on every plain
Where Britain's power is known, or far or near,
    That freedom there may have an endless reign!
Then though she die, in some revolving year,
    A race may rise to make her live again!
The future slave may lisp the patriot's name
    And his breast kindle with a kindred flame!*

Lang's idea of naming places in honour of heroes or episodes in the struggle for freedom is a good one. I am reminded that in

* From "Colonial Nomenclature" by John Dunmore Lang. There are six stanzas in the poem, the last two having been omitted.

1913, when there was much public discussion about a name for the Commonwealth capital city, the North Melbourne branch of the Australian Labor Party wrote to Andrew Fisher, Labor Prime Minister, suggesting that it be called "Eureka"—"in order to perpetuate the memory of that historical event which in 1854 at the Eureka Stockade struck a blow at military tyranny, and established democratic rule in Australia." Nothing more was heard of the suggestion.

On the whole, official place-namers have been cautious or time-serving, inspired by nostalgic thoughts of "home" or merely dull-witted. Not always so, of course. Surveyor J. G. W. Wilmott of Victoria had the happy gift of choosing names that were apt and sometimes witty.

But it was the ordinary people, apart altogether from the Aborigines, who found most inspiration in naming Australian places. Judge Advocate David Collins noted "a happiness that is sometimes visible in the allusions of the lower order of people." Who but convicts could have thought up such a name as "Pinchgut"? That little outcrop of rock in Sydney Harbour, known officially as Fort Denison, was famed for hangings and for hunger from the very earliest months of settlement. Convicts who had stolen food or other items from the supply stores were sent to this island prison either to be executed or to be put on a term of bread and water. Out of human misery, and an irrepressible sense of humour, the name Pinchgut was born. Governor Phillip called it Rock Island. But it is as Pinchgut that the people know it to-day.

Australian nomenclature was greatly enriched with the arrival of thousands of immigrants when the gold rushes started in 1851. The colour and vigour of that period are expressed in many of the local place names.

But old habits do not die easily. Surely the good Dr. Dunmore Lang must have turned in his grave in March, 1952, when the South Oakleigh District Progress Association (the area is a part of the Melbourne metropolis) requested the Oakleigh City Council to re-name postal district S.E.13, "Beechcroft." "It was explained," says the *Oakleigh and Caulfield Times*, "that the name had been selected because, while it is devoid of association with names of people, places, or clubs, it was considered very British in character."

1. PLACE NAMES

FISHER'S GHOST CREEK

Soon I came to a tiny bridge and a creek which is, perhaps, the only creek in the world to bear the name of a ghost—Fisher's Ghost Creek. Only in heavy rain could it now bear any resemblance to a real creek, for time and erosion had filled its bed with a mass of jumbled rubbish and reedy mud; at this dry time a child could have jumped across it. Nevertheless, this creek is associated with one of the strangest stories in the annals of Australian crime, the story of how a ghost brought a murderer to justice (or so they say).

Fisher's Ghost had its origin in 1826, soon after the corporeal Frederick Fisher had departed from the pain and sorrow of this world. In the intervening century and more, it has become the subject of countless articles, a fantastic range of legends, and a film. The framework of the story differs little from scores of similarly sordid and undramatic crimes . . . the story of how Frederick Fisher, then an emancipist, but formerly a convict, lived in a little hut at Campbelltown with a man named George Worrall; how Fisher disappeared about the middle of 1826, while Worrall took over all his possessions and accounted for it by telling the good folk of Campbelltown that Fisher had left the colony. But it is here that the story becomes unique in the criminal calendar, with the introduction of an unexplained excursion into the supernatural.

In October, 1826, a man named Farley was driving in his horse and trap one evening over a bridge where the present bridge stands (though remember the details are encrusted with legend, one account being that he was driving past a paddock which Fisher had formerly owned, though this was also near the bridge, and so the differing legends broadly agree, while the essentials stand out with curious clarity), when his horse jibbed; then, "frozen stiff with horror," Farley saw, sitting on the top rail (either of the bridge or the fence) the gleaming, unsubstantial, ghostly figure of a man whom he recognised as Fisher.

When he finally shook himself free of the paralysis induced by this luminous apparition, Farley went home convinced he had received a sign from another world, and that Fisher's disappearance was due to a migration not of his body but merely of his soul. Next day, after bracing himself to meet the inevitable jeers of the unbelieving, Farley betook himself to the local constable, who was sufficiently impressed to accompany Farley to the spot. There, in the broad light of normal day, a close inspection disclosed a curious, though possibly quite irrelevant, fact—there were bloodstains on the rail exactly at the spot where Farley swore he had seen Fisher's ghost.

One thing led to another—possibly there was a shadow of suspicion already in the police mind—so finally a black-tracker was brought to the scene, and told to find what he could.

The tracker worked slowly along the banks of the creek, until he came to a spot where he declared he could smell "white man's fat."

A little farther along, the now eager and almost-convinced police party came to a fairly deep pool, where, after a bit of dragging, they found the months-dead body of Frederick Fisher. Soon afterwards George Worrall was apprehended, questioned, confessed, tried, and hanged—hanged, the legend says, on the village green where now the children play, and the roses nod to the evening winds.

Apparently the ghost was never officially mentioned at the trial —it is a nice point of law whether a ghost is competent to give evidence, or be used in evidence—though Worrall's confession made any serious attempt at independent evidence unnecessary; but Fisher's Ghost was the unseen witness present in everybody's mind, a dramatic, if shadowy, figure of retribution and justice.

WARREN DENNING, *The Road to Canberra.*

OLD-TIME BENDIGO GULLIES

A reader has assured me that the following places were once hives of industry in Bendigo, but are now—many of them—just names. Here they are: The Pup's Hill; Emu Point; Beelzebub Gully; Snob's Hill; Brandy Gully; Fiddler's Green; Sand Fly Gully; Psalm Singing Gully; One Eye; Let Him Sleep Gully; Red Jacket Gully; Butcher's Hill; Derwent Gully; Pinchgut; Elysian Flat; Robinson Crusoe Gully (now Crusoe); Adelaide Hill; Solomon's Hill; Drunken Scotchmen's Gully; Dead Dog Gully; and Tin Pot. I might say that on receipt of this information I made it my business to verify the facts and found them correct. However, I also found something else, and this was an old-time example of judicial wit. The paragraph was dated 1860, and appeared in the Bendigo *Advertiser*. I quote it for you.

"In the case concerned, evidence concerning shares and mining companies was being given, and the names of Specimen Hill, Tin Pot and Dead Dog companies were referred to; whereupon His Honour facetiously suggested that the 'Tin Pot' should be tied to the 'Dead Dog's' tail. A person of unsound mind here laughed, and was taken out of court immediately, suffering from an hysterical affection."

"Observer" in the Bendigo *Advertiser*, June 11, 1949.

BIG JACK

Few men have a mountain named after them. Jack Mountain, Southern N.S.W., was named after big Jack Heydon, claimed as the local strong man. Many stories are told of his amazing feats. He was not a showman and did not perform these feats for wagers, but just in the ordinary way of living. He once carried a sack of flour from Eden to Bega, about 50 miles, without putting it down. Big Jack mountain barred the way from Monaro to the coast for many years because it was considered impossible to put a road over it, but a road was built—one of the steepest roads in Australia.

BREAD AND DRIPPING VALLEY

In the Parkes (N.S.W.) district there is a deserted gold mining area that for many years was known as Bread and Dripping Valley. It received that name because the miners there were having such bad luck that they lived for months on bread and dripping. Bread, dripping and possibly a roasted onion was once known as "the fossicker's dinner."

SOME VICTORIAN PLACE NAMES

Surveyor Wilmott's habit of punning was responsible for some quaint names. He is said to have named such places as Katamatite (because an earlier settler driving home drunk kept asking his wife, "Kate, am I tight?"); Miepoll (after a police magistrate who had a habit of saying "My Poll says this . . ." and "My Poll says that . . ."); Willaura, Dundonnell, Dunworthy, and others. He might even have been responsible for naming Bandiana, named after a bandy-legged lubra named Anna.

Adavale owes its name to Mrs. Ada Stevens, who lost her veil when crossing a creek there in 1870. Her husband shouted "There goes Ada's veil" as the veil landed on the water and was lost. It sounds incredible that a place should get its name from such an unimportant incident.

Chewko derives its name from the Chewko Tobacco Company, and Drayton from the simple fact that many drays were seen there in the early days. Ravenshoe was so named because someone found a copy of Henry Kingsley's *Ravenshoe* in a tree there; while Greymare owes its name to an old grey mare which used to graze about the locality.

Tinaroo is a corruption of an exclamation by a man named Atherton when he discovered tin there. Throwing his hat in the air he shouted "Tin, hurroo!" That reminds me of a little New South Wales town in which I once lived. This town was called Candelo, and is said to have been named because a man lost in the bush saw a light in a settler's window and shouted, "Candle, oh!" Why he did not shout "Kerosene lamp, oh!" is not recorded.

A. T. in the Melbourne *Age,* June 2, 1945.

2. LOCAL ALLUSIONS

ROCKHAMPTON AND THE THREE S'S

Rockhampton was known as the town of three S's—sin, sweat and sorrow.

MOUNT MORGAN AND THE FOUR G'S

Mount Morgan might be known in the mining world for its once-rich gold mines, but old-timers speak of it as the town of four G's—girls, goats, galahs, and glass bottles.

BOURKE—WHERE YOU NEVER GET SICK

You never get sick in Bourke. It's too hot for the germs to live.

THE NEVER-NEVER

Beyond the farthest Gov'ment tank, and past the farthest bore—
The Never-Never, No Man's Land, No More, and Nevermore—
Beyond the Land o' Break-o'-Day, and Sunset and the Dawn. . . .

HENRY LAWSON, "Marshall's Mate."

OLD JACK ROBERTSON ON VICTORIA

New South Wales and Victoria have laughed at each other, mostly with good humour but sometimes in a spirit of animosity from very early times, but especially following the separation of Victoria from the mother colony in 1851.

Sir John Robertson, N.S.W. politician, said of the southern colony:

"Victoria! What the hell do I care for Victoria? A b—— country to the south of the Murray inhabited by b—— savages!"

"HAPPILY . . . NOT A VICTORIAN."

David Gaunson, M.L.A., was briefed to defend Ned Kelly at his trial in Melbourne. The Age, Melbourne newspaper, was politically opposed to Gaunson, and took the opportunity of attacking him in a leading article, for "prostituting his profession" by defending the famous bushranger. See Max Brown's Australian Son.

"Has he not disgraced his position as Chairman of Committees of the Legislative Assembly of Victoria? . . . Looked at critically there is not an incident of Kelly's career to plead a passing word of pity. . . . Happily, Mr. Gaunson is not a Victorian, his instincts having been formed amid the associations of the sister colony of N.S.W.—a fact which should be remembered by those distinguished strangers who will doubtless carry the story of his adventures with them to Europe.

TAKING SIDES

Victoria, originally a portion of N.S.W., was not created a separate State until 1851. Up to that time, and even after, distinctions were made between those who lived on the Melbourne *side* of the colony and those on the Sydney *side*. Thus, in *Robbery Under Arms,* Boldrewood alludes to "Our side of the country" (i.e., the Sydney side) and again to "Melbourne . . . we all liked that side of the country." Although modern usage has tended to limit the use of *Sydneysider* to describe a resident or native of Sydney, its correct use is to describe any person in N.S.W.

SIDNEY J. BAKER, *The Australian Language.*

MELBOURNE—PRO AND CONTRA

Melbourne, Queen City of the South.

Life does not simply stand still of a Melbourne Sunday; it falls down into a stupor.

Melbourne, City of the Cabbage Garden (old saying).
Melbourne, the City of Dreadful Knights.
Melbourne, the only cemetery that's lit up at night.
Melbourne's Yarra, the only river that flows upside down.

Racing pressman, Ossie Imber, was bemoaning the incessant rain in Melbourne during the Cups carnival.
"You ought to be here in winter," remarked one of the locals.
"What?" Imber asked. "You don't mean that people live here all the year!"

POPULAR LABELS

Queenslanders were, or are, frequently called Canecutters, Bananalanders, Banana-eaters.
New South Wales folk—Cornstalks, Sydneysiders (both becoming obsolete).
Victorians—Yarra-yabbies, Cabbage-patchers, Cabbage-landers. (The latter two are almost obsolete.)
Tasmanians—Tassies, Apple-islanders, Vandemonians (almost obsolete), Mountain-devils, Taswegians.
South Australians—Crow-eaters.
Western Australians—Sandgropers, Groperlanders, Westralians.
Northern Territory folk—Territorians.

"THE PLACE FOR A VILLAGE"

John Batman's excursions through the area which was eventually to become Melbourne, led him to explore the lower reaches of the Yarra River. The entries in his journal for June, 1835 contain a phrase which has long since passed into our folklore:

"The boat went up the large river I have spoken of, which comes from the east and, I am glad to state, about six miles up found the river all good water and very deep. This will be the place for a Village."

THE BEECHWORTH HORSESHOES

One of the most valuable pairs of horseshoes with which any horse was ever shod was that attached to Jorrocks, a prize show pony owned by Tinker Brown's circus. The circus was in the Beechworth district during the goldfields fever in 1858, and Brown hit upon a novel advertising idea.

A pair of horseshoes made out of gold—weighing 7 oz. 4 dwt. each—were hammered on the front hooves of Jorrocks, the pony. They were made so that they could be detached and put on again for each performance. Regular weighing proved that little weight was lost from them.

When Tinker Brown died, the circus was disbanded. His widow preserved the famous golden horseshoes, hidden in a specially made mat, on her Wagga (N.S.W.) home's front doorstep. Many years later she decided to sell them, with gold prices soaring, and the Mint paid £96/16/- for them. Tinker Brown's grave is in Wagga Cemetery.

N. WINDSOR in the Melbourne *Argus*, July 22, 1950.

THE MAN WHO RODE THE BULL THROUGH WAGGA

The emphasis on the "ah" has always been enjoyed by the citizens of Wagga Wagga.

The saying of the man who rode the bull through Wagga is just as familiar to the people of the country as is the saying of the dog on the tucker box.

Many years ago a very prominent and respected citizen was invited to open the Wagga Wagga agricultural show. In the course of his speech he declared that the fertility of the Murrumbidgee River would some day build a great city in Wagga-Wog-ah!

> Years ago, back ever so far,
> A bull was ridd'n through Wagga-Wog-ah;
> The fact was known in Tar-cut-ta,
> And cooeed to Car-pen-tar-iar.
> And round the world wherever you are
> You'll hear of the bull of Wagga-Wog-ah,
> How Bidgee Bill with great eclat
> Rode the famous bull through Wagga-Wog-ah.

Chorus:

> So we'll toss a toast in the Widow's bar:
> To the jockey and bull of Wagga-Wog-ah!
> Wagga-Wog-ah, Wagga-Wog-ah,
> Give three cheers for Wagga-Wog-ah.
> Hip-pip-pip, Hip-Hoorah!
> Shake it up for Wagga-Wog-ah,
> For beautiful girls—oh, what a star!—
> Fill 'em again for Wagga-Wog-ah!

In those days of bullocks and drays,
Before they came with a motor car,
Happy we were, Tra-la-la-la,
Ere the train rumbled to Tumba-rum-bah.
Happy we were, Tra-la-la-la,
When teamsters camped in Wagga-Wog-ah;
Before the streets were smeared with tar,
The bull was ridden through Wagga-Wog-ah.

JACK MOSES, *Nine Miles from Gundagai.*

THE DOG ON THE TUCKER BOX

Air: "Camooweal Races"

I'm used to punchin' bullock teams
   Across the hills and plains,
I've teamed outback this forty years
   In blazin' droughts and rains,
I've lived a heap of troubles down
   Without a bloomin' lie,
But I can't forget what happened me
   Nine miles from Gundagai.

'Twas gettin' dark, the team got bogged,
   The axle snapped in two,
I lost me matches and me pipe,
   So what was I to do?
The rain came on, 'twas bitter cold,
   And hungry too was I,
And the dorg sat in the tucker box
   Nine miles from Gundagai.

Some blokes I knows has stacks o' luck
   No matter 'ow they fall,
But there was me, Lor' luv a duck,
   No blessed luck at all.
I couldn't make a pot o' tea,
   Nor get me trousers dry,
And the dorg sat in the tucker box
   Nine miles from Gundagai.

I can forgive the blinkin' team,
   I can forgive the rain,

I can forgive the dark an' cold,
    An' go through it again.
I can forgive me rotten luck,
    But hang me till I die,
I can't forgive that plurry dorg,
    Nine miles from Gundagai.*

Traditional, collected by the Sydney Folklore Society.

THE MAN FROM SNOWY RIVER

There was movement at the station, for the word had passed
    around
    That the colt from old Regret had got away,
And had joined the wild bush horses—he was worth a thousand
    pound,
    So all the cracks had gathered to the fray.
All the tried and noted riders from the stations near and far
    Had mustered at the homestead overnight,
For the bushmen love hard riding where the wild bush horses are,
    And the stock-horse snuffs the battle with delight.

There was Harrison, who made his pile when Pardon won the
    cup,
    The old man with his hair as white as snow;
But few could ride beside him when his blood was fairly up—
    He would go wherever horse and man could go.
And Clancy of the Overflow came down to lend a hand,
    No better horseman ever held the reins;
For never horse could throw him while the saddle-girths would
    stand—
    He learnt to ride while droving on the plains.

And one was there, a stripling on a small and weedy beast;
    He was something like a racehorse undersized,
With a touch of Timor pony—three parts thoroughbred at least—
    And such as are by mountain horsemen prized.
He was hard and tough and wiry—just the sort that won't say die—
    There was courage in his quick impatient tread;
And he bore the badge of gameness in his bright and fiery eye,
    And the proud and lofty carriage of his head.

* "Sat" is obviously a euphemism. See the volume of verses, *Nine Miles from Gundagai*, by Jack Moses.

But still so slight and weedy, one would doubt his power to stay,
    And the old man said "That horse will never do
For a long and tiring gallop—lad, you'd better stop away,
    Those hills are far too rough for such as you."
So he waited, sad and wistful—only Clancy stood his friend—
    "I think we ought to let him come," he said:
"I warrant he'll be with us when he's wanted at the end,
    For both his horse and he are mountain-bred.

"He hails from Snowy River, up by Kosciusko's side,
    Where the hills are twice as steep and twice as rough;
Where a horse's hoofs strike firelight from the flint-stones every
      stride,
    The man that holds his own is good enough.
And the Snowy River riders on the mountains make their home,
    Where the river runs those giant hills between;
I have seen full many horsemen since I first commenced to roam,
    But nowhere yet such horsemen have I seen."

So he went; they found the horses by the big mimosa clump,
    They raced away towards the mountain's brow,
And the old man gave his orders, "Boys, go at them from the
      jump,
    No use to try for fancy riding now.
And, Clancy, you must wheel them, try and wheel them to the
      right.
    Ride boldly, lad, and never fear the spills,
For never yet was rider that could keep the mob in sight,
    If once they gain the shelter of those hills."

So Clancy rode to wheel them—he was racing on the wing
    Where the best and boldest riders take their place,
And he raced his stock-horse past them, and he made the ranges
      ring
    With the stockwhip, as he met them face to face.
Then they halted for a moment, while he swung the dreaded lash,
    But they saw their well-loved mountain full in view,
And they charged beneath the stockwhip with a sharp and sudden
      dash,
    And off into the mountain scrub they flew.

Then fast the horsemen followed, where the gorges deep and black
    Resounded to the thunder of their tread,

And the stockwhips woke the echoes, and they fiercely answered
    back
  From cliffs and crags that beetled overhead.
And upward, ever upward, the wild horses held their way,
  Where mountain ash and kurrajong grew wide;
And the old man muttered fiercely, "We may bid the mob good-
    day,
  No man can hold them down the other side."

When they reached the mountain summit, even Clancy took a
    pull—
  It well might make the boldest hold their breath;
The wild hop scrub grew thickly, and the hidden ground was full
  Of wombat-holes, and any slip was death.
But the man from Snowy River let the pony have his head,
  And he swung his stockwhip round and gave a cheer,
And he raced him down the mountain like a torrent down its bed,
  While the others stood and watched in very fear.

He sent the flint-stones flying, but the pony kept his feet,
  He cleared the fallen timber in his stride,
And the man from Snowy River never shifted in his seat—
  It was grand to see that mountain horseman ride.
Through the stringybarks and saplings, on the rough and broken
    ground,
  Down the hillside at a racing pace he went;
And he never drew the bridle till he landed safe and sound
  At the bottom of that terrible descent.

He was right among the horses as they climbed the farther hill,
  And the watchers on the mountain, standing mute,
Saw him ply the stockwhip fiercely; he was right among them still
  As he raced across the clearing in pursuit.
Then they lost him for a moment, where two mountain gullies
    met
  In the ranges—but a final glimpse reveals
On a dim and distant hillside the wild horses racing yet,
  With the man from Snowy River at their heels.

And he ran them single-handed till their sides were white with
    foam;
  He followed like a bloodhound on their track,
Till they halted, cowed and beaten; then he turned their heads
    for home,
  And alone and unassisted brought them back.

But his hardy mountain pony he could scarcely raise a trot,
  He was blood from hip to shoulder from the spur;
But his pluck was still undaunted, and his courage fiery hot,
  For never yet was mountain horse a cur.

And down by Kosciusko, where the pine-clad ridges raise
  Their torn and rugged battlements on high,
Where the air is clear as crystal, and the white stars fairly blaze
  At midnight in the cold and frosty sky,
And where around the Overflow the reed-beds sweep and sway
  To the breezes, and the rolling plains are wide,
The Man from Snowy River is a household word to-day,
  And the stockmen tell the story of his ride.

A. B. ("Banjo") Paterson.

MARK TWAIN ON MARYBOROUGH (VIC.)

When Mark Twain, celebrated American humorist, visited
Maryborough (Victoria) towards the close of last century, he was
credited with designating the town as "a railway station with a
town attached." The illustration has frequently been quoted,
both in terms of criticism and praise. . . . After all we would not
be stretching the imagination so far as our railway station is concerned, because it is a structure which still stands as a monument
to its builders and gives the town more than ordinary distinction.

From the Maryborough *Advertiser*, November 14, 1949.

MARK TWAIN ON THE BLUE MOUNTAINS

. . . the growing day and the early sun exposed the distant range
called the Blue Mountains. . . . A resident told me that these were
not mountains; he said they were rabbit-piles. And explained
that long exposure and the over-ripe condition of the rabbits was
what made them look so blue. This man may have been right, but
much reading of books of travel has made me distrustful of gratis
information furnished by official residents of a country. The facts
which such people give to travellers are usually erroneous, and
often intemperately so. The rabbit plague has indeed been very
bad in Australia, and it could account for one mountain, but not
for a mountain range, it seems to me. It is too large an order.

Mark Twain, *Following the Equator*.

A TALE OF DROUGHT

Ernestine Hill in her excellent book *Water into Gold* mentions the sad fate of a town in Central Victoria during a year of drought in the eighteen eighties. To the misery of drought was added the horror of a full-scale rabbit invasion of the area. Indeed, so great was this rabbit-wave that it measured ten miles wide and ten feet high, and carried the town away with it in its onward rush.

There was only one survivor. He said "that he had been lofted far out on to a sandy plain, where the wave broke, and let him down lightly with a few bruises." Having told this strange tale he shortly afterwards expired.

THE *GEM'S* CABINS

The *Gem* was one of the famous paddle wheelers of the last century, plying up and down the Murray river.

It was said of her cabins that they were built small purposely to ensure that as few mosquitoes as possible could enter them.

MELBA AND THE BENDIGO CHIMES

A Brighton (England) publican will pay £2 a week to cover the cost of stopping and starting chimes in a nearby clock-tower just so he can get an undisturbed night's sleep. He couldn't have known that he'll pay as much in six months as would cover his fare to Bendigo, Victoria, where the citizens have had the same service gratis ever since Dame Nellie Melba complained that the post-office chimes kept her awake. For years the booming chimes have cut out at 11 p.m., not to speak again until Bendigonians are munching their early-morning toast and marmalade.

From the Melbourne *Sun*, May 23, 1949.

HUMOUR IN SIGNS

A story used to be told about a signpost, at the junction of two roads, which read: "This way to Timbuctoo—If you can't read inquire at the blacksmith's opposite." While it is doubtful if ever such a notice did exist, I have seen other notices which were just as stupid. For instance, near the top of Big Jack Mountain, on the south coast of N.S.W., there was a sign at a creek crossing which read: "When this sign is under water the crossing is dangerous."

In the Parramatta (N.S.W.) district is a large sign reading "The Home of the Big Loafer." However, this sign appears on a bakery. One would imagine that Sydney pedestrians were savage and dangerous creatures if one looked at the "Beware of Pedestrians" notice which was erected at Circular Quay. It was intended as a warning to motorists to keep a sharp lookout for pedestrians at a blind crossing, made necessary during the construction of the underground railway.

One of the most apt signs I ever saw was at the main entrance to a large cemetery. This sign read: "One-way Traffic." Of course it was intended as a notice for vehicular traffic.

A farmer attached to his gate a notice reading: "Beware of the Agapanthus—Enter at Your Own Risk." It was surprising the number of people who did not know that an agapanthus was an African lily.

In front of a little shop at a popular fishing village there was a notice reading: "I have Worms To-day." The worms mentioned were for fish bait. On the Blue Mountains of N.S.W. someone erected a small notice at a lookout reading: "Keep Still and Listen to the Silence." I have seen a number of people there listening intently, and it was not uncommon to hear one say to the other, "I cannot hear anything, can you?"

A hairdresser and tobacconist in a Sydney suburb has made good use of the Australian's love of a gamble. In his window appears a sign reading "We do S.P. here." The average Australian thinks only of starting price betting when "S.P." is mentioned, but in tiny letters readable only on going close to the window, you learn that S.P. stands for "Shave Perfectly."

Instead of the usual "Shut the Gate" notice, an old man who was having trouble with people leaving his gate open painted this on the gate: "You Left it Open Before."

Near the number plate of a motor car I noticed a small sign reading: "If you can read this notice you are too close," while on the back of another car appears: "Please don't scratch my back."

A. T. in the Melbourne *Argus*, December 24, 1948.

PART FIVE

AUSTRALIANISMS

PHRASES, TERMS AND LOCAL REFERENCES

"THE BOTANY BAY DOZEN"

Perhaps the first authentic example of convict slang in Australia was the use of *scrubbing brushes* for bread containing more chaff and bran than flour—noted by D. Collins in his *Account of N.S.W.* (1802). It is not recorded in overseas slang dictionaries. Nor is *red shirt* for a back scarified by flogging. Nor, though they are formed on English slang terms for coins, are *tester,* a flogging of twenty-five lashes (also known as a *Botany Bay dozen*); *bob,* fifty lashes; *bull,* seventy-five lashes; and *canary,* one hundred lashes. Nor are *old fake,* a convict on his second probation; *logs,* a prison (Collins refers to "log prisons" at Sydney and Parramatta); a *clean potato,** a free man; *wheelbarrow,* a bullock waggon taking supplies to men in an *iron gang*; and *domino,* the last lash in a flogging.

SIDNEY J. BAKER, *The Australian Language.*

---

* Clean potato: In the old bush ballad, "Sam Holt", occurs the line, "You were not the cleanest potato, Sam Holt".

THE CURRENCY LADS AND LASSES

In the early days (of Australian settlement—Ed.) a great variety of specie was in circulation, English silver, American and Spanish dollars, johannes, ducats, mohurs, pagodas, rupees, guilders, as well as paper money of different kinds and notes of hand issued by established tradesmen. Such notes and other paper were called *currency notes* and the various coins were called collectively *currency*. English gold pieces were called *sterling*, as opposed to the mixed colonial *currency*. Figuratively, the two words were applied to immigrants and the native-born respectively.

> Joshua Lake, in his *Webster's Dictionary* supplement of 1898, quoted by Sidney J. Baker, *The Australian Language.*

"I AM STERLING"

Our colonial-born brethren are best known here by the name of "currency" in contradistinction to "sterling," or those born in the mother country. The name was originally given by a facetious paymaster of the 73rd Regiment quartered here—the pound currency being at the time inferior to the pound sterling. Our currency lads and lasses are a fine interesting race, and do honour to the country whence they originated. The name is sufficient passport to esteem with all the well-informed and right-feeling portion of our population; but it is most laughable to see the capers which some of our drunken old sterling madonnas will occasionally cut over their currency adversaries in a quarrel. It is then "You saucy baggage, how dare you set up your currency crest at me? I am sterling, and that I'll let you know."

To all acquainted with the open manly simplicity of character displayed by this part of our population, its members are the theme of universal praise; and, indeed, what more can be said in their favour than that they are little tainted with the vices so prominent among their parents? Drunkenness is almost unknown with them, and honesty proverbial; the few of them that have been convicted having acted under the bad auspices of their parents or relatives. . . . The currencies grow up tall and slender, like the Americans, and are generally remarkable for that Gothic peculiarity of fair hair and blue eyes which has been noticed by other writers. Their complexions when young are of a reddish-yellow, and they are, for the most part, easily distinguishable—even in more advanced years—from those born in England. Cherry cheeks are not accompaniments of our climate, any more than that of America, where a blooming complexion will speedily draw upon you the observation, "You are from the Old Country, I see?" ... "The Currency Lad" is now a popular standing toast, since it was first given by Major Goulburn at the Agricultural dinner, while "The Currency Lasses" gives name to one of our most favourite tunes.

SURGEON PETER CUNNINGHAM, *Two Years in New South Wales* (1827).

OAKES' OATH

A once-familiar figure around whom the mists of legend have gathered is the man who gave rise to the old expression, "Oakes' oath."

There used to be a saying current in parts of New South Wales, "I'll chance it, as Oakes did his oath." The story goes that Oakes, a Parramatta identity, once prosecuted a neighbour for stealing some of his cattle.

In the Court case that followed, a pair of horns was produced—alleged to have been found in the prisoner's possession.

When asked if he was prepared to swear that the horns had belonged to one of his beasts, Oakes thought carefully a moment, then said bluffly, *"Well, I'll chance it! Yes!"*

Australasian Post, June 7, 1956.

THE SHEARERS' VOTE

Spring shearing is the season of a unique ballot. From the far Barcoo in Queensland to the Western District of Victoria, it is known simply as "the shearers' vote."

Rain wet the sheep yesterday and it is doubtful if they'll be fit for to-day's shearing.

The only way to find out is to test them. So shearing starts as usual. At the top of the long line of the shearers the station-owner watches anxiously.

He hopes that the sheep will be dry, and there will be no delay —for delay means missing markets, prolonged shearing with added expenses, and overtaxing pastures when the even flow of sheep from paddock to shed is interrupted.

The shearer, too, is anxious. Delays mean hard cash to him. A day lost means an average loss of £10 a man.

And the shearer has his health to consider. Nothing can bring on pneumonia quicker than constant handling of wet sheep.

By now each shearer has shorn two sheep. Immediately all

K

activity ceases. Quiet reigns. The vote is on. It's a serious business. The "rep" (shearers' spokesman with the management) pads silently up the board.

He gives two pieces of paper to each shearer. On one is written "dry"; on the other "wet."

He has a tin with a slot in the top.

The shearer decides whether his sheep are wet or dry, and drops in his paper accordingly.

Whatever the decision, it is final. There can be no appeal. But if the sheep are found wet in the morning, there could be another test in the afternoon.

The vote can have its lighter side. There may be some attraction in town at the week end. So sometimes on the Friday, a vote will be called even though there may not have been rain for weeks.

JOHN DUNN in the Melbourne *Herald*, October 14, 1952.

A BURKETOWN MOSQUITO NET

I got a job with the only white man in the Northern Territory who would not employ Chinamen. His name was Johansen, a huge Norwegian sailor. Every night I would go down to the sly-grog shanty run by Greenhide Bill, and listen to tales about Klondike, Woodlark Island and Hannan's, and also to arguments upon religion, philosophy, and politics.

I was young and impressionable in those days, and wherever men talked I would listen. I did not drink but I used to delight to hear old Greenhide lay down the law. Greenhide was a bush lawyer; he knew everything, and he settled all arguments by force of personality.

Greenhide was a cripple and very fat; all he could do was to hobble about on a crutch. When Greenhide ran out of gin (it was all gin in those days), he used to send me over to get some "Sarm-su" from the Chinamen. "Sarm-su" is an evil-smelling home-made poison which the Chinamen distil from rice. Greenhide would laugh and say to me: "I will give them all Burketown mosquito-nets to-night."

A "Burketown mosquito-net" is to be too drunk to feel the mosquitoes. Men used to say that the mosquitoes dropped dead from old Greenhide, he was so saturated with square gin.

Still, those talks in the old mining sly-grog shanty helped to instruct and educate me.

I have been in many small rushes in the Northern Territory and Kimberley, and have always met the same type of man. It goes without saying that prospectors are radical in their politics. They are not afraid to take a chance. The future is always alluring to them; they show the wisdom of being "ever new to life."

"Olof" in the *Australian Worker*, March 14, 1928.

THE LARRIKIN

The Australian "larrikin" or "tug" is the counterpart of the English "hoodlum" or "tough." The word "larrikin" has its origin in the Hibernian pronunciation by one Dalton (a police-sergeant of an earlier Melbourne) of the word "larking." "What was the accused up to, Sergeant?" "Just larrakin', your Worship!"*

J. ALEX. ALLAN, *Men and Manners in Australia.*

THE LARRIKIN "PUSHES"

The larrikin . . . is not the product of any one period in our history. He dates back to the *cabbageites* and *cabbage-tree mobs* of the early nineteenth century. He was the original *currency lad*, tough, defiant, reckless. When our capital cities began to grow he came into his own as a member of the *pushes*. His heyday was probably in the 1880's when the power of the push held communities in terror and when one of the larrikin's greatest delights was to kick a man to death. This ruffian's teeth were drawn and his brutality curbed, but as an individual he is by no means extinct. As long as there is an Australian city's backstreets for him to find a place in there will be a larrikin.

SIDNEY J. BAKER, *The Australian Language.*

PORTRAIT OF THE LARRIKIN

Let me give you a description of a typical male specimen as he may be found at the street corners about seven o'clock in the evening, expectorating tobacco juice and talking blasphemy. He is generally a weedy youth, undersized and slight, but like all Australians, who are cast in a lanky not thickset mould, he is wiry and active. He has a repulsive face, low forehead, small eyes, a colourless skin, and irregular discoloured teeth. His hat is either small, round and hard, or a black slouch. He pays attention to his dress, which is always of dark colour and very tight-fitting, the coat of the shortest, the trousers like fleshings, and his boots very high-

* See Baker's *The Australian Language* for a discussion on the origin of this word.

neeled and small, the impress of every toe being clearly distinguishable *en repousse.*

Knots of these creatures collect in the evening, and the streets are not the more pleasant to walk in for their presence. They call themselves "pushes," and there are often conflicts between those who infest different parts of the town. The larrikin is a coward. He is only courageous when there are numbers present, and he prefers his adversary in a minority of one to ten, or thereabouts.

Throwing lumps of blue metal is one of his favourite modes of attack. The agility with which he will discharge his missile and then dart round the nearest corner to avoid the return shot is wonderful.

EDWARD KINGLAKE, *The Australian at Home* (1891).

LARRIKIN LANGUAGE

For they spoke the gutter language with the easy flow that comes
Only to the men whose childhood knew the gutters and the slums.

HENRY LAWSON, "The Captain of the Push."

'Tis the everyday Australian
  Has a language of his own,
Has a language, or a slanguage,
  Which can simply stand alone.
And a "dickin pitch to kid us"
  Is a synonym for "lie,"
And to "nark it" means to stop it,
  And to "nit it" means to fly!

And a bosom friend's a "cobber,"
  And a horse a "prad" or "moke,"
While a casual acquaintance
  Is a "joker" or a "bloke,"
And his ladylove's his "donah,"
  Or his "clinah" or his "tart,"
Or his "little bit o' muslin,"
  As it used to be his "bart."

And his naming of the coinage
  Is a mystery to some,
With his "quid" and "half-a-caser"
  And his "deener" and his "scrum."

And a "tin-back" is a party
   Who's remarkable for luck,
And his food is called his "tucker"
   Or his "panem" or his "chuck."

A policeman is a "johnny"
   Or a "copman" or a "trap,"
And a thing obtained on credit
   Is invariably "strap."
A conviction's known as "trouble,"
   And a gaol is called a "jug,"
And a sharper is a "spieler"
   And a simpleton's a "tug."

If he hits a man in fighting
   That is what he calls a "plug,"
If he borrows money from you
   He will say he "bit your lug."
And to "shake it" is to steal it,
   And to "strike it" is to beg;
And a jest is "poking borak,"
   And a jester "pulls your leg."

Things are "cronk" when they go wrongly
   In the language of the "push,"
But when things go as he wants 'em
   He declares it is "all cush."
When he's bright he's got a "napper,"
   And he's "ratty" when he's daft,
And when looking for employment
   He is "out o' blooming graft."

And his clothes he calls his "clobber"
   Or his "togs," but what of that
When a "castor" or a "kady"
   Is the name he gives his hat!
And our undiluted English
   Is a fad to which we cling,
But the great Australian slanguage
   Is a truly awful thing!

W. T. GOODGE, "The Great Australian
Slanguage" (1897).

"SUCH IS LIFE!"

Ned Kelly is said to have made the comment, "Such is Life!" as he stepped on to the drop, just before his hanging, in 1880.

In his review of Frank Clune's reprint of an early pamphlet, A Noose for Ned, *Mr. Clive Turnbull writes:*

Mr. Clune has been at pains to try and trace the origin of the phrase, "Such is life." In the *Bulletin* of November 20, 1880, appeared a homily on the hanging, he says, in which Kelly is credited with "an unconscious paraphrase of the historical dying remark of blind King George, 'Such is life.'"

The blind king was George III; but none of his biographies, says Mr. Clune, makes any mention of death-bed remarks. The final court of appeal, the British Museum Library, dismissed the story as "unreliable hearsay."

So, says Mr. Clune, until it is proved wrong, he will credit Kelly with having originated the phrase (used later by Tom Collins as the title of his great novel).

Melbourne *Argus*, October 15, 1949.

THE BUSHMEN'S BIBLE

The *Bulletin*—which for thirty-five years was known as the "Bushmen's Bible" . . .*

RANDOLPH BEDFORD, *Naught to Thirty-three.*

THE BRADDON BLOT

The name of Sir Edward Nicholas Braddon, Premier of Tasmania during the greater part of the nineties, is associated with one of the most famous expressions to arise out of Australian politics.

Braddon was active in supporting the principles of Federation, and was appointed one of Tasmania's representatives to the 1897 Convention which met to frame the clauses of the Commonwealth's Constitution.

Each colony, while it remained separate, had the power to levy its own Customs duties. Federation meant that this power would pass to the Commonwealth Government, and the States would thus lose their main source of revenue.

Sir Edward Braddon proposed that 75% of all Customs and

* The Sydney *Bulletin*, founded in 1880, was widely read by bullockies, shearers, stockmen, and other bush workers.

excise revenue collected by each State should be returned to it, and the remaining 25% should go towards the cost of Federation.

This proposal, which was carried despite strong opposition from New South Wales, became known as the "Braddon Clause." It was operative for a period of 10 years. In that time, opponents continually referred to it as the "Braddon Blot."

Sir Henry Braddon, son of Sir Edward, in an address to the Royal Australian Historical Society in 1933, told a story of his younger days which is relevant here.

"My father," said Sir Henry, "was very much amused when I told him how the 'Braddon Blot' had saved me from a fine of fifty shillings and costs.

"One morning I was anxious to get into town quickly from Ashfield, but as I ran into the station the train was already in full motion. I swung on to the last carriage, to find myself opposite the train guard, who pulled out the inevitable pocket-book and asked me my name and address.

"When I gave my name a gleam came into his eye and he said, 'Any relation to the *Blot*?'

"I said, 'I suppose so, since my father was the author of both.'

"To my great relief he then said that in that case he did not propose to make any report; and so the family was saved fifty shillings and costs!"

Australasian Post, June 7, 1956.

BUCKLEY'S CHANCE

"He hasn't got Buckley's chance" is a phrase still used to describe the million to one chance. It may have derived from the experience of William Buckley "the wild white man," who escaped from a convict party landed on the Victorian coast in 1803, and who managed to keep alive with the help of Aborigines for thirty-two years until found by John Batman's party. Or, more likely, it may refer to a well-known Melbourne firm, Buckley and Nunn, and derive from the old saying: "He's got two chances—Buckley's and none," that is, no chances at all.

TOM COLLINS

Tom Collins was a synonym for idle rumour. This Tom was a mendacious fellow at whose door was laid the leg-pulling that flourished in hotel bars and wherever men gathered to gossip. A newcomer, breasting the bar of a hotel in Little Collins or Little Bourke Street, Melbourne, would be greeted with the latest scandal uttered against him. The victim, trying to run it to earth, would be told that Tom Collins said it, and Tom had always just gone to do the block in the pub line. A wowser side to Tom is suggested by a topical rhyme (*Bulletin*, August 19, 1893) sent to Furphy by A.G.S.* on May 22, 1905.

Tom Collins

Who never drinks and never bets,
But loves his wife and pays his debts
And feels content with what he gets?
Tom Collins.

Who has the utmost confidence
That all the banks now in suspense
Will meet their paper three years hence?
Tom Collins.

Who reads the *Herald's* leaders through
And takes the *Evening News* for true,
And thought the *Echo's* jokes were new?
Tom Collins.

Who is the patriot renowned
So very opportunely found
To fork up Dibbs's thousand pound?†
Tom Collins.

By a humorous coincidence the name of Furphy during the war of 1914-18 came to signify idle rumour.

MILES FRANKLIN and KATE BAKER, Joseph Furphy, The
Legend of a Man and his Book.

FURPHY

At the outbreak of World War I the metal-bodied carts used in Victorian military camps for water and sanitary purposes were supplied by the foundry established by John Furphy‡ at Shep-

---

* Joseph Furphy, author of *Such is Life*, and A. G. Stephens, famous Australian critic. Furphy wrote *Such is Life* under the pseudonym of "Tom Collins".

† "Dibbs's thousand pound": Sir George Dibbs, "protectionist" leader in the N.S.W. in 1890. "Going to England at the expense, so he thought, of the colony, he quite forgot that it was necessary for Parliament to consent to the appropriation of public funds. But he was saved from parliamentary censure by a last-minute repayment to the Treasury of the sum of £1,000 expended by him abroad. It is almost unnecessary to add that Dibbs himself did not provide any of the £1,000." H. V. Evatt: *Australian Labour Leader*.

‡ John Furphy, brother of the famous Joseph, author of *Such is Life*.

parton (Vic.) in 1874. The name of Furphy appeared on each vehicle, with the slogan,

> "Good, better, best;
> never let it rest,
> till your good is better,
> and your better best."

Camp rumours or latrine rumours came to be known as "furphies," and from its original military use it spread into popular speech.

Sydney *Bulletin*, May 18, 1949.

JIMMY WOOD

A Bar-Room Ballad

There came a lonely Briton to the town,
  A solitary Briton with a mission,
He'd vowed a vow to put all "shouting" down,
  To relegate it to a low position.

Transcendantly British in his dress,
  His manners were polite and slightly formal
And—this I mention with extreme distress,
  His put-away for liquid was abnormal.

He viewed this "shouting" mania with disgust,
  And being generosity perverted,
When any of the "boys" went on the bust,
  He strove his best that they might be converted.

He wouldn't take a liquor with a man,
  Not if he was to be hanged, drawn and quartered,
And yet he drank—construe it as you can—
  Unsweetened gin, most moderately watered.

And when the atmosphere was in a whirl,
  And language metaphorical ran riot,
He'd calmly tender sixpence to the girl,
  And drink his poison—*solus*—nice and quiet.

Whenever he was asked to breast the bar,
  He'd answer with a touch of condescension:
"I much regret to disoblige so far
  As to refuse your delicate attention.

131

"That drink's a curse that hangeth like a leech—
    A sad but indubitable fact is,
Mankind was made to drink *alone,* I preach,
    And what I preach invariably practise.

"I never pay for others, nor do I
    Take drink from them, and never, never would, sir—
One man one liquor! though I have to die
    A martyr to my faith, that's Jimmy Wood, sir.

"My friend, 'tis not a bit of use to raise
    A hurricane of bluster and of banter,
I preach the humble gospel in the phrase—
    Similia similibus curantur.

"Which means: by drinking how and when I like,
    And sticking to the one unsweetened sample,
I hope in course of time that it will strike
    All men to follow up my good example."

In course of time it struck all men that Jim
    Was fast developing into a soaker—
The breath of palsy on his every limb,
    A bleary face touched up with crimson ochre.

Yet firmly stood he by the sinking ship,
    Went down at last with all his colours flying;
No hand but his raised tumbler to his lip,
    What time J. Wood, the Martyr, lay a-dying.

Misunderstood reformer! gallant heart!
    He gave his path to Death—the great collector;
Now . . . in Elysian fields he sits apart
    And sips his modest "Tommy Dodd" of nectar.

His signature is on the scroll of fame,
    You cannot well forget him though you would, sir,
The man is dead, not so his homely name,
    Who drinks alone—drinks toast to Jimmy Wood,
        sir.*

BARCROFT BOAKE in the Sydney *Bulletin,* May 7, 1892.

* The *Bulletin* appends the footnote: "A man who drinks by himself is said to take a 'Jimmy Woodser'." "Shouting": Buying drinks for other persons.

THE OLD JIMMY WOODSER

The old Jimmy Woodser comes into the bar
  Unwelcomed, unnoticed, unknown,
Too old and too odd to be drunk with, by far;
So he glides to the end where the lunch-baskets are
  And they say that he tipples alone.

. . . . . .

And I thought—there are times when our memory trends
  Through the future, as 'twere, on its own—
That I, out-of-date ere my pilgrimage ends,
In a new-fashioned bar to dead loves and dear friends
  Might drink, like the old man, alone.

HENRY LAWSON, "The Old Jimmy Woodser."

WOWSERS

Australia has a word for the Anthony Comstocks, a word that should be used the world over to describe a killjoy, and that word is "wowser."*

RANDOLPH BEDFORD, *Naught to Thirty-three.*

SUNDOWNERS

There is a species of tramp found nowhere but in Australia that spends its whole life travelling from station to station, getting a night's lodging and "rations" (a measure of flour, tea, and sugar) at each. He carries a swag containing all his personal property wrapped in a blue blanket which is folded like a horse collar. The swag is called in the vernacular a "bluey," and the tramp is elegantly said to "hump it." From his invariable habit of making his appearance just before the sun sets, this personage has got the name of "sundowner," by which he is universally known.

EDWARD KINGLAKE, *The Australian at Home* (1891).

"WALTZING MATILDA," HUMPING THE BLUEY, WHALING, ETC.

*The swagman, sundowner, bagman, battler and whaler
were itinerant Australians of varying kinds who roamed*

---

* The word "wowser", according to Sidney J. Baker, appeared in the Sydney journal, *Truth*, probably for the first time, on October 8, 1899. It was used in a heading: "Willoughby Wowsers Worried". "Legend has it," writes Baker in *The Australian Language*, "that John Norton, politician and owner of the journal, invented *wowser* from the slogan, 'We Only Want Social Evils Remedied (Righted or Rectified)', but this amiable theory lacks confirmation."

the tracks of the bush either in search of work, or merely seeking enough food and nutriment to keep themselves alive. The whaler usually kept to the banks of the larger rivers like the Darling and Murrumbidgee. Most of these outback types have almost disappeared. There were considerable numbers of them from the time of the sixties— after the alluvial gold had petered out in the main fields —onwards until the first world war period.

They had this in common: they carried a "swag," "drum," or "matilda," which Henry Lawson described as being "usually composed of a tent 'fly' or strip of calico (a cover for the swag and a shelter in bad weather ...), a couple of blankets, blue by custom and preference ... and the core is composed of spare clothing and small personal effects."

To "hump the bluey," "hump the drum" or "waltz matilda" meant simply to carry such a swag.

The origin of the term "matilda" is not known.* It was not coined by Banjo Paterson for his famous song, "Waltzing Matilda" (probably written at the close of the last century) but it does not seem to have had a wide currency before that song really made it nationally known.

Of the song itself, much has been written. The following shows the extent to which it has travelled beyond its native shores.

Banjo Paterson, the Australian troubador who wrote the words of "Waltzing Matilda," died in 1941 when his great Australian ballad was sweeping through bombed Britain. We didn't know when we sang about the defiant swagman in the "locals" of Bethnal Green, Tiger Bay, Jarrow, and Govan, that the minstrel boy of the bush country had just passed on and left us this legacy, a drinking song that went as well with old and mild as it does with Australian ale.

All we knew was that we couldn't sing "Waltzing Matilda" without thinking of brown faces under wide-brimmed Digger hats, of Tobruk "Rats" and guest aircrews of the R.A.A.F., of narrow blue-jean collars and those spitting alleycats of the Mediterranean—the "Scrap Iron" destroyer flotilla of the R.A.N.

For many of us, this wryly gay, sadly rollicking Australian song was the first stimulus to a new curiosity about the far-flung land.

* However, see my notes in *The Argus*, Melbourne, April 3, 24, 27, 1956.

I first heard it from the tender throat of a 13-year-old Derry boy, the star cathedral treble of the whole Six Counties. He had learned "Waltzing Matilda" from an Australian sailor, and he sang it like a hymn, sadly, in the last sweet swan-song of adolescence.

It was years afterwards before I heard it sung in what has now become the traditional way—to the tramp of marching feet.

To the un-Australian—or pre-Australian—ear, "Waltzing Matilda" is strange and fascinating. For migrants it is the Excelsior of their great adventure. They sing it on the ships that sail from Tilbury, San Francisco, Bremerhaven and Genoa.

LARRY BOYS in *Tomorrow's Australians*, February 14, 1949.

ORIGIN OF THE BUNYIP

The bunyip had its origin in the folk tales of the blacks.

Long before the white man came, the natives believed in the existence of some dark creature of monstrous size that lived in the swamps, lagoons and billabongs of their tribal lands.

Their descriptions of it varied, but they were all in agreement in describing its shining, baleful eyes, and its bellowing voice.

It had a huge body, either covered with fur or feathers, and where its legs should have been there were flippers that thrashed the water when it was angry.

It devoured human beings, coming upon them in silence and when least expected.

The blacks I questioned about the bunyip always added, with some satisfaction, that it favoured women.

In a drawing of the bunyip made by a Murray River black in 1848, the creature is depicted as having a body resembling that of a hippopotamus and a head like that of a horse.

However, another drawing made by a Victorian black showed it with the head and neck of an emu.

ALAN MARSHALL in the Melbourne *Argus*, December 14, 1951.

LIKE A BABOON, AN EMU, AND A MAN

The Veritable Bunyip has been seen at last! We are informed by Mr. Edwards, the managing clerk at the office of Messrs. Moor and Chambers, that during his late trip, and making the circuit of Phillip Island, he and his party were astonished at observing an animal sitting upon a bank in a lake.

The animal is described as being from six to seven feet long and, in general appearance, half man and half baboon.

Five shots were fired, and the last discharge was replied to by a spring into the air, and a contemptuous fling out of the hind legs, and a final disappearance in the placid waters of the lake. A somewhat long neck, feathered like an emu, was the peculiar characteristic of the animal.

Melbourne *Morning Herald*, October 29, 1849.

A RECENT BUNYIP

Far back in historical ages,
   The people could not understand
How creatures that baffled the sages
   Were found in Australia's fair land.

The platypus—strangest of creatures—
   With fur like a mole—has webbed feet:
A bill like a duck are queer features,
   An egg laying mammal unique.

Now Jimmy and Lionel Moser,
   Their brother-in-law Andy Rice,
Have found in the Murray a poser
   On which they are seeking advice.

It swims like an Olympic sprinter,
   And spouts in the air like a whale;
It whistles like steamers in winter,
   When giving the station a hail.

A big head, with neck long and slender,
   With eyes extraordinarily bright;
Are details they clearly remember,
   As seen in the fast-fading light.

These lads are not users of "pinky"*
   I think their impressions are real—
It may be from pointers so skimpy,
   A cross twixt a bunyip and seal.

"Silky Oak" in the Swan Hill *Guardian*, September 23, 1947.

COINAGE—AUSTRALIAN STYLE

One penny—a copper, brown, bronze, or bronck.
Threepence—a trey or trizzie.

* "Pinky": Cheap wine.

Sixpence—a zak, a tanner, a kick, or a sprat.
One shilling—a bob, or deener.
Two shillings—a florin, or swye (two bob or two deeners).
2/6—half-a-crown, half-a-dollar, half-a-caser, two-and-a-kick.
Five shillings—a crown, a dollar, or a caser.
Ten shillings—half-a-note, a half-note, or ten bob.
One pound—a quid, a greenback, fiddley or frog.
Five pounds—five quid, a fiver, a spin, a toadskin.
Ten pounds—a tenner, a brick.

Salt, February 2, 1942.

WHY "DRONGO"?

Like Mary's little lamb, "drongo"* went wherever Australians
went during the war.

Drongo became famous and most of us know that Drongo was
a poorly performed racehorse.

How many really know all the facts? Mr. Cliff Graves, turf
editor of the Sydney *Daily Telegraph* gives us the gen.

"Drongo was the name of a horse which failed to win a race.
He raced twenty-three years ago. He was foaled in 1921 and always
tailed off hopelessly in his races.

"However, over a distance he finished fast, and ran second in
the Victoria Derby and Leger, and was placed in ten other races.
He was a clumsy creature, ungainly as a dromedary.

"Bobby Lewis once said of him that if a jockey tried to hurry
him early in a race he would fold his legs and fall down.

"The horse retired in 1925 and after that anybody or anything
slow or clumsy became a drongo."

Next time anybody calls you a drongo you'll know just what
they mean.

Salt, April 8, 1946.

DEAR BILL!

Dear Bill! Ain't it a bastard!
(An expression, largely used by Australian soldiers, to denote the
deepest feelings of exasperation and disgust.)

"DIGGER"

> *How much the term "digger" has a flavour of Eureka and
> how much it is merely suggestive of excavating trenches in the
> first world war— this will always be argued and it is not just*

* Drongo is also the popular name for a bird found in parts of northern
Australia, especially Queensland.

a matter of word derivation; it is a part of the nation's tra-
dition. I frankly like to think of it in terms of the diggers at
Ballarat in 1854. I am quite sure that in the minds of many
other Australians, too, the flavour of Eureka is a part of that
special flavour of the word "digger." A. G. Butler, D.S.O., dis-
cusses the whole question in his interesting essay, The Digger,
A Study in Democracy *(Angus and Robertson, Sydney, 1945).*
Here are two opinions on the term by soldiers of the second
A.I.F.

When was the term "digger" first applied to the Anzacs? . . .
Just before the last war (1914-18 war—Ed.) I was employed in
the P.W.D. Tasmanian Railway Construction Branch. In one of
the day-labour gangs a typical old bowyanged navvy (ex-N.Z. gum
digger), "Digger" Cowley, always greeted you with "Good-day,
digger." The timekeeper on these works, W. H. Sandy, and I
drifted to World War I.

After Gallipoli we went to France. On a typical grey sloppy
Flanders morn, early 1917, Captain Sandy (now Lt.-Col. Sandy,
D.S.O.), and I were plodding through Poperinghe near the origi-
nal Toc H building. I was surprised and impressed by "old
Sandy's" greeting to each passing lad—"Good-day, digger." Like
magic the term became mass-produced. From every estaminet,
urged by the vin rouge or vin blanc plonk, oozed the expression,
"Good-day dig.", or, more slangishly, "How's she, dig."

I often think of "old Sandy," that cheerful unorthodox soldier
with the persistent bubble in his Adam's apple, and I feel that
many, knowing him, will say: "Well, now you come to think of
it, he is just the likeliest old b—— within the first A.I.F. to have
been the originator of 'digger'."

LT.-COL. C. DENNIS HORNE in *Salt*, April 24, 1944.

I must join issue with Lt.-Col. Horne on the origin and application of the word "digger" in the first A.I.F. At least two years
prior to 1917 this greeting was in general use, and I submit that
its origin may be traced to the later days of Gallipoli.

Following the unsuccessful battles of early August, 1915, the
bulk of the Australian forces was engaged in constructing and
improving trenches. The 7th Brigade (2 Division) was on Che-
shire Ridge, The Apex and Durrant's Post, and it was a general
source of merriment to other units to inquire of our boys their
"present occupation," to which the reply was generally "Digging,
digging, always b—— well digging." My own battalion (27 Bat-

talion) became well known as the "3 D's" ("Dellman's Dugout Diggers"), to which we added the then popular "dinkum," and so caused the battalion to be known as "Dellman's Dinkum Dugout Diggers."

I suggest that the greeting "digger" originated at this time and not, as suggested by Lt.-Col. Horne, in the early part of 1917.

MAJOR T. A. O'CONNOR, in *Salt*, June 5, 1944.

THE TWO-UP GAME

Although described as Australia's national game, *two-up* is a closed book to many of the public. This in spite of the fact that the *Australian Encyclopaedia* (1926) devotes a special section to it, and in spite of the fact that there are countless (illegal) *swy-up schools* or *swy schools* where the necessary education may be obtained at reasonable expense.

The origin of the game has been traced to China and to English provincial sport. It is scarcely necessary, however, to go much farther back in history than our own early days. In an article on the evils of gambling, we find the Sydney *Gazette* of April 15, 1804, recommending "the dispersion of the Little Chuck-farthing mob that generally assembles at one of the wharves in the course of the afternoon."

If you saunter down to the docks in almost any Australian port to-day you will find the descendants of chuck-farthing days indulging in a practically identical game played with pennies. These are, of course, mainly casual schools formed when the men find the time; the orthodox school, run on organised lines and under strict control, is called an *alley*. . . .

Figures in the two-up world are the *centre, centre man* or *ringie,* the ringkeeper; the *spinner* who tosses the coins;* the *alley clerk,* a battler who arranges bets for a player, especially if the latter is inexperienced; the *sleeper catcher,* a person who picks up bets that have been left on the floor too long (this is regarded as a legitimate perquisite, the *sleeper* being a bet or winnings not picked up by a tardy backer); *alley loafers,* moneyless players who are never allowed a seat round a ring; the *toe-rag,* a hobo or deadbeat; a *head,* a professional gambler; a *grouter,* a gambler who passes until the chances are in his favour and then bets that the spinner will throw out on the main; and, of course the *virgin* or *mug,* as any nonprofessional player of the game is known among the experts.

* Hence the famous expression, "Come in, spinner".—Ed.

"You've got to protect the mugs" is an old two-up saying usually observed in organised schools, since the casual *two-upper* (another Australian term) brings a good deal of money to the game. . . .

The small piece of board upon which the two pennies are rested for spinning is called the *kip, stick, bat* or *kiley*. This *kip* is not always what it seems. It is sometimes slotted or grooved so that a double-headed penny (a *jack*) or a double-tailed penny (a *gray*) can be inserted. The kip is then known as a *lannet*. When the coins are tossed in the air, the spinner palms one of the pennies and, with a deft twist of the lannet, allows the jack (or the gray, as the case may be) to spin into the air. The same form of trickery can be worked from an ordinary kip, by palming alone.

SIDNEY J. BAKER, *The Australian Language.*

PART SIX

SOME PERSPECTIVES

Never allow the thoughtless to declare
That we have no tradition here. . . .

MARY GILMORE, *Battlefields.*

Intolerance of oppression and sympathy with
the underdog are among the most attractive
features of the Australian character.

PROFESSOR W. K. HANCOCK, *Australia.*

To keep Australia Australian we have got to
understand Australia and resist to the utmost
all movements which, by design or accident,
threaten its essential character.
You and I must not only be ever-watchful
but ever-critical.
We need not be ashamed of being patriots.

CLIVE TURNBULL.

COMMENT

My aim, in this final part, has been to gather together some of the stories, references, ballads and sayings which throw light on the historic traditions of the Australian people.

Two threads run and intertwine throughout these sections. Firstly, the movements of the people, expressed in many hard-won battles, towards a democratic form of government. Secondly, the growing love of the people for their homeland, their gradual loosening of the ties which had at first closely bound them to Britain, and the emergence, in the eighteen seventies, eighties and nineties of a strong nationalism, an "aggressively Australian" sentiment which aimed at political, economic and cultural independence.

1. Convicts and Governors

The old fallacy about the convicts being "the worst types that the English prison system could throw together" (I quote from Sidney Baker's *The Australian Language*) is still widely believed. History records otherwise. The vast majority were sent out for minor thefts and were victims of the land enclosure acts and the industrial revolution, which together consolidated the wealth of England in a few hands in the eighteenth century.

It has been often enough stated that among the convicts were men and women of the finest calibre—the Irish rebels, the Scottish martyrs, such eminent men as Francis Greenway, the architect, and Hall, the editor, the Tolpuddle men, and many others.

The early governors were autocrats.

The great struggles in this period, from 1800 to the end of the eighteen forties, were waged around the question of who would control the legislature. The squatters, the largest landholders, eventually gained supremacy and the powers of the governors were considerably reduced. By the time of the gold rushes in the early fifties, the squatters were the virtual lawmakers. They attempted to keep up the flow of convicts, their main source of cheap labour. When public pressure brought an end to the convict system in New South Wales in 1840, they made strong efforts to revive it. The people again defeated them.

The smaller settlers allied themselves with other groups—traders, artisans, and emancipated convicts—in their opposition to the "squattocracy." They demanded a more representative form of government, an end to the governor's censorship powers and a more democratic judicial system. The convicts also, within the limits of their fetters, did much to end the system of which they were the victims. They fought, too, to gain better conditions from the squatters who were their main employers.

Unable to rely on a steady flow of convict labour after 1840, the squatters encouraged a scheme of assisted immigration; large numbers of English and Irish poor came to Australia in the eighteen forties. Among them were Chartists and Irish republicans, who exerted a considerable influence on the main trends of Australian political thinking.

2. THE GOLD DIGGINGS

Gold discoveries in New South Wales and Victoria in the early fifties brought hundreds of thousands of new colonists to Australia.

The squatters had attempted to keep these discoveries quiet, but failing in this, they put every obstacle in the way of the diggers, fearing loss of labour and encroachment on their lands.

Squatter-controlled legislatures in the two states devised a licensing system by which the miner had to pay an exorbitant monthly fee for his "right" to dig, whether he struck gold or not. This and other harsh measures led to revolts of the miners on several of the diggings. The culmination of the struggle took place at Eureka Lead, Ballarat, in December, 1854. (See The Men of Fifty-four in Part One.)

A new and fuller measure of democracy came from the agitation on the goldfields. By 1860 representative parliaments were a feature of the respective colonies. The squatters, however, still had control of the "upper houses"—the Legislative Councils.

While democrats from many lands were prominent among the gold-rush immigrants, there were features of life on the diggings that were far from progressive. The treatment of the Chinese miners, for instance, showed that passions and racial sentiments could be aroused without just cause. The Chinese were accused by the diggers of lowering their hard-won conditions. In actual fact it was the squatters and traders who first fanned this antagonism into open flames. The Chinese were in the habit of living frugally and sending the gold they won back to their homeland; hence the opposition to them from those who hoped to get the major share of it. The diggers lost nothing through the presence of the Chinese on the fields. Nevertheless this resentment continued until the end of the century, and became one of the bases of the so-called "White Australia" policy, the object of which was to exclude from Australian shores certain nationals, especially those of Asiatic birth.

3. SQUATTERS AND SELECTORS

I have already referred to the demands by the diggers for the unlocking of the lands when the alluvial gold had petered out. (See Bushrangers in Part One.) Legislation in New South Wales in 1861,* and later in Victoria, attempted to set up small-scale agricultural and dairy farming, but without great success for almost half a century. The "selectors," as I have pointed out, fared badly at the hands of the squatters and for the most part eked out a poor existence on the least fertile land. Their condition was further aggravated by droughts, bush fires and floods.

The selectors were often forced off their land by natural calamities and by the foreclosures of the banks. The big land companies, largely capitalised from England, gradually acquired some of the best of the selectors' properties.

Yet the selectors and their wives, with a courage and optimism almost beyond belief, added greatly to the tradition of mateship and never-say-die which Australia had known since convict times. They and their children came to know and love their country despite its frequent harshness. They gave a strong impetus to the forward march to nationhood.

4. IMMIGRANTS

The "new chums" or "chooms" were English migrants who settled in Australia from early times, but especially following the introduction of assisted passages in the eighteen forties.

It is hardly necessary to point out that the "new chums" played a major part in the settlement of Australia. But on their arrival they were frequently treated as figures of fun and practical jokes were a feature of their "initiation" into the new life. It was the old, old story of the local-born or "currency lads" getting a little of their own back on those pompous Englishmen who came to Australia with strong superiority complexes. The feelings of the native Australians towards the newcomers went deeper than this, however. In the latter half of the nineteenth century, nationalism

* Known as the Robertson Land Act, after Premier John Robertson, who introduced it.

was a powerful unifying force among the local-born. There was a tendency to regard the immigrant with suspicion as one who might help to break down living standards and democratic traditions. Slogans like "Australia for the Australians" and poems like Lawson's "A Word to Texas Jack" were the outcome of this deeply-held nationalist outlook. In one of Banjo Paterson's verses about Saltbush Bill, the author refers to "a jackeroo that came from a foreign strand" (meaning England). When Bill and the jackeroo come to blows:

> *Now the new chum fought for his honour's sake*
> *and the pride of the English race,*
> *But the drover fought for his daily bread with*
> *a smile on his bearded face.*

5. EARLY TRADE UNIONISM

Attempts to improve their working conditions were made in several instances by groups of convicts. However, it was not until the end of transportation to New South Wales in 1840 that trade unions could be formed on an effective basis.

Carpenters and joiners set up a friendly society in Sydney in 1845. Following the formation of the Operative Stonemasons' Society in 1850 there was a steady growth of trade union activity. The Eight Hours' Day movement, Chartist-inspired and led by the stonemasons, had won its objective by 1856. By the end of the eighties most trades had organised on some sort of union basis.

The great economic struggles of the nineties, following the boom period of the previous decade, showed the Australian workers their weakness without some form of political organisation to back up their demands on a parliamentary level, and to give them unifying objectives. Various socialist theories, the establishment of what was to become the Australian Labor Party, the introduction of I.W.W. theories and objectives from the United States, the One Big Union scheme, contributed to the ferment of the developing Labor movement in the period from 1890 to the outbreak of the war in 1914.

Many Labor Party members and followers felt that their principles were betrayed when Labor Prime Minister Fisher pledged the country "to our last man and our last shilling" in support of Britain's defence in the event of war. Again, after war had broken out and another Labor Prime Minister, W. M. Hughes, tried to introduce conscription for overseas service, tremendous opposition was aroused, spearheaded by the I.W.W. and other anti-conscription bodies. It would be a mistake to assume that only Labor Party supporters and industrial workers were opposed to this measure. When in 1916 a referendum was held to decide the conscription issue, a substantial majority of people in all walks of life voted against the proposal.

The end of the first world war saw the emergence of the Australian Labor Party as a weakened, though still powerful, political force. The I.W.W. ceased to have any effective influence. Soon, the question of socialist objectives for the party was to stir widespread discussion and to raise new issues of political organisation throughout the whole Australian Labor movement.

6. Republicanism and Nationalism

The earliest Irish convicts, most of them connected with the rebellion of 1798, had strong republican sympathies, and their influence, strengthened by the flow of Irish immigrants in the forties, and by the ideas of such men as the Scottish Presbyterian, Dr. John Dunmore Lang, gave to the trend of Australian republicanism a more than passing significance.

At Eureka, some of the rebellious diggers proposed setting up a Republic of Victoria. Again, during the period from 1860 to 1900 there were widespread discussions on the questions of monarchy versus republicanism. The famous journal, the Sydney *Bulletin*, began its life in 1880 with a declaration in favour of an Australian republic.

With the federation of the colonies into a Commonwealth in 1901, republicanism gradually died out as a political trend. Nationalism, on the other hand, and its implication of an Australia independent of British political and economic control, grew in vigour.

Love of the country went back to the days of the currency lads. As immigrants became absorbed into the Australian environment they ceased to think of England as "home." The "colonial" resented the patronising and often arrogant visitor from Britain and sought in the new land forms of culture corresponding to the deep sense of pride and achievement which it invoked.

The Sydney *Bulletin* met this need with its essentially nationalist approach to the local scene. It encouraged writers and artists to speak in terms and in language that would appeal to the shearer and the stockman as well as the city-dweller. It encouraged writers like Lawson, Paterson, Furphy, Brady, Victor Daley and A. G. Stephens, who knew their country and its people well, and shared their democratic aspirations.

The eighteen nineties saw the flowering of the richest literary and artistic expression the country has yet known. Australia had reached cultural maturity, and had begun to assert its voice as a nation in its own right.

1. Convicts and Governors

"THE SCHEMERS ABOVE"

Let us drink a good health to our schemers above
Who at length have contrived from this land to remove
Thieves, robbers and villains, they'll send 'em away,
To become a new people at Botany Bay.

Some men say they have talents and trades to get bread,
Yet they sponge on mankind to be cloathed and fed,
They'll spend all they get, and turn night into day,
Now I'd have all such sots sent to Botany Bay.

There's monopolizers who add to their store,
By cruel oppression and squeezing the poor,
There's butchers and farmers get rich quick in that way,
But I'd have all such rogues sent to Botany Bay.

There's whores, pimps, and bastards, a large costly crew,
Maintained by the sweat of a labouring few,
They should get no commission, place, pension or pay,
Such locusts should all go to Botany Bay.

And that we may sweep our foul nation quite clean,
Send off the shop-tax promoters so mean,
And those who deprive the light of the day,
Should work for a breakfast at Botany Bay.

The hulks and the jails had some thousands in store,
But out of the jails are ten thousand times more,
Who live by fraud, cheating, vile tricks, and foul play,
Should all be sent over to Botany Bay.

Now, should any take umbrage at what I have writ,
Or here find a bonnet or cap that will fit,
To such I have only this one word to say,
They are all welcome to wear it at Botany Bay.

> "Botany Bay, A New Song," a rare broadsheet of which
> there is a copy in the Mitchell Library, Sydney.

TRUE PATRIOTS ALL

From distant climes o'er widespread seas we come,
Though not with much eclat or beat of drum,
True patriots all; for be it understood,
We left our country for our country's good.*

BOTANY BAY

Farewell to Old England for ever,
　　Farewell to my rum culls as well,
Farewell to the well-known Old Bailee
　　Where I used for to cut such a swell.

Chorus:

Singing too-ral, li-oor-al, li-addity,
Singing too-ral, li-oor-al, li-ay;
Singing too-ral, li-oor-al, li-addity,
Singing too-ral, li-oor-al, li-ay.

There's the captain as is our commandier,
　　There's the bo'sun and all the ship's crew;

* From the prologue "by a Gentleman of Leicester", spoken at the opening
of Australia's first theatre "at Sydney, Botany Bay", by George Barrington,
pickpocket. In the play that followed, all the parts were played by convicts.
The year was 1796.

There's the first and the second class passengers
  Knows what we poor convicts goes through.

'Taint leaving Old England we cares about,
  'Taint cos we mis-spells wot we knows,
But becos we light-finger'd gentry
  Hops around with a log on our toes.

Oh, had I the wings of a turtle-dove!
  I'd soar on my pinions so high;
Slap bang to the arms of my Polly love,
  And in her sweet presence I'd die.

Now all my young dookies and duchesses,
  Take warning from what I've to say:
Mind all is your own as you toucheses,
  Or you'll find us in Botany Bay.

FLORIAN PASCAL, *Little Jack Sheppard.**

THE CONVICTS' OATH OF MATESHIP

. . . And then, at Jones's suggestion, or rather command, for
none disputed his assumption of the leadership, they took the
Convict Oath. They chanted the eight verses, which began:

Hand to hand
  On Earth, in Hell,
  Sick or Well,
On Sea or Land,
  On the Square, ever.
And ended—the intervening verses dare not be quoted—
  Stiff or in Breath,
  Lag or Free,
  You and Me,
In Life, in Death
  On the Cross, never.

They chanted them with crossed and re-crossed hands, and the
foot of each pressed to the foot of another. And after the verses,
the "loving-cup" of blood. Not a very copious draught—to provide
a hearty drink would have weakened them, and their leader was
too much of a general to occasion an unnecessary demand on their

* A musical play of the eighteen eighties. The song was for many years
extremely popular among Australians and is still frequently sung.

strength—only a drop or two from each man's open vein, sucked by every other man. So was fealty to their leader, honour to one another plighted. The Convict Oath was a terrible thing; it was never broken, without occasioning death to someone—not necessarily to the violator. . .

PRICE WARUNG in the Sydney *Bulletin*, July 4, 1891.

A RECKLESS MAGISTRATE

A story illustrating the reckless manner in which prisoners were flogged is told by the Launceston *Advertiser*. "A prisoner was found guilty of absconding, and sentenced to receive fifty lashes, when some circumstances were disclosed which proved that the prisoner was innocent, but had lost his pass. 'Never mind,' said the Launceston magistrate, 'the warrant is signed, let him be punished now; I will forgive him the next time he's brought up.' "

GEORGE E. BOXALL, *History of the Australian Bushrangers.*

THE CONVICT'S LETTER

The convicts, so far from having been ashamed of being flogged, boasted of it But nothing pleased them better than the relation of stories about the flogging of "freemen," as those settlers who had gone to the colonies neither as convicts nor officials were called.

One story, which may or may not be true, has been told as having occurred in every convict district in Australia. It was to the effect that a master one day gave a letter to an assigned servant and told him to take it to the nearest gaol. The servant, surmising that the letter was somewhat to the following effect: "Dear Sir,— Please give the bearer fifty for absconding (or what not), and oblige, yours truly, etc.", told a plausible tale to the first freeman he met and induced him to deliver the letter. The point of the story generally lay in the ingenuity with which the convict induced the freeman to deliver the letter for him, but the astonishment of the freeman when he was seized up to the triangles in spite of his struggles and protestations, and given the "fifty," was a perpetual source of joy and hilarity to the convicts who heard the story.

ibid.

"TASMANIAN JUSTICE"

Magistrates in 1827 were not always willing to spare the time required for a patient investigation. Some curious examples of magisterial equity are often told. One magistrate rose from the bench when he heard his waggon in the street, and delivered his sentence in his progress towards the door—"I can't stop; give him fifty."

JOHN WEST, History of Tasmania.

LIEUTENANT DAWES AND THE HEADHUNTERS

The picture of the English colonists at Sydney Cove as "guests" of the aboriginal inhabitants of the land may raise a smile to-day, but Governor Phillip used the word in all seriousness. He had the typical eighteenth century English notion of the "noble savage," dear to the romancers and poets, tamed by the civilising rod of empire. Such happy notions served, like Nelson's blind eye, to help the English to see only what they wanted to see. The plundering and rape of the native peoples was not a particularly pleasant picture.

"I shall think it a great point gained," wrote Phillip, "if I can proceed in this business without having any dispute with the natives, a few of which I shall endeavour to persuade to settle near us, and who I mean to furnish with everything that can tend to civilise them, and to give them a high opinion of their new guests."

He went about the job with his usual thoroughness, ordering all convicts to keep away from the aboriginal camps. Some convicts who attacked a party of natives were ordered one hundred and fifty lashes each and were kept in irons for a year. He imposed his civilising kindness on a young native named Benelong, set him up in grand style, and afterwards took him to England with another of Benelong's tribesmen, to be presented to the king. By the time Governor Hunter had brought him back to his homeland he was thoroughly surfeited with "civilisation" and took to the bush.

In a despatch of May 15, 1788, Phillip wrote, "Every precaution that was possible has been taken to prevent their receiving any insults and when I shall have time to mix more with them, every means shall be used to reconcile them to live amongst us, and to teach them the advantages they will reap from cultivating land."

Humanitarian as the aims of the first governor undoubtedly were, they were based upon a complete lack of understanding of the aboriginal mode of living; nor did Phillip have the means of keeping Englishman and Aborigine apart. There were persistent attacks on the native camps and interference with the aboriginal women. Friendly and warm-hearted at first, the dark people soon had good reason to be suspicious of the motives of their "guests." They were slowly becoming dispossessed of their hunting grounds. When the English officers went out duck-shooting they employed natives to swim out and retrieve the birds that fell into the river waters. In return for this service they received "the offals, and now and then a half-picked bone." They soon became surly and unco-operative.

The death of Phillip's gamekeeper at the hands of an Aborigine, decided the governor that kindness towards his "hosts" should on occasion be tempered by firmness. He ordered Lieutenant William Dawes and a party of soldiers to go down to Botany Bay and bring back ten aboriginal heads—male heads, because he was averse to hurting women. Dawes refused. The threat of arrest and probable repercussions would not persuade him to change his mind; however, after a talk with the Reverend Johnson, he decided to join the party.

Phillip's headhunters returned without their "bag"; and Dawes made it clear that he would never be induced to go on such an expedition again. A year later he was still of the same mind. It became necessary, for the proper upholding of authority, to have him sent back to England.

Professor G. A. Wood has described Dawes as "the first conscientious objector in Australian history." And the words which he is said to have spoken, "I will *not* cut off anyone's head and bring it home in a bag," echo bravely across the years.

THE FLOGGING OF PADDY GALVIN

> *In 1800, nineteen convicts were charged with conspiring to upset the government. Among those arrested, but not charged, was General Joseph Holt, one of the leaders of the Irish rebellion of 1798, who was sent out to Sydney in the following year with a number of other insurgents. Holt describes in his* Memoirs *how he was ordered to Toongabbie to witness the flogging of the nineteen convicts.* Attempts were made to get information from them as to where their pikes and other alleged arms were hidden.*

The next prisoner who was tied up was Paddy Galvin, a young

* This extract and the following are from the *Memoirs of Joseph Holt, General of the Irish Rebels in 1798*, edited by T. Crofton Croker, London, 1838. Croker's editing is heavy-handed and much of the original colourful writing has been lost. Part of Holt's holograph manuscript is in the Mitchell Library, Sydney. See *True Patriots All* by Geoffrey C. Ingleton.

lad about twenty years of age. He was also sentenced to receive three hundred lashes.

The first hundred were given on his shoulders, and he was cut to the bone between the shoulder blades, which were both bare. The doctor then directed the next hundred to be inflicted lower down, which reduced his flesh to such a jelly that the doctor ordered him to have the remaining hundred on the calves of his legs.

During the whole time Galvin never whimpered or flinched, if, indeed, it had been possible for him to have done so. He was asked, "Where the pikes were hid?" Galvin answered that he did not know, and if he did, he would not tell. "You may hang me," he said, "if you like; but you shall have no music out of my mouth to make others dance upon nothing."

JOSEPH HOLT, *Memoirs*.

THE CASTLE HILL REBELLION

"At half past eleven o'clock on Sunday night, 4th of March, 1804, an express was received by His EXCELLENCY, from Captain ABBOTT, Commanding Officer at Parramatta, with the intelligence that the Prisoners at Public Labour at Castle Hill, and the Settlers' men, were in a state of Insurrection, and had committed many daring outrages."

In these words the Sydney Gazette *of March 11, 1804, opened its account of the stirring events known as the Battle of Vinegar Hill. It was the most powerful of the convict rebellions. Its leaders were mainly Irish and their followers numbered several hundreds.*

On the 4th of March, 1804, when returning home through Parramatta, I saw several men standing about in little gangs, and, recollecting what had been told me, I suspected something was going on, but said nothing. I met Timothy Holster, taskmaster of the Government men. He and I seldom met but we drank together, and on this occasion we called for a decanter of rum. He was an Englishman, and when we were drinking he said to me, "Mr. Holt, take my advice, and do not be out late to-night, as I should be sorry to hear of anything against you."

I asked what he meant, and he told me that the Irishmen were to break out that night, and that the Government were in possession of their plans.

I immediately proceeded to Mr. Cox with my wife and child, and told him what I had heard. He asked me my opinion of the business. I answered that I knew nothing more than what I had heard and told him; but that I should be ready to defend his house and keep off any assailants. He gave Sergeant King, who was his clerk, orders to prepare some cartridges, and we were all upon the alert. . . . In the morning Mr. Cox rode over to inquire the cause of the proceedings of the night. He returned, and gave the following account: About 300 men had assembled on Castle Hill, and chosen one Cunningham, as their leader. Captain George Johnston went towards them and demanded what they wanted. They replied, "Death or liberty." A soldier named Laycock, who stood six feet six inches, a quartermaster in the corps, came up, and with one blow killed Cunningham on the spot. On this the whole mob took to their heels, and many were shot.

Ten of the leaders were hung, and three more hung the same evening at Parramatta. A party of 40 soldiers and some of the loyal settlers arrested some of the unfortunate wretches who tried to escape by flight, and brought them back before a court-martial. It was arranged that lots should be drawn from a hat, and that every third man whose name was drawn should be hanged. The arrival of the Governor put an end to this extraordinary proceeding.

JOSEPH HOLT, Memoirs.

The alarm began at Castle Hill about 8 o'clock on Sunday night where there are upwards of 200 Irish Prisoners (sent here for Seditious Practices in Ireland), by setting a House on fire and ringing the Bell, when Cunningham appeared as the avowed leader, vociferating the cries of "DEATH OR LIBERTY!" and assuring those who were joining him (and others who say they were compelled), that Sydney and Parramatta were in their possession, that they had nothing to do but obey his orders and plunder the Settlers of their Arms (for which purpose parties were sent off in different directions), and after being united, to march to Hawkesbury, where they were assured of their force being augmented to 1,100 men, with which they were to return to Castle Hill on Tuesday morning to breakfast, march to Parramatta, for the possession of which two well known disaffected persons were to be answerable. After planting the Tree of Liberty at Government House, they were to proceed to Sydney, the possession of which was also supposed secured by three disaffected characters, and then embark on board the ships, which would also be ready to receive them.*

Sydney Gazette, March 11, 1804.

* In reading the above, Patrick Henry's famous utterance comes to mind: "Is life so dear or peace so sweet as to be purchased at the price of chains and slavery? Forbid it, Almighty God! I know not what course others may take, but as for me, give me liberty, or give me death!"

RUM REBELLION

The New South Wales Corps, brought originally to Australia for garrison duties, and large landowners like John Macarthur, living profitably at the expense of small settlers, traders and convicts, were determined that Governor Bligh should no more interfere with their monopoly of the colony's rum sales than the two previous viceroys. Bligh was equally determined to act on his commission and put an end to the power of the "rum barons." Inevitably, clashes occurred, culminating in the arrest and trial of Macarthur on charges of importing a still illegally, and other malpractices. Macarthur refused to be tried by a court which included his enemy, Judge Advocate Atkins.

The corps sided with Macarthur, military insurrection followed, and the rebels, under Major Johnson, released Macarthur from jail and then marched on Government House. Bligh himself was arrested. He was eventually recalled to England where he ably defended himself. Lachlan Macquarie, who took his place as governor, allowed the rum monopoly to flourish for a time, but with the expansion of settlement, especially after 1815, land became an even more profitable means of monopoly investment.

This dastardly Junto—disgrace to the sword
  Which dangles beside them, ne'er before drawn in anger
Till the King's Captain General to them did accord
  A discipline more brisk than their grog-selling langour—
          They then caught flame
          Of revenge out of shame
In a body assembled their cowardly swords drawn
          'Gainst the person of Bligh
          Whose station is high
Involved in his seizure the rights of the Crown.

   .   .   .   .

The noise of the rebellion resounds o'er the Plain
  The anarchist Junto have pulled down the banner
Which monarchical Government sought but in vain
  To hold as the rallying standard of honour.
          The Diadem's here fled
          From off the King's head

His royal appointment by force they depose
        But the time it draws nigh
        When magnanimous Bligh
Will triumph with honour and prostrate his foes.

              "Song on New South Wales Rebellion."*

THE CONVICTS' RUM SONG

    Cut yer name across me backbone,
      Stretch me skin across a drum,
    Iron me up on Pinchgut Island
      From to-day till Kingdom Come!

    I will eat yer Norfolk dumpling
      Like a juicy Spanish plum,
    Even dance the Newgate Hornpipe
      If ye'll only gimme RUM!

                    Traditional.

CRAWLERS—KEEP OUT!

On getting sight of Sydney you see a waterside town scattered wide over upland and lowland, and if it be a breezy day the merry rattling pace of its manifold windmills here and there perched on the high points, is no unpleasing sight. It gives, even from the distance, a presage of the stirring, downright earnest life (be it for good or evil) that so strongly characterises the race that lives, and breathes, and strives around: a race with whom it is one of the worst reproaches to be *a crawler*.

    "ALEXANDER HARRIS", *Settlers and Convicts* (1847).

MUSQUITO ON HANGING

When the famous aboriginal convict, Musquito, was sentenced to death in Hobart Town in 1824, he said to his gaoler, Mr. Bisdee: "Hangin' no bloody good for blackfellow."

"Why not as good for blackfellow as for whitefellow?" Mr. Bisdee asked him.

"Oh," said Musquito, "very good for whitefellow. He used to it."

* Quoted, from the Bligh Papers, Mitchell Library, Sydney, by H. V. Evatt, in *Rum Rebellion*. Evatt's is the fullest and best-documented account of the insurrection.

GOVERNOR ARTHUR AND THE PROCLAMATION—
THE "BLACK WAR"

Tasmania's "Black War," which led to the complete anni-
hilation of a race of fine, gentle Aborigines, began soon after
the landing of Europeans and the setting up of the penal
establishments of Van Diemen's Land. At first friendly and
hospitable, the native tribes soon learned to despise and hate
the new occupiers of their soil. The military, the settlers and
many of the escaped convicts treated the Aborigines with an
inhumanity, a cold, ruthless cruelty that can have few paral-
lels in history. That the Aborigines were not the first offenders
and provokers of this developing hostility is clearly shown in
a letter written by Governor Arthur in 1828.

"On my succeeding to the government," he wrote, "I found
the quarrel of the Natives with the Europeans, occasioned by
an unfortunate step of the officer in command of the garrison
on the first forming of the settlement, was daily aggravated
by every kind of injury committed against the defence-
less Natives by the stock-keepers and sealers, with whom it
was a constant practice to fire upon them whenever they
approached, and to deprive them of their women whenever
the opportunity offered."

The Aborigines, with a courage which no English firearms
could quell, defended as best they could their families and
their tribal hunting grounds. They would not submit tamely
to Governor Arthur's order that they should be herded into
small reserves.

Finally, the Governor issued a proclamation, copies of
which were posted in the woods, warning the tribes away
from the settled districts: "I do hereby strictly command and
order all Aborigines immediately to retire and depart from,
and for no reason, or on no pretense, save as hereinafter provided, to re-enter such settled districts." One can imagine the
effect of these words on a people who could neither read nor
write!

When the proclamation failed, the official "Black War"
commenced in earnest with full-scale military operations. The
red-coats achieved nothing and they returned from their
"campaigns" to face a storm of ridicule. But what they were
unable to accomplish, the settlers achieved with method and
efficiency. Black men, women and children were shot down
mercilessly, or bayoneted, or burned alive. Out of the several

thousands who, thirty years earlier, were a laughing, happy, kindly people, only two hundred had survived by 1835. These were taken to Flinders Island in storm-swept Bass Strait, and their remnants had completely died out in 1860.

The following is an authentic record of a conversation between Tom, an Aborigine, and Governor George Arthur.

Tom: A'nt your stock-keeper bein' a kill plenty black fellow?

Governor: But your countrymen kill people that never did them any harm—they even kill women and children.

Tom: Well, a'nt that all same's white un? A'nt he kill plenty black un, a woman, an little picaninny too?

Governor: But you know, Tom, I want to be friendly and kind to them, yet they would spear me if they met me.

Tom (laughing): How he tell you make a friend along him? A'nt he all same a white un? 'Pose black un kill white fellow, a'nt you send all your constable after him? You say, dat black a devil kill a nurra white man; go—catch it—kill it—a'nt he then kill all black fellow he see, all picaninny too? A'nt dat all same black fellow—a'nt you been a take him own kangaroo-ground? How den he like?

(The Proclamation was then read, particularly those references to Aborigines having to apply for passports to travel through certain areas.)

Tom: You been make a proflamation—I never see dat foolish. When he see dat? He can't read; who tell him?

Governor: Can't you tell him, Tom?

Tom: No! me like you tell him yourself. They very soon spear me.

JOHN WEST, *History of Tasmania.*

THE FEMALE FACTORY

"There's plenty of flash molls in Sydney Town, but don't go near 'em is my advice," says Sam Clift to Benjamin Hall, in Wild Colonial Boys.* *"Just go straight to Parson Marsden in Parramatta and tell him you want a good gal, a straight goer—one not afraid o' work. He'll fix you up with a bride, I'll warrant, in next to no time. There's plenty of decent young females sent out for small offences, as ye were yourself, and they make dang good wives when they settle down with a steady-going young fella like you. . . . Marriage is only a*

* *Wild Colonial Boys,* by Frank Clune. The Benjamin Hall referred to was father of the famous bushranger.

matter of luck and you're as likely to get a good wife from the Female Factory as from anywhere else. . . ."

The Female Factory at Parramatta was set up as a reception house for convict women. Here in the most appalling conditions, they picked wool, made clothing or wove a coarse woollen cloth, until they were assigned as servants or were able to marry.

" *. . . it was from this place,"* wrote J. H. M. Abbott in Out of the Past, *"that the ancestress of many a good Australian went to the hut of the man who had chosen her to be his bride and his helpmate in the conquest of the wilderness. Indeed, Australia owes much to many of the women from the Factory whom emancipated prisoners took to wife because they could get no others. Most of them valiantly pioneered the new, wild country with their men, and played their parts nobly. Many a splendid 'Hawkesbury Native' whose manhood helped to make the Commonwealth could look back with loving pride to the woman whom the Factory had provided him with as a mother. In what she did after she left it she generally gave abundant proof that even the Factory couldn't keep a good girl down."*

BOTANY BAY COURTSHIP*

The Currency Lads may fill their glasses,
And drink to the health of the Currency Lasses;
But the lass I adore, the lass for me,
Is a lass in the Female Factory.

O! Molly's her name, and her name is Molly,
Although she was tried by the name of Polly;
She was tried and was cast for death at Newry,
But the Judge was bribed and so were the Jury.

She got *"death recorded"* in Newry town,
For stealing her mistress's watch and gown;
Her little boy Paddy can tell you the tale,
His father was turnkey of Newry jail.

The first time I saw the comely lass
Was at Parramatta, going to mass;
Says I, "I'll marry you now in an hour,"
Says she, "Well, go and fetch Father Power."

* "An excellent new Song, as it ought to be sung in the Theatre Royal, Sydney, by Mr. Bert Levy, in the character of THE TICKET-OF-LEAVE HOLDER."

But I *got into trouble* that very same night!
Being drunk in the street I got into a fight,
A constable seized me—I gave him a box—
And was put in the watch-house and then in the stocks.

O! it's very unaisy as I may remember,
To sit in the stocks in the month of December;
With the north wind so hot, and the hot sun right over,
O! sure, and it's no place at all for a lover!

"It's worse than the tread-mill," says I, "Mr. Dunn,
To sit here all day in the *hate* of the sun!"
"Either that or a dollar," says he, "for your folly,"—
But if I had a dollar I'd drink it with Molly.

But now I am out again, early and late
I sigh and I cry at the Factory gate,
"O! Mrs. R——, late Mrs. F——n,
O! won't you let Molly out very soon?"

"Is it Molly McGuigan?" says she to me,
"Is it not?" says I, for she know'd it was she.
"Is it her you mean that was put in the stocks
For beating her mistress, Mrs. Cox?"

"O! yes and it is, madam, pray let me in,
I have brought her a half-pint of Cooper's best gin,
She likes it as well as she likes her own mother,
O! now let me in, madam, I am her brother."

So the Currency Lads may fill their glasses,
And drink to the health of the Currency Lasses;
But the lass I adore, the lass for me,
Is a lass in the Female Factory.

Sydney *Gazette,* July 14, 1832.

JIM JONES

Air: "Irish Molly, Oh!"

Oh, listen for a moment, lads,
    And hear me tell my tale;
How, o'er the sea from England's shore,
    I was compelled to sail.

The jury says, "He's guilty, sir!"
  And says the judge, says he—
"For life, Jim Jones, I'm sending you
  Across the stormy sea.

"And take my tip, before you ship
  To join the iron gang,
Don't be too gay at Botany Bay,
  Or else you'll surely hang.

"Or else you'll hang," he says, says he,
  "And after that, Jim Jones,
High up upon the gallows tree
  The crows will pick your bones.

"You'll have no chance for mischief then—
  Remember what I say.
They'll flog the mischief out of you
  When you get to Botany Bay!"

The waves were high upon the sea,
  The winds blew up in gales;
I'd rather be drowned in misery
  Than go to New South Wales.

For night and day the irons clang,
  And like poor galley slaves
We toil and moil and when we die
  Must fill dishonoured graves.

But by and by I'll break my chains;
  Into the bush I'll go;
And join the brave bushrangers there—
  Jack Donahoe and Co.*

And some dark night when everything
  Is silent in the town
I'll kill the tyrants one and all
  And shoot the floggers down.

I'll give the law a little shock—
  Remember what I say.

* Jack Donahoe, famous convict bushranger. See the next ballad.

162

They'll yet regret they sent Jim Jones
In chains to Botany Bay!

Quoted in FRANK CLUNE, *Wild Colonial Boys*.

BOLD JACK DONAHOE

In Dublin town I was brought up, in that city of great fame—
My decent friends and parents, they will tell to you the same.
It was for the sake of five hundred pounds I was sent across the main,
For seven long years in New South Wales to wear a convict's chain.

Chorus:

Then come, my hearties, we'll roam the mountains high!
Together we will plunder, together we will die!
We'll wander over mountains and we'll gallop over plains—
For we scorn to live in slavery, bound down in iron chains.

I'd scarce been there twelve months or more upon the Australian shore,
When I took to the highway, as I'd oft-times done before.
There was me and Jacky Underwood, and Webber and Webster, too.
These were the true associates of bold Jack Donahoe.

Now Donahoe was taken, all for a notorious crime,
And sentenced to be hanged upon the gallows-tree so high.
But when they came to Sydney gaol he left them in a stew,
And when they came to call the roll they missed bold Donahoe.

As Donahoe made his escape, to the bush he went straightway.
The people they were all afraid to travel night or day—
For every week in the newspapers there was published something new
Concerning this dauntless hero, the bold Jack Donahoe!

As Donahoe was cruising, one summer's afternoon,
Little was his notion his death was near so soon,
When a sergeant of the horse police discharged his car-a-bine,
And called aloud on Donahoe to fight or to resign.

"Resign to you—you cowardly dog! a thing I ne'er will do,
For I'll fight this night with all my might," cried bold Jack Dona-
hoe.
"I'd rather roam these hills and dales, like wolf or kangaroo,
Than work one hour for government!" cried bold Jack Donahoe.

He fought six rounds with the horse police until the fatal ball,
Which pierced his heart and made him start, caused Donahoe to
fall.
And as he closed his mournful eyes, he bade this world adieu,
Saying, "Convicts all, both large and small, say prayers for Dona-
hoe!"*

Traditional.

* This convict bushranger died in 1830. An account of his exploits will be
found in Boxall's *History of the Australian Bushrangers.* It will be noted
that the chorus is identical with that of the much later ballad, "The Wild
Colonial Boy". In another version of the Bold Jack Donahoe ballad this
chorus is not used.

2. THE GOLD DIGGINGS

A CONVICT'S DISCOVERY

In August, 1788, a convict named James Daley declared that he had found gold and, in proof of his story, displayed a piece of stone which appeared to be impregnated with the precious metal. At first, even under coercion, he flatly refused to reveal to the authorities where the find had been made. Later, Governor Phillip appeared and compelled Daley to walk before him, threatening instant death should he attempt to run away or deceive His Excellency. The wretched man, being fearful of the lash, made a confession—that he had filed down a portion of a yellow metal buckle, mixed with the filings particles of gold filed off a guinea piece, and then blended the whole with clay which he baked, or otherwise made stone-like. It is not improbable that Daley was the first discoverer of gold in this country. His confession, as some believe, may have been untrue; certainly it was extorted through fear, not of death, but the lash.

CHARLES BARRETT, *Gold*.

A MEMORABLE DAY

I took the pick and scratched the gravel off a schistose dyke which ran across the creek at right angles with its side and, with a trowel, I dug a panful of earth which I washed in the waterhole. The first trial produced a little piece of gold. "Here it is!" I exclaimed; and then I washed five panfuls in succession, obtaining gold from all but one. . . . What I said on the instant—though, I must admit, not warranted as the language of calm reflection—has since been much laughed at. . . . "This," I exclaimed to my guide, "is a memorable day in the history of New South Wales. I shall be a baronet, you will be knighted, and my old horse will be stuffed, put into a glass case, and sent to the British Museum."

EDWARD HAMMOND HARGRAVES describes his discovery of gold on the Turon River, N.S.W., on February 12, 1851.

THE DIGGERS

When first I left old England's shore,
    Such yarns as we were told,
As how folks in Australia
    Could pick up lumps of gold;
So, when we got to Melbourne town,
    We were ready soon to slip
And get even with the captain—
    All hands scuttled from the ship.

We steered our course for Geelong town,
    Then north-west to Ballarat,
Where some of us got mighty thin,
    And some got sleek and fat;
Some tried their luck at Bendigo,
    And some at Fiery Creek;
I made a fortune in a day
    And spent it in a week.

From "With My Swag On My Shoulder," an old bush
song.

GOLD FEVER

The gold fever of the colony was renewed in intensity. Many who had resisted the temptations of Ballarat succumbed to those of Mount Alexander; and when the eager flood of prospectors unearthed the still richer deposits of Bendigo Creek, some twenty miles to the north, the last touch was given that upset the stoicism of the coolest head. The turnkeys of all the gaols resigned, the warders of the lunatic asylum decamped. Out of forty police who were stationed in Melbourne, thirty-eight sent in their resignations for the end of December; and the New Year's holiday found a city of twenty thousand people with two constables to keep order. There were fifty-nine vessels lying in the Bay. They had 1,029 seamen; 521 of these disappeared for the diggings, and the others had to be watched. . . . Some vessels that had only two men apiece offered £80 a man for a crew to take them home, but that could induce nobody; £100 had as little effect; and it was only by the payment of £120 that a vessel which was bound to return to England within a given time could bribe a common seaman to ship for a voyage, for which the ordinary rate would have been £8. The resignations of those in the civil service flowed in at such a rate that La Trobe had, on his own responsibility, and with many misgivings, to increase the salaries all round by about a half.

ALEXANDER SUTHERLAND, quoted in CHARLES BARRETT,
Gold.

THE ROARING FIFTIES

Excitement in Melbourne increased when several thousands of lucky diggers returned to the city for the Christmas holidays. They had money to spend, and they spent it so liberally that shopkeepers reaped a very rich harvest. Profiteering of course was rampant. Prices of goods were doubled and trebled. The diggers cheerfully paid whatever prices were demanded by greedy vendors. There was no price-fixing in those wonderful days. Men were known to light their pipes with blazing bank-notes, and even to eat notes sandwiched between slices of buttered bread. When the governor's wife, choosing a ball dress in a Melbourne shop, hesitated over paying the extravagant price demanded for the material she fancied, a digger, who was standing by the counter, said to the attendant, "Put it up for *my* missus."

BARRETT, op cit.

GOLDEN CRADLES (A Gold Diggers' Song)

> In bush attire let each aspire
>   By noble emulation,
> To gain a digger's chief desire
>   Gold, by wise regulation.
>
> With spades and picks we work like bricks
>   And dig in gold formation;
> And stir our cradles with short sticks
>   To break conglomeration.

This golden trade doth not degrade
  The man of information,
Who shovels nuggets with the spade
  Of beauteous conformation.

What mother can her infant stock
  View with more satisfaction
Than we our golden cradles rock,
  Which most love to distraction.

Let those who dare try thwart our care
  At our gold occupation;
They with bewilderment will stare
  At golden incubation.

We dig and delve from six to twelve,
  And then for relaxation,
We wash our pans and cradles' shelves,
  And turn to mastication.

JAMES BONWICK, *Notes of a Gold Digger, and Gold
Diggers' Guide* (1852).*

DIGGERS' JINGLE (*circa* 1854)

On the goldfields of Ballarat
You're scarce allowed to wear your hat;
Thrice lucky he who in its stead
Will long get leave to wear his head.

Traditional.

"WHERE'S YOUR LICENCE?"

Now a tall ugly trap,
Espied a young chap,
Up the gully cutting like fun;
  So he quickly gave chase,
  But 'twas a hard race—
I assure you the digger could run.

* Bonwick has this note: "Amusements are not in harmony with the diggings. Men come here usually to work in earnest, and they have no time for play. Yet now and then a song is heard, with the notes of a flute or violin. At Bullock Creek a sick friend was charmed on the one side by Kate Kearney, and on the other by the whole range of Wesley's hymns proceeding from a most indefatigable Burra songstress. In one tent near me there was an occasional concert of a fife, a dish-bottom drum, and a primitive sort of triangles. As a sample of a diggings song, a selection may be given (the above—Ed.). It is said to be set to the air of 'Coronation'."

Down a hole he went pop,
Whilst the bobby up top,
Says, "just come up," shaking his staff:
"Young man of the crown,
If you want me, come down;
For I'm not to be caught with such chaff."

CHARLES THATCHER.*

"JOE!"

The diggers called the police "the Joes," they being the tools of "law and order" for Charles Joseph La Trobe; in the same way, the English police under Charles Fox were called "Charlies," and under Sir Robert Peel "peelers" or "bobbies."

The police retaliated with "digger dogs."

"Right, up, my noble bloody digger dog, out with your licence. Don't keep me here all day." That was their style.

From an unpublished MS. by MONTY MILLER, veteran of Eureka.

POLICE ON THE DIGGINGS

They let the thief escape—notorious!
They capture the poor digger—glorious!
They are not men, yet they're the police,
And doubtless help to keep the peace.
Tell me, La Trobe, of all the breed,
How many can the licence read?

"GOLDDIGGER": *Laughing a Crime or Twenty Pounds No Comedy* (1853).

THE SQUATTOCRACY

The squatters now have grown so great,
You cannot reach their high estate;
The mutton growers take their stand,
The would-be nobles of the land. . . .

ibid.

* From " 'Where's Your Licence?' A celebrated parody on 'The Gay Cavalier', and sung by Mr. Thatcher, on the Gold Fields, with great applause." In *Eureka, Freedom's Fight of '54*, Robert Ross refers to a statement that the above lines were composed by Mr. Mulholland, Ballarat's first town clerk. This is, of course, incorrect.

THE DIGGERS' DEMANDS

> And why, ye councillors of the land,
> Who spend our gold with liberal hand,
> Should we not have the franchise, too,
> And soil to till, as well as you?

ibid.

THE MINERS' OATH—1854

The "Southern Cross" was hoisted up the flagstaff—a very splendid pole, eighty feet in length, and straight as an arrow. This maiden appearance of our standard, in the midst of armed men, sturdy, self-over-working gold diggers of all languages and colours, was a fascinating object to behold. There is no flag in old Europe half so beautiful as the "Southern Cross" of the Ballaarat miners, first hoisted on the old spot, Bakery-hill. The flag is silk, blue ground, with a large silver cross, similar to the one in our southern firmament; no device of arms, but all exceedingly chaste and natural.

Captain Ross, of Toronto, was the bridegroom of our flag, and sword in hand he had posted himself at the foot of the flagstaff, surrounded by his rifle division.

Peter Lalor, our commander-in-chief, was on the stump holding with his left hand the muzzle of his rifle, whose butt-end rested on his foot. A gesture of his right hand signified what he meant when he said, "It is my duty now to swear you in, and to take with you the oath to be faithful to the Southern Cross. Hear me with attention. The man who, after this solemn oath does not stand by our standard, is a coward in heart.

"I order all persons who do not intend to take the oath, to leave the meeting at once.

"Let all divisions under arms 'fall in' in their order round the flagstaff."

The movement was made accordingly. Some five hundred armed diggers advanced in real sober earnestness, the captains of each division making the military salute to Lalor, who now knelt down, the head uncovered, and with the right hand pointing to the standard exclaimed in a firm measured tone:

"We swear by the Southern Cross to stand truly by each other, and fight to defend our rights and liberties."

An universal well-rounded *Amen,* was the determined reply; some five hundred right hands stretched towards our flag.

The earnestness of so many faces of all kinds of shape and colour; the motley heads of all sorts of size and hair; the shagginess of so many beards of all lengths and thicknesses; the vividness of double the number of eyes electrified by the magnetism of the Southern Cross; was one of those grand sights, such as are recorded only in the history of "the crusaders in Palestine."

CARBONI RAFFAELLO, *The Eureka Stockade.*

MARK TWAIN ON EUREKA

By and by there was a result; and I think it may be called the finest thing in Australasian history. It was a revolution—small in size, but great politically; it was a strike for liberty, a struggle for a principle, a stand against injustice and oppression. It was the Barons and John over again; it was Hampden and Ship-Money; it was Concord and Lexington. . . . It is another instance of a victory won by a lost battle.

MARK TWAIN, *More Tramps Abroad.*

THE REMOVAL OF INSPECTOR LOBBS FROM BALLAARAT TO MELBOURNE

(After the style of "The Soldier's Tear.")

Upon the hill he turned,
    To take a last fond look,
Of the diggers who were washing up,
    Near the bridge, there, at the brook;
He heard the cradles rock,
    So familiar to his ear;
And th' inspector leaned against the fence
    And wiped away a tear.

Around the blessed creek,
    Some diggers took a sight
Of the inspector standing there,
    And joed with all their might.
But he was too far off,
    Their insolence to hear;
And he still kept leaning 'gainst the fence,
    And brushed away a tear.

He turned and left the spot—
    Oh, do not deem him weak,
For new were the inspector's togs,
    And quite plump was his cheek.

Go watch the jolly style,
   These coves live in up here;
Be sure that those who have to leave,
   Will wipe away a tear.*

CHARLES THATCHER, Colonial Songster (1857).

PASSING OF THE ALLUVIAL GOLD DAYS

*Pint*pots were once filled from rich ground,
   And in gold bags they *sacked* it,
Now strange to say in *quartz* 'tis found,
   But it's harder to extract it;
To *pick* it up's the work of weeks,
   And it requires great vigour,
And *blasting* rocks and *damming* creeks
   Is done by every digger.

CHARLES THATCHER, Thatcher's Colonial Minstrel (1864).

No. 2 REEF, BEFORE CRUSHING

"Alexander Forbes," says Douglas B. W. Sladen in the introduction to his anthology, A Century of Australian Song, *" . . . was a wild fellow, who ran away to sea from college; and at last coming to Queensland, became a 'swagman' of every trade by turns—stockman, drover, butcher, miner, and what not. In all these capacities he seems to have been a prime favourite with his mates, and really was a man of very considerable powers. His rhymes have a value, because he wrote from his own experiences, and his experiences were such as do not ordinarily befall writers, so that there is very little first-hand writing about them. Here, for instance, is 'No. 2 Reef,' a rhyme, which was not poetical enough to be worth considering in the text, but which yet is a characteristic piece of miners' humour. . . ."*

Now, if this claim turns out an ounce,
   Right joyful I shall be;
I'll walk into the Morinish,
   And have a jolly spree.

* This fine little satire on the comforts enjoyed by the police on the gold diggings is a parody on the maudlin poem, "The Soldier's Tear", by Thomas Haynes Bayly (1797-1839). The strong dislike of the diggers for the police is brought out in the second verse. The cry of "Joe!" invariably went up when the "traps" approached. One of the victories gained at Eureka was the recall of the gold commissioners. Hence, the popularity of this song among the diggers can be well imagined.

And if two ounces it should run,
    By jove! that would be glorious;
Rockhampton I'd turn upside down,
    And spend a month uproarious.

And if three ounces we should get,
    That just would suit my kidney;
I'd take my passage in a boat,
    And have a trip to Sydney.

If we four ounces should obtain,
    No longer here I'd tarry;
The steamer which takes home the mails,
    This male should also carry.

And if a duffer it should prove—
    But, Lord! I'll say no more now;
I have a guardian angel,
    And he's stuck to me before now.

A REMARKABLE ESCAPE

It rarely comes to the writer of goldfields stories to have the privilege of recording for the first time one that happened as long ago as June 13, 1893. It was told to me by Mr. J. G. Thomas who came over from N.S.W. to see his daughter and build up his health.

The pioneer prospector and later manager on the Mulga Queen Mine on the Edistoun field was at Coolgardie soon after the rich bonanza, Bailey's Reef, was discovered by Tommy Talbot, whose death occurred recently, and his mates Dick Fosser and Harry Baker. Like many other youths, Thomas joined in the rush to the supposed find near Mount Yuille, having hurriedly packed some stores on to his horse and joined the rush. But it was a false alarm . . . not even a billycan of gold that gave the name to that dud rush.

He was returning to Coolgardie to replenish his stores and lit a fire and put his billy on at a clay pan near Mt. Robinson (not the one near Hannan's Lake). He had his gun handy, hoping to pot some bird or animal as a change from tin dog; he spied what he took to be an emu. He allowed the object to come nearer through the bush but keeping his aim. To his consternation it proved to be a man! His heart gave a jump. *He might easily have shot the little be-whiskered man who had a blanket over his shoul-*

ders to keep off the rain, the corners hanging down like the small wings of an emu!

Instead of shooting him, Thomas asked him to share his billy. He was *Paddy Hannan* and he was glad to accept the tea and to realise that Providence had indeed been good to them. He was to *make history next day.*

They were both on the way to Coolgardie. Before they started, the little man in his quiet way said, "You have been very kind to me. I am going to report our find to the warden's office and as soon as I do so and claim the reward, there will be a rush. You had better pick up some more tucker and hurry back to a point on the western slope of the centre of three small hills." (They are known as Mt. Charlotte, Hannan's Hill and Cassidy Hill.)

"Tell my mates," Paddy Hannan went on, "Dan O'Shea and Tom Flannigan, that I told you to peg out next to our Reward Claim."

As suggested, J. G. Thomas hurried back, found the two mates, pegged out his claim and did fairly well, the beginning of good and bad runs of luck . . . prospector's luck!

"Diorite" in the *Western Mail,* August 28, 1952.

3. SQUATTERS AND SELECTORS

COLONIAL CURIOSITIES: THE SQUATTER

*In this ballad, Charles Thatcher, "the Colonial Minstrel,"
lists a number of strange features of Australian life which he
proposes should be sent to England and shown at the British
Museum.*

> The first one I've got on my list
>   Would be viewed with surprise by the nation—
> 'Tis the squatter who never complains
>   And who doesn't require compensation.

CHARLES THATCHER, *Thatcher's Colonial Minstrel* (1864).

PORTRAIT OF A SQUATTER, 1857

> Oh, you stupid, grumbling chap,
> At you I means to have a rap;
> For you always are complaining
> Of your bad luck here, and feigning
> That by the discovery of gold,
> You fellows are completely sold;
> But had not gold been found out here,
> You all might then have, p'raps, looked queer,

And found no customers, I fear,
    For that bad, scabby mutton.
But now you sell your crops like fun;
Hay at an awful price per ton;
And that's the way we coves are done,
    You avaricious glutton.

Signed, BILLY NUTTS.

"Lines upon a Squatter after the style of *Hogg*, improved by *Lamb*," From THATCHER's *Colonial Songster* (1857).

THE SQUATTER'S MAN

This old ballad belongs to the period of the eighteen sixties.

Come, all ye lads an' list to me,
That's left your homes an' crossed the sea,
To try your fortune, bound or free,
    All in this golden land.
For twelve long months I had to pace,
Humping my swag with a cadging face,
Sleeping in the bush, like the sable race,
    As in my song you'll understand.

Unto this country I did come,
A regular out-and-out new chum.
I then abhorred the sight of rum—
    Teetotal was my plan.
But soon I learned to wet one eye—
Misfortune oft-times made me sigh.
To raise fresh funds I was forced to fly,
    And be a squatter's man.

Soon at a station I appeared.
I saw the squatter with his beard,
And up to him I boldly steered
    With my swag and billy-can.
I said, "Kind sir, I want a job!"
Said he, "Do you know how to snob,
Or can you break in a bucking cob?"
    Whilst my figure he well did scan.

"'Tis now I want a useful cove
To stop at home and not to rove.

The scamps go about—a regular drove—
    I suppose you're one of the clan?
But I'll give ten, ten, sugar an' tea;
Ten bob a week, if you'll suit me,
And very soon I hope you'll be
    A handy squatter's man.

"At daylight you must milk the cows,
Make butter, cheese, an' feed the sows,
Put on the kettle, the cook arouse,
    And clean the family shoes.
The stable an' sheep yard clean out,
And always answer when we shout,
With 'Yes ma'am,' and 'No, sir'; mind your mouth,
    And my youngsters don't abuse.

"You must fetch wood an' water, bake an' boil,
Act as butcher when we kill;
The corn an' taters you must hill,
    Keep the garden spick and span.
You must not scruple in the rain
To take to market all the grain.
Be sure you come sober back again
    To be a squatter's man."

He sent me to an old bark hut,
Inhabited by a greyhound slut,
Who put her fangs through my poor fut,
    And snarling, off she ran.
So once more I'm looking for a job,
Without a copper in my fob.
With Ben Hall or Gardiner I'd rather rob,
    Than be a squatter's man.*

            Collected by A. B. PATERSON, *Old Bush Songs.*

GIVE EVERY POOR MAN A HOME†

        Oh, Government, hear our petition,
            Find work for the strong willing hand,

---

* Paterson gives these explanations: "Do you know how to snob?"—A snob
in English slang is a bootmaker, so the squatter wanted his man to do a bit of
boot repairing. "I'll give ten, ten, sugar an' tea."—The "ten, ten" refers to the
amount—ten pounds weight—of flour and meat that made up the weekly ration
on the stations. For Ben Hall and Gardiner, see under "Bushrangers".

† From "'Hurrah for Australia', New Original Song, on the Land Question,
as written and sung by Thatcher, with immense applause."

Our dearest and greatest ambition
  Is to settle and cultivate land;
Australia's thousands are crying
  For a home in the vast wilderness,
Whilst millions of acres are lying
  In their primitive wild uselessness.

Upset squatterdom domination,
  Give every poor man a home,
Encourage our great population,
  And like wanderers no more we'll roam;
Give, in mercy, a free scope to labour
  Uphold honest bold industry,
Then no one will envy his neighbour,
  But contented and happy we'll be.

CHARLES THATCHER, Thatcher's Colonial Minstrel (1864).

THE FREE SELECTOR

(A song of 1861)

Ye sons of industry, to you I belong,
And to you I would dedicate a verse or a song.
Rejoicing o'er the victory John Robertson has won
Now the Land Bill has passed and the good time has come,
  Now the Land Bill, etc.

No more with our swags through the bush need we roam
For to ask of another there to give us a home;
Now the land is unfettered, and we may reside
In a home of our own by some clear waterside,
  In a home of our own, etc.

On some fertile spot which we may call our own,
Where the rich verdure grows, we will build up a home,
There industry will flourish and content will smile,
While our children rejoicing will share in our toil,
  While our children, etc.

We will plant our garden and sow our own field,
And eat from the fruits which industry will yield,
And be independent, as long we have strived,
Though those that have ruled us the right long denied,
  Though those that have ruled us, etc.

Traditional.

DESCRIPTION OF A "COCKY"

A "cocky" is a small farmer. He usually selects himself a three-hundred- or five-hundred-acre holding, clears it, fences it, pays for it, ploughs it, sows wheat in it—and then goes to bed to wait for his crop. The next morning he gets up and finds the paddock white with cockatoos grubbing up his seed. He is there to plough and sow and reap—cockatoos. And that, they say, is how he got the name of a cockatoo farmer—a cocky.

C. E. W. BEAN: *On the Wool Track.*

THE NEW ENGLAND COCKY

'Twas a New England cocky, as of late I've been told,
Who died, so 'tis said, on account of the cold;
When dying, he called to his children "Come here!
As I'm dying, I want my fortune to share.

"Dear children, you know I've toiled early and late,
I've struggled with nature, and wrestled with fate.
Then all do your best to my fortune repair;
And to my son John I leave a dear native bear.

"To Mary I give my pet kangaroo,
May it prove to turn out a great blessing too;
To Michael I leave the old cockatoo,
And to Bridget I'll give the piebald emu.

"To the others whatever is left I will leave—
Don't quarrel, or else my poor spirit will grieve;
There's the fish in the stream, and the fowl on the lake,
Let each have as much as any may take.

"And now, my dear children, no more can I do,
My fortune I've fairly divided with you,"
And these were the last words his children did hear—
"Don't forget that I reared you on pumpkin and bear."

Traditional.

THE SHEEP-WASHER'S LAMENT

Air: "The Bonnie Irish Boy."

Come now, ye sighing washers all,
Join in my doleful lay,

Mourn for the times none can recall,
  With hearts to grief a prey.
We'll mourn the washer's sad downfall
  In our regretful strain,
Lamenting on the days gone by
  Ne'er to return again.

When first I went a-washing sheep
  The year was sixty-one,
The master was a worker then,
  The servant was a man;
But now the squatters, puffed with pride,
  They treat us with disdain;
Lament the days that are gone by
  Ne'er to return again.

From sixty-one to sixty-six
  The bushman, stout and strong,
Would smoke his pipe and whistle his tune,
  And sing his cheerful song,
As wanton as the kangaroo
  That bounds across the plain.
Lament the days that are gone by
  Ne'er to return again.

Supplies of food unstinted, good,
  No squatter did withhold.
With plenty grog to cheer our hearts,
  We feared nor heat nor cold,
With six-and-six per man per day
  We sought not to complain.
Lament the days that are gone by
  Ne'er to return again.

With perfect health, a mine of wealth,
  Our days seemed short and sweet,
On pleasure bent our evenings spent,
  Enjoyment was complete.
But now we toil from morn till night,
  Though much against the grain,
Lamenting on the days gone by,
  Ne'er to return again.

May bushmen all in unity
  Combine with heart and hand,
May cursed, cringing poverty
  Be banished from the land.
In Queensland may prosperity
  In regal glory reign,
And washers in the time to come
  Their vanished rights regain.

                                        Traditional.

A "COCKY'S" WORK

On some farms I have come across an old tool-shed built of slabs—once the home of a settler in the days of the pit saw. I have pulled the bootlace latch as so many before me and, entering the gloom, have noted the broad hearth and the rusted camp oven, and up against the wall a rough-hewn stool; and it has not then been so difficult to hear again the voices of the selector and his wife, and the chatter of the barefoot children. I have asked the old man who showed me around: "Did you work hard in the old days?" And with the ghost of a hearty laugh he has replied: "Work hard? Why, they used to put a bag over the sun so we wouldn't see it go down."

                          MAX BROWN, *Australian Son.*

JACK DOW

Jack Dow of Toganmain station (N.S.W.), was a quaint bush character. His fame to eccentricity rested on the stupid jobs he used to give men looking for work. One was to set a man turning a grindstone. If the man stopped, Dow, who was watching, would call, "Keep her moving!" As the stone wasn't being used for any purpose the worker couldn't see the use of turning it, and usually turned the job in without even waiting for rations.

"HUNGRY TYSON," SQUATTER

Starting business with his brother, he (James Tyson) once found himself on a bank of the Murrumbidgee with only a shilling in his pocket. This was demanded by the punt-man to ferry him across. Tyson saved the money by swimming.

        A. E. MARTIN, *Place Names in Queensland, New Zealand*
                                              and the Pacific.

181

A TALE OF TYSON

A broad-shouldered man, he was, standing near six feet four in his socks; and keen-eyed as a duckhawk. They say Jimmy was a vegetarian, and mean enough to eat boiled grass when short of tucker, though he could have bought a feed easy enough. One night, he rode up to a homestead and asked for a shakedown. The boss was away and his missus, who recognised Jimmy, wasn't one of the giving sort. She'd heard about Jimmy liking vegetables better than mutton and beef. And what does she say to him? "Go out and hobble yourself. There's plenty of grass in the horse paddock."

CHARLES BARRETT, *The Sunlit Land, Wanderings in Queensland.*

KILEY'S RUN

.   .   .   .

Old Kiley seldom used to roam,
He liked to make the run his home;
The swagman never turned away
With empty hand at close of day
    From Kiley's Run.

.   .   .   .

But droughts and losses came apace
    To Kiley's Run,
Till ruin stared him in the face;
He toiled and toiled while lived the light,
He dreamed of overdrafts at night:
At length, because he could not pay,
His bankers took the stock away
    From Kiley's Run.

Old Kiley stood and saw them go
    From Kiley's Run,
The well-bred cattle marching slow;
His stockmen, mates for many a day,
They wrung his hand and went away.
Too old to make another start
Old Kiley died—of a broken heart
    On Kiley's Run.

.   .   .   .

The owner lives in England now
    Of Kiley's Run.

He knows a racehorse from a cow;
But that is all he knows of stock:
His chiefest care is how to dock
Expenses, and he sends from town
To cut the shearers' wages down
     On Kiley's Run.

.   .   .   .

The name itself is changed of late
     Of Kiley's Run.
They call it "Chandos Park Estate."
The lonely swagman through the dark
Must hump his swag past Chandos Park—
The name is English, don't you see;
The old name sweeter sounds to me
     Of Kiley's Run.

     From A. B. PATERSON, "On Kiley's Run."

THE PREMIER WHO WENT TO BOURKE

Just before one big drought broke, the people of Bourke had received a visit from their Premier. A deputation waited on him there to ask for a few more concessions in railway freights or something. It was hardly necessary to put the case to him, because even people on the other side of the world knew by the cables in the papers what the case along the Darling was just then. The grass had long since disappeared; the face of the country was shifting red and grey sand, blowing about wherever the wind carried it. The fences were covered; dead sheep and fallen trunks had become sand-hills. Millions of trees were killed; the birds had been dropping dead. Except where there were trees, the West was literally not different from the Sahara Desert. Some men's nerves had broken down under the conditions, and they had had to flee from the back-country in fear for their sanity. The rest of the world had been watching the fight against that calamity as people in war follow the struggle at the front. All the rest of Australia, and even Europe, had given signs of their sympathy. What little comfort the men and women out there had, they drew from this. So there was really no need to put the case to their Premier.

However, just for form's sake, they put to him for about three-quarters of an hour some of the urgencies which had been filling the newspapers for months, and which presumably had been worrying the government into white hairs. He seemed to be listening. When they had pretty well finished he suddenly looked up.

"What do you do with the country in these parts?" he said, waving his hands towards the window. "What—er—what use d'yer make of it?"

They were a little surprised. They had just been telling him for three-quarters of an hour.

But they said:

"Oh, well, we put sheep on it—that is, when there is any grass on it. . . ."

"D'jever think of dairyin'?" asked the Premier.

C. E. W. BEAN, *On the Wool Track.*

4. IMMIGRANTS

THAT'LL TELL YOU ABOUT EMIGRATION

Air: "Drops of Brandy."

What a curious country this is,
    And what changes it's now undergoing,
For since the gold-fields started first,
    In importance each day it's been growing:
Five years ago sheep were boiled down
    For their fat upon many a station,
But each animal's now worth twelve bob—
    That'll tell you about emigration!

The gold age now is gone by,
    As regards high extravagant prices—
Shopkeepers are civil and meek,
    And a moderate profit suffices:
They don't come it now on the bounce,
    They're civil in their conversation,
And they're all now obliged *to give change*—
    That'll tell you about emigration!

CHARLES THATCHER, *Thatcher's Colonial Minstrel* (1864).

COLONIAL EXPERIENCE

(By a New Chum)

Air: "So Early in the Morning."

When first I came to Sydney Cove
And up and down the streets did rove,
I thought such sights I ne'er did see
Since first I learnt my ABC.

Chorus:

Oh! it's broiling in the morning,
It's toiling in the morning,
It's broiling in the morning,
It's toiling all day long.

Into the park I took a stroll—
I felt just like a buttered roll.
A pretty name "The Sunny South!"
A better one "The Land of Drouth!"

Next day into the bush I went,
On wild adventure I was bent,
Dame Nature's wonders I'd explore,
All thought of danger would ignore.

The mosquitoes and bull-dog ants
Assailed me even through my pants.
It nearly took my breath away
To hear the Jackass laugh so gay!

This lovely country, I've been told,
Abounds in silver and in gold.
You may pick it up all day,
Just as leaves in autumn lay!

Marines will chance this yarn believe,
But bluejackets you can't deceive.
Such pretty stories will not fit,
Nor can I their truth admit.

Some say there's lots of work to do.
Well, yes, but then, 'twixt me and you,
A man may toil and broil all day—
The big, fat man gets all the pay.

Mayhap such good things there may be,
But you may have them all, for me,
Instead of roaming foreign parts
I wish I'd studied the Fine Arts!

Traditional.

PADDY MALONE IN AUSTRALIA

Och! my name's Pat Malone, and I'm from Tipperary,
  Sure, I don't know it now, I'm so bothered, Ohone!
And the gals that I danced with light-hearted and airy,
  It's scarcely they'd notice poor Paddy Malone.
'Tis twelve months or more since our ship she cast anchor
  In happy Australia, the emigrant's home,
And from that day to this there's been nothing but canker,
  And grafe and vexation for Paddy Malone.
    Oh, Paddy Malone! Oh, Paddy, Ohone!
    Bad luck to the agent that coaxed ye to roam.

Wid a man called a squatter I soon got a place, sure;
  He'd a beard like a goat, and such whiskers, Ohone!
And he said—as he peeped through the hair on his faitures—
  That he liked the appearance of Paddy Malone.
Wid him I agreed to go up to his station,
  Saying "Abroad in the bush you'll find yourself at home,"
I liked his proposal, and wi'out hesitation
  Signed my name wid a X that spelt Paddy Malone.
    Oh, Paddy Malone, you're no scholard, Ohone!
    Sure, I made a criss-cross that spelt Paddy Malone.

A-herding my sheep in the bush, as they call it—
  It was no bush at all, but a mighty great wood,
Wid all the big trees that were small bushes one time,
  A long time ago, faith! I s'pose 'fore the flood.
To find out this big bush one day I went further,
  The trees grew so thick that I couldn't, Ohone!
I tried to go back then, but that I found harder,
  And bothered and lost was poor Paddy Malone.
    Oh, Paddy Malone, through the bush he did roam!
    What a babe in the wood was poor Paddy Malone.

I was soon overcome, sure, wid grafe and vexation,
  And camped, you must know, by the side of a log;

o

I was found the next day by a man from the station,
  For I coo-eed and roared like a bull in a bog.
The man said to me, "Arrah, Pat! where's the sheep now?"
  Says I, "I dunno! barring one here at home,"
And the master began and kicked up a big row too,
  And swore he'd stop the wages of Paddy Malone.
  Arrah! Paddy Malone, you're no shepherd, Ohone!
  We'll try you with bullocks now, Paddy Malone.

To see me dressed out with my team and my dray too,
  Wid a whip like a flail and such gaiters, Ohone!
But the bullocks, they eyed me, and seemed for to say, too
  "You may do your best, Paddy, we're blest if we go."
"Gee whoa! Redman! come hither, Damper!
  Hoot, Magpie! Gee, Blackbird! Come hither, Whalebone!"
But the brutes turned round sharp, and away they did scamper,
  And heels over head turned poor Paddy Malone.
  Oh, Paddy Malone! you've seen some bulls at home,
  But the bulls of Australia cow Paddy Malone.

I was found the next day where the brutes they did throw me
  By a man passing by, upon hearing me groan;
And, wiping the mud from my face till he knew me,
  Says he, "You're name's Paddy?" "Yes! Paddy Malone,"
I thin says to him, "You're an angel sent down, sure!"
  "No, faith, but I'm not; but a friend of your own!"
And by his persuasion, for home then I started,
  And you now see before you poor Paddy Malone.
  Arrah, Paddy Malone! you are now safe at home.
  Bad luck to the agent that coaxed ye to roam.

Traditional.

PLAYING THE NEW-CHUM JACKEROO

The young arrival from England who lands here with a small
amount of money with which he intends starting a cattle "ranch"
or "sheep farm" goes first to a station to learn what is called
"colonial experience." In this stage of existence he is known as a
"new chum" or "jackeroo," and often his life is not a happy one.
A jackeroo is fair game for everyone, but if he takes a few practical
jokes good humouredly, and bears no malice, he will soon be left
in peace by his companions. A good temper is the key that unlocks
the Australian heart before anything. Those who pass their lives

in the bush generally have their heart in the right place, though they do love to play a new chum.

EDWARD KINGLAKE, *The Australian at Home* (1891).

Jackeroos are always given some old rogue of a horse which can be depended on for a few accurate "bucks" whenever he is mounted. . . . "Bring up the old horse, Bill," the manager will say to the stockman, "Mr. Newcome had better ride him." "Been used to riding much?" he will ask the pink-cheeked English boy who had perhaps been on horseback half-a-dozen times in his life.

And so on. He has to try and catch Old Scrubber, and having at last done so, amidst general laughter, he has to mount him. Seemingly quiet, the horse goes "into figures."

Down with his head, up with his back, a sudden contraction and expansion, and Mr. Newcome is kissing his maternal earth with a vigour which, had it only been voluntary, would have been accepted as proof of the keenest sense of filial duty. Vastly amused are all the spectators and poor Newcome does not know which is the most exasperating, their sham commiseration or their roisterous merriment.

ibid.

JIMMY SAGO, JACKEROO

Air: "Wearing of the Green."

If you want a situation, I'll just tell you the plan
To get on to a station, I'm just your very man.
Pack up the old portmanteau, and label it Paroo,
With a name aristocratic—Jimmy Sago, Jackeroo.

When you get on to the station, of small things you'll make a fuss,
And in speaking of the station, mind, it's we, and ours, and us.
Boast of your grand connections and your rich relations, too,
And your own great expectations, Jimmy Sago, Jackeroo.
They will send you out on horseback, the boundaries to ride;
But run down a marsupial and rob him of his hide,
His scalp will fetch a shilling and his hide another two,
Which will help to fill your pockets, Jimmy Sago, Jackeroo.
Yes, to fill your empty pockets, Jimmy Sago, Jackeroo.

When the boss wants information, on the men you'll do a sneak,
And don a paper collar on your fifteen bob a week.
Then at the lamb-marking a boss they'll make of you.
Now that's the way to get on, Jimmy Sago, Jackeroo.

A squatter in the future I've no doubt you may be,
But if the banks once get you, they'll put you up a tree.
To see you humping bluey, I know, would never do,
'Twould mean good-bye to our new chum, Jimmy Sago, Jackeroo.
Yes, good-bye to our new chum Jimmy Sago, Jackeroo.*

Traditional.

THE LONDON SWELL

There's nothing that exasperates a true Australian youth,
Whatever be his rank in life, be he cultured or uncouth,
As the manner of a London swell. Now it chanced, the other day,
That one came out, consigned to me—a cousin, by the way.

(The Australian and his cousin stroll along Collins Street, Melbourne.)

As we strolled along that crowded street, where Fashion holds
    proud sway,
He deigned to glance at everything, but not one word did say;
I really thought he was impressed by its well-deserved renown
Till he drawled, "Not bad—not bad at all—for a provincial town."

.   .   .   .

But, unmindful of my agonies, in the slowest of slow drawls,
He lisped away for hours of the Abbey and St. Paul's,
Till those grand historic names had for me a hateful sound,
And I wished the noble piles themselves were levelled to the
    ground.

My young bright life seemed blasted, my hopes were dead and
    gone,
No blighted lover ever felt so gloomy and forlorn;
I'd reached the suicidal stage—and the reason of it all,
This supercilious London swell, his eye-glass and his drawl.

ARTHUR PATCHETT MARTIN, *Fernshawe: Sketches in Prose
and Verse* (1881).

* "A Jackeroo," says C. E. W. Bean, "is a young man, usually from Great
Britain or from the Australian cities, serving on a station in order to gain experience." They were frequently unpopular with the shearers and station hands
because they were "favoured workers", serving as "cadets" or apprentices and
supposedly above them on the social plane. Henry Lawson gives a sympathetic
picture of these men in his poem, "New-Chum Jackeroos".

THE "RAW" NEW-CHUMS—1888

The immigrants were fine, burly fellows, but "raw" and absolutely useless till they got acclimatised.

They remained at the depot a few weeks, and if no one wanted them they were given passes along the line while looking for work.

Duaringa was our rail station, and the runs on which we were contracting were seventy or a hundred miles distant. I always felt sorry for the poor newcomers who walked those distances on the off-chance of getting a job for which they were not fit.

Their clothing was totally unsuited for Queensland climate—thick, heavy woollen suits and small, hard black hats with narrow rims. They were red raw with sunburn, and the sandflies and mosquitoes recognised them as choice morsels, and added to their miseries—sandflies by day and "skeeters" all night.

Even the old hands suffered from the insect pests, but I always "cracked hardy." I told them once about the dog that bit a man, and the dog died. I said the mosquitoes bit me and died, and that it was a nuisance sweeping the heaps of dead insects out of my camp every morning. (Those were my truthful days.)

Generally, after a few years, the men from the old country hardened, and could hold their own with all-comers, being mostly healthy and of good physique.

During the Christmas spell one young fellow became blind on the track through sandy blight or sandflies, and we gave another new-chum £1 a week to look after him in the travellers' hut till he could see again (the highest wages he had received till then).

Sometimes we sublet a part of the work to them—post-cutting, boring, or post-hole sinking—but they always chucked it after a day or two, with blistered hands and parboiled faces, so we would load them up with tucker and part the best of friends.

JULIAN STUART.

(From an undated cutting from *The Australian Worker*,
Sydney, supplied by MRS. LYNDALL HADOW.)

NEW-CHUMS BECOME "DINKUM AUSSIES"

In 1887 (Queen Victoria's jubilee year) the people in our district gathered to see an ox roasted to celebrate fifty years of the queen's beneficent reign and to rejoice accordingly.

Loyal speeches were made and loyal cheers given. The bullock was eaten, and there was free beer for all who cared to drink it, but some of us who were of an inquisitive turn of mind wanted to know what particularly the queen had done more than any other woman that we should get up early to make a fuss about her?

Of course, we were hushed down and suppressed, even when we tried to quote Bobby Burns to our elders in support of our youthful opinions. The mountains did not fall on us, nor did the bears come out of the caves and eat us up when we told those elders that they were as backward and benighted at the end of fifty years' reign as they had been at the beginning of it.

John Farrell had addressed to the queen a poem, in which he used some very plain language, and we had been reading it. There was a rumour that he was to be arrested for it for lese-majesty, or treason felony, and we should not have been surprised if he had been beheaded for it.

When the carnival was over and we were on the boat home-ward bound, an argument arose as to monarchy versus republican-ism. To men advanced in years it seemed nothing short of terrible that we should think of altering the form of government "under which we enjoyed so many liberties."

There was a stranger present—a young American-Irishman—and he laughed at the idea that the form of government made any difference.

He told us that he had left republican America because he was wanted by the police in connection with a strike at Pittsburgh, where he had been an ironworker. He had left America because men were getting life sentences on flimsy evidence, and said he did not want to die in jail.

He was the first striker we had ever seen, and we were glad when he became naturalised, took up land near our farm, married an Australian girl, and became a good Australian.

Many a night he had eager listeners to the tales he could tell of the doings between "master and man" on the other side of the world, and from him we first got our ideas of what unionism meant.

In 1888 I was on a fencing contract on the Upper Dawson, and on the same station were some young Scotchmen, who told us they had been mixed up with the stonecutters' strike. They had been granite workers and when, after about eight months' strike against a reduction, their union had been beaten, rather than go back at the low rates they had emigrated. They had turned their backs on Scotland and gave Australia a show.

They were a fine sturdy lot, and Australia was not treating them well for a start. One of them had brought his wife along, and she was doing the cooking for the camp, and that was the principal reason why we amalgamated with them. The young Scotchwoman was a splendid cook.

While they were becoming acclimatised, getting used to the Queensland weather, we were getting to know from them at first-hand something of the suffering and privation endured by the workers in the old land through protracted and unsuccessful labour troubles.

They were determined to succeed, and made light of all their troubles while learning the Australian way of doing things. Often at night "Scots Wha Hae" and "Bonnie Doon" echoed among the Dawson hills. After a few lean, hard years, good times came to them, and I often saw their names associated with Labour activities, too.

In 1889 I met an Englishman in a stockman's hut on the Belyando. He was well-read and intelligent, and a great talker. He seemed glad to have someone who would listen to him. He talked nearly all night. He had some English papers, in one of which was an article by Bernard Shaw, of whom I had never heard before, and of whom he seemed to think very highly.

Though living like a hatter on a backblocks run, he seemed to be an advanced thinker, and came in very handy when we were forming the Central Queensland Labourers' Union.

Very few of us were capable of making an organising speech, so we got him on the job, and it was a success from the word "go".

JULIAN STUART.

(From an undated cutting from The Australian Worker,
supplied by MRS. LYNDALL HADOW.)

5. EARLY TRADE UNIONISM

We are hoboes and scamps and tired tramps,
  But we love our Union well;
Our spirit won't fail, we will die in gaol,
  And smile in the flames of hell.

TOM McMILLAN in *Direct Action.*

8-8-8

*In 1883, the Melbourne Trades Hall Committee paid trib-
ute to a sick, prematurely aged man, James Stephens, Chartist
and veteran of the Operative Masons' Society:*
"... *Australians ... who have always exhibited a noble
example of spontaneous generosity, will, we feel sure, be quick
to recognise living worth, nor leave to future generations to
discharge a great national obligation which we owe for the
promulgation and achievement of one of the greatest of
modern reforms that has blessed the working classes of these
colonies, viz., the Eight-Hours' system of labour. James Stephens, a working mason, who is called 'one of the pioneers of
the Eight-Hours' system in Australia,' was the man who, over*

a quarter of a century ago, first conceived the idea of this great national reform for the abridgement of the hours of labour. Working one day during the summer of 1855, under an almost tropical sun and with seared hands driving the burning tools over hard Victorian stone, his mind was suddenly seized with the simple but now dearly prized blessing of the subdivision of the wage-earner's day into three parts, viz., eight hours' labour, eight hours' recreation, eight hours' rest, and calling upon his fellow-workmen in language well remembered to-day, exhorted them to lay the foundations of that principle, the complete achievement of which is now nearly accomplished by every class of labour throughout Australia.

"James Stephens, who with others struggled hard to achieve this great boon, is now an old man, almost sightless and maimed for life with both his arms broken by a fall from a scaffold, and thereby rendered totally unable to provide for himself and his wife during the inevitably short remainder of his life. The Trades Hall Committee of Melbourne therefore appealed to the public and their fellow-workmen throughout the colonies to regard this effort for a National Testimonial to this veteran of labour, not so much from a charitable point of view, as from a consciousness of the obligations we owe to one within whose breast was born the germ, and who devoted the best years of his life to mature the scheme for the emancipation of his fellow-men from excessive hours of toil."

There is a monument to those who won the Eight-Hours day, opposite the Trades Hall in Melbourne. For many years, an Eight-Hours procession marched with banners through the city streets; it was essentially a craft-unions parade and in time, when Labour Day had taken the place of the old Eight-Hours day as a public holiday, the march drew less and less support. The growth of heavy industry after the first world war, and the consequent emergence of the big industrial unions, brought about changes in the procession. Strong political slogans were introduced and the current demands of the workers stressed. Finally, the Trades Hall Council abandoned the Labour Day procession and the militant workers transferred their procession to May Day.

AN AUSTRALIAN PAEAN—1876

Our April bears no blossoms,
No promises of spring;

Her gifts are rain and storm and stain,
    And surges lash and swing.
No budded wreath doth she bequeath,
    Her tempests toss the trees;
No balmy gales—but shivered sails,
    And desolated seas.

Yet still we love our April,
    For it aids us to bequeath
A gift more fair than blossoms rare,
    More sweet than budded wreath.
Our children's tend'rest memories
    Round Austral April grow;
'Twas the month we won their freedom, boys,
    Just twenty years ago.

.   .   .   .

We hear the children's voices
    'Mid the rattle of its looms,
Crying "Wherefore shut God's heaven
    All our golden afternoons?"
Though here the English April
    Nor song nor sun imparts,
Its spring is on our children's lips,
    Its summer in their hearts!

We've left the land that bore us,
    Its castles and its shrines;
We've changed the cornfields and the rye
    For the olives and the vines.
Yet still we have our castles,
    Yet still we bow the knee;
We each enshrine a saint divine,
    And her name is Liberty.

Liberty! name of warning!
    Did'st thou feel our pulses beat
As we marching, moved this morning
    All a-down the cheering street?
In our federated freedom,
    In our manliness allied,
While the badges of our labour
    Were the banners of our pride.

> Did our fancies speak prophetic
>   Of a larger league than this—
> With higher aims and nobler claims
>   To grasp the good we miss;
> When in freer federation
>   In a future yet to be,
> Australia stands a nation
>   From the centre to the sea.

MARCUS CLARKE.

Written to celebrate the anniversary of the Eight Hours Day.

EIGHT-HOURS DAY RHYME

> Eight hours to work, eight hours to play,
> Eight hours to sleep, and eight bob a day.

THE NEW UNIONISM

Unionism came to the Australian bushman as a religion. It came bringing salvation from years of tyranny. It had in it that feeling of mateship which he understood already, and which always characterised the action of one "white man" to another. Unionism extended the idea, so a man's character was gauged by whether he stood true to union rules or "scabbed" it on his fellows. The man who never went back on the union is honoured to-day as no other is honoured or respected. The man who fell once may be forgiven, but he is not fully trusted. The lowest term of reproach is to call him a "scab."

Experience has taught that the man who sells himself to the employer at a time of strike is a man of weak character, if not worse. At many a country ball the girls have refused to dance with them, the barmaids have refused them a drink, and the waitresses a meal.

Unionists have starved rather than accept work under other conditions. Hundreds of men have worn their boots and clothes to tatters seeking work upon union terms; and not finding it, have gone without for a year—remaining penniless, but independent and proud that they had not degraded themselves. It was such men who made the union a success, and enabled it to hold its own against well-organised capitalism aided by friendly governments. Men imbued with such a spirit put the cause above personal self-interest. They needed no prompting—no exciting by fiery orators —but stood loyal to principle, no matter what the consequences might be. Rough and unpolished many of them may be; but manly, true and "white" all the time, and the movement owes them much.

W. G. SPENCE, Australia's Awakening (1908).

A TALE OF THE PAROO

Loyalty to Labor's ideals was . . . aroused by many incidents of courage and self-sacrifice on the part of the workers. Thus, in the Paroo country, an old swagman came to the Brindingabba hut, weak and ill. He was alone and had no money to buy food. Endeavouring to reserve his fast-failing strength, he was intent on one thing, to vote for the Labor candidate. "I want to give Hughie a vote," he said, "I suppose it will be my last." But half of his journey to the electorate was still to be traversed and his condition was desperate. "I have knocked all around these creeks this many year," he said, "and I could never get a vote. But I did get in on a vote this time, and when I got it, I said: 'This belongs to Hughie Langwell.' " That night the old man died. His name was Martin Farrell. The only papers found on him were his union ticket and a receipt for a subscription to the Broken Hill strike fund.*

H. V. EVATT, Australian Labour Leader.

JUDGE HIGINBOTHAM AND THE STRIKE FUND

These two sides of him, the modest but lively human being and the austere office-holder, were just as marked when he left politics and sat on the Bench. He was rigid about procedure in court, sternly rebuking a witness who stood with his hands in his pockets, and insisted on respect being paid to his high office. And, though he refused a knighthood, he stayed away from a public dinner because the Speaker of the House was to take precedence of the Chief Justice. But, deep within him, was the democrat who lived in hopes of social justice: who revelled, as he confessed to an English visitor, in the growing solidarity of Labor, and believed in its future. When, in 1890, the great maritime strike took place, and the Employers' Union refused the Trades Hall Council's request for a conference, he forsook the traditional aloofness of the Bench and wrote:

* The first colonial labour parties came into existence in 1891, following the maritime strike of 1890, in which not only seamen and waterside workers were involved, but shearers, coal-miners, drivers, carters, and other workers as well. The lesson the Australian Labor movement had learned from this first great clash of the nineties was that political as well as industrial action was necessary to win the workers' demands.

"The Chief Justice presents his compliments to the President of the Trades Hall Council, and requests that he will be so good as to place the amount of the enclosed cheque of £50 to the credit of the strike fund. While the United Trades are awaiting compliance with their reasonable request for a conference with the employers, the Chief Justice will continue for the present to forward a weekly contribution of £10 to the same object."

VANCE PALMER, *National Portraits* (Third Edition, September, 1954).

JOCK McPHAIL

(A Tale of the 1891 Shearers' Strike)

"Woolshed burned, and eight men injured in a most unequal fight."
>   That was what the papers stated
>   In a telegram undated,
When the blacklegs came to Brenda, thief-like, at the dead of night;
And the inference accepted by the city journalists
Found expression in the headline, "Outrage by the Unionists";
But the gods' ungarnished gospel is this bold and bitter tale
From the Never-Never Classics, headed simply, "Jock McPhail."

    .   .   .   .

Now the Brenda shed was Union when the Brownings held the run,
Never shark or blackleg working under Browning sire or son;
But, beneath the broker's hammer, Brenda went to "Angel" Gray,
And a stronghold of the Union with the freehold passed away.

For the Angel was a mongrel with a sanctimonious air,
Who had earned a reputation by his aptitude at prayer;
And he spoke with ceaseless longing of the harp and of the crown,
So it wasn't any wonder that he cut the wages down.

But the men who shore at Brenda when old Browning bossed the board
Took a solemn oath and binding, every one in stern accord,
That unless the full agreement in the Union terms was made,
Not a man on Brenda station should so much as sharpen blade.

Never word they said to super., never threat made Angel Gray,
Till he posted up a notice at the shed one Saturday—

"Brenda shearing starts on Thursday. P.U. terms."*
    They read the news;
Then they formed a deputation to make manifest their views.

But that shearers' deputation had no leader eloquent,
And it simply kept repeating, when it lacked an argument—
"Brenda shed has been a stronghold of the Union in the past;
Brenda shed shall be a stronghold while the bonds of Union last."

And the Angel heard and answered: "I have taken this in prayer
To the footstool of the Father, humbly wrestling with it there,
And you have my ultimatum; take or leave it as you like."
"We'll announce the benediction," said McSweeney:
    "Let us strike!"

So they formed a camp at Brenda, and they picketed the gates,
Picketed the route and roadways, watchful as the sleepless Fates,
And the men the boss imported never entered Brenda shed,
And the station hands he threatened joined the shearers' camp
    instead.

And the Angel's heart was troubled, for, although his ways were
    deep,
Whatsoever thing he ventured, lo! the shearers held him cheap;
And, at last, one Monday morning when a month had passed
    away,
Came a notice of submission from the hands of Angel Gray.

It was posted at the woolshed, and the pickets farthest out
Caught the ringing exultation of the shearers round about,
And the cheer that thrilled through Brenda, with its fervid
    euphony,
Was the loud amen of Labour loyal unto victory.

There was gathering of outposts in a wild confusion then,
Joy of hard-won battle beaming in the eyes of half-fed men;
And the sentiments of Logan were re-echoed far and wide
When he said, "Let's celebrate it at the Cattle Drovers' Guide."

So they journeyed to the shanty, and they drank like warriors bold
When the flagons of our fathers filled the board in days of old.

    * "P.U. terms": Pastoralists' Union rates and conditions for shearers, as
opposed to the shearers' own demands.

Drank and feasted; but when midnight found them full of maud-
lin glee,
Jock McPhail rode through the darkness Brendawards with Red
McGee.

Something crooked Jock was fearing, so they sought the gloom of
trees
In a wide half-circle northward of the tell-tale southern breeze,
Riding cautiously and quickly till a broken shaft of light,
Shining from the shearers' humpy, told them that McPhail was
right.

Spectre-footed, then, and eager to the humpy door they crawled,
Peered through chinks, wild-eyed with anger, listening like men
enthralled;
For they heard the Brenda super. to a stranger hoarsely say—
"There'll be bloodshed here to-morrow sure as God made Angel
Gray!"

Silently the door they opened, silently as shadows passed,
Seized the super. and the stranger, fought with them and bound
them fast;
Then they forced the Angel's purpose from the super., and McGee
Mounted horse to warn the others of the boss's treachery.

But Red Mac could scarce have reached them when along the
homestead track
Angel drove toward the humpy with the blacklegs at his back;
"Open up!" he cried the super., "It is I! You need not fear!"
Jock McPhail alone made answer—"Never scab shall enter here!"

But they broke the door and rushed him. Still McPhail stood firm
and true;
With his back against a door-post blood with every hit he drew.
Right and left they fell before him, right and left on either hand,
And the mark on Angel's forehead is the Union shearers' brand.

And, perchance, the Cause had conquered, but a "scab" with
blood aflow,
Climbed the hut and with a sapling struck McPhail a coward's
blow,
And with one great cry of anguish dying out into a groan
Sank the man who fought for Brenda, loyal-hearted and alone.

And the Angel, watching grimly, shouted when he saw him fall;
Shouted and, with hot blood-hunger, showed his baseness then to
all;
"Hound of hell and spawn of harlot! this for you, and this!" he
cried,
And he struck the prostrate shearer, spurning him with foot aside.

And he left him bleeding, senseless, seeking for him later on
When the blacklegs' swags were settled, but the Unionist was
gone.
Broken-boned and blind and feeble, maddened by his awful pain,
Spitting blood in gurgling mouthfuls, Jock had striv'n to rise in
vain.

But he crawled towards the woolshed, hand by hand and knee by
knee,
Blood-trailed in the dusty salt-bush, crooning ever painfully—
"Brenda shed a Union stronghold always was in years gone past;
Brenda shed shall still be Union while the bonds of Union last."

Foot by foot he struggled onward where the silent darkness lay;
Foot by foot, the hot blood flowing swiftly with his life away;
Foot by foot, until—Eureka! he could feel the woolshed door;
Then a thought of earth's tomorrow troubled Jock McPhail no
more;

For beneath the woolshed creeping, coat and shirt and bark in
hand,
Only this his heart was crying as he slowly made a brand—
"Brenda shed a Union stronghold always was in years gone past;
Brenda shed"—the brand was lighted—"shall be Union to the
last."

Gleams of light that grew and gathered; burst of flame that wing-
like spread,
Smiting all the bush with terror, all the sullen sky with dread!
What though Unionist and blackleg worked like heroes at the
well—
Limned in flame and robed in glory Brenda shed to ashes fell.

And the smoke-grimed Union shearers gathered mournfully
around,
Treading lightly o'er the ashes, for they trod on holy ground;

And they swore on oath, bareheaded, by a slow and bloody trail,
Still to fight and yet to conquer for the sake of Jock McPhail.

E. S. EMERSON ("Milky White"): *A Shanty Entertainment.*

STRIKERS AND NEW-CHUMS—1891

Press reports from the special representative of a Melbourne
daily, written "in the field" in 1891, tell us that while visiting the
Sandy Creek strike camp, outside Clermont (Queensland), he
found about 300 men controlled by a committee enforcing strict
rules of conduct.

Liquor was not permitted; leave passes were required before
visits could be made to the township and a curfew was imposed.
The men had arms and were all well mounted.

These observations are supported by the publication in 1927 of
the reminiscences of the chairman of the Sandy Creek camp committee.

The "swaggies" of the period appear to have been not skilled
colonial shearers but the "new-chums," tempted to Australia by
the propaganda of government immigration officers in London.
Throughout England's villages and towns there appeared this
notice:

"Immigrants wanted for Australia—a land flowing with milk
and honey—there to gain an independence. All that is wanted is
the will."

It brought thousands of "new-chums" to Queensland in the
eighties and until labour organised in the nineties for better conditions in the pastoral industry, this unskilled labour pool constituted the greater part of the swaggies immortalised by "Matilda."
(Paterson's "Waltzing Matilda."—Ed.)

In 1887, for instance, the Quetta brought some hundreds of
British immigrants to Rockhampton. Some, after tramping many
miles in search of work, found it months later—burr-cutting and
prickly-pear clearing at £1 a week. In those days there was no
"week's notice or week's pay" given in the pastoral industry—
men could be "tramped" at a moment's notice, hundreds of miles
from the next chance of work, without a shilling to their names.
The Quetta burr-cutters got this raw deal, and in Barcaldine a
meeting of shearers held around a wool-waggon outside O'Reilly's
pub, having heard the cutters' story from a colonial, who afterwards was elected chairman of Sandy Creek camp, passed a resolution denouncing the misrepresentations of the immigration

authorities "at Home." The resolution was tabled to *Reynolds' Newspaper,* London.

A jingle improvised by the camp leader, which gives an idea of conditions prevailing in the Queensland outback, ran:

> On the far Barcoo
> Where they eat nardoo,
> Jumbuck giblets and pigweed stew,
> Fever and ague
> And scurvy plague you
> And the Barcoo rot;
> But worst of the lot
> Is the Bel-y-ando spew.*

LYNDALL HADOW in the Melbourne *Herald,* May 13, 1944.

"SOCIALISM IS BEING MATES"

Many men who want to do what is right object to socialism because they think it will tend to turn the state into a tyranny and the citizens of the state into mere machines. Seeing that the state of to-day is of the grossest kind, and the average workman of to-day a machine which, directly it gets out of order, is flung out to rust—to starve—I cannot see that this should be a very serious objection to a change. . . . I am sure that socialism—true socialism—will destroy tyranny, and make men what they should be—*mates.*

WILLIAM LANE in the *Hummer,* January 16, 1892.

THE SINKING OF THE *RODNEY*

In the shearers' fight with the pastoralists in 1894, all sorts of characters were raked up . . . to fill the places of unionists. A body of these were shipping on the *Rodney,* a steamer trading on the Darling and Murray rivers. These boats carry goods on barges which trail behind whenever the river is navigable, and take wool-laden barges down stream in the wool season.

At Swan Hill, on the Murray, there was a camp of union men, and as the *Rodney* steamed past, the "scabs" jeered and hooted the men in the camp. They were very brave when out of danger. The *Rodney* travelled on to the junction, and then made away up the River Darling. The captain's orders were that he should stop at Pooncarrie all night. He, however, pushed beyond Marara,

* "Belyando Station," said Julian Stuart, "is noted for its bad tucker, though not alone in that."

and selected a spot where there is a small island in a big reedy swamp, tying up his craft to a gum tree. Though he felt sure no one could get on board, nevertheless he kept up his fires and placed a watchman on deck.

The boat and its attached barges had, however, been seen by the "enemy." No doubt word had been sent from Swan Hill. A number of men borrowed a boat from higher up the river, and quietly carried it on their shoulders along the river bank, out of sight of the watchman. With muffled oars they pulled across the river. Originally about twenty-five had agreed to join in the capture, but only about a dozen really did the work. Some of those who backed out wanted to batten down the "scabs" under the hatches and burn them, but the leaders refused to hear of any such terrible vengeance.

The men who formed the boarding party turned all their clothing inside out, and covered face, head, hair and clothes with mud until recognition was impossible. About four o'clock in the morning they waded through the mud-swamp to the side of the tied-up boat. The watchman on his beat soon saw a muddy head appear over the side of the steamer. He gave the alarm to Captain Dickson, who cursed him because he had not tomahawked the head. The captain rushed aft and tackled the first man he met. This happened to be a good lightweight boxer, and science told, though he admitted that the captain was a tough snag. In a few minutes the steamer was captured. The crew tried to cut her adrift, but had no chance.

The forty "scabs," who had been so bold at Swan Hill, played a different tune now. Roused out of sleep, they evidently thought their end had come. They fell on their knees and begged for mercy. They were removed from the boat and taken ashore without harm. Two of those who had boarded the boat were below on a hunt for more "scabs." They had finished their search, when "the means to do ill deeds" in the shape of many tins of oil and other inflammable material caused one to remark suddenly to the other:

"What say if we burn the blanky boat?"

No sooner said than done. Quickly the reeds in the swamp glistened with the shimmer of flame; the water, the bank, and the big eucalyptus trees reflected the unwonted glare; whilst on the river bank, opposite the burning *Rodney*, sat a young man with a concertina, playing "After the Ball is Over."

W. G. SPENCE, *Australia's Awakening.*

FREEDOM ON THE WALLABY

Australia's a big country
    An' Freedom's humping bluey,
An' Freedom's on the wallaby,
    Oh! don't you hear 'er cooey.
She's just begun to boomerang
    She'll knock the tyrants silly,
She's going to light another fire
    And boil another billy.

Our fathers toiled for bitter bread
    While loafers thrived beside 'em,
But food to eat and clothes to wear,
    Their native land denied 'em.
An' so they left that native land
    In spite of their devotion,
An' so they came, or if they stole,
    Were sent across the ocean.

Then Freedom couldn't stand the glare
    Of Royalty's regalia,
She left the loafers where they were
    An' come out to Australia.
But now across the mighty main
    The chains have come to bind her,
She little thought to see again
    The wrongs she left behind her.

Our parents toiled to make a home,
    Hard grubbin' 'twas and clearin',
They wasn't troubled much with lords
    When they was pioneerin'.
But now that we have made the land
    A garden full of promise,
Old Greed must crook 'is dirty hand
    An' come to take it from us.

So we must fly a rebel flag
    As others did before us,
And we must sing a rebel song
    And join in rebel chorus.
We'll make the tyrants feel the sting
    O' those that they would throttle;

They needn't say the fault is ours
If blood should stain the wattle.

HENRY LAWSON in the Sydney *Worker*, October 6, 1894.

THE WOLF IN SNAKE'S CLOTHES

The mills of the gods grind slowly,
But they grind exceedingly small,
So to hell with the lane entirely
That hasn't a turning at all.

Old Saddlestrap, a loquacious identity, noted for his Labor activities up and down the Barcoo in the days when unionism was young, generally managed to get his classical quotes a bit tangled.

The above will do as a sample.

It was his summing-up after he had been acting as spokesman for the rouseabouts at a roll-call, at which the boss had been in a bad temper, on account of an argument with the shearers which had delayed the start for a few weeks.

They had refused to sign the agreement till they had submitted it to a Brisbane lawyer, and this took up a lot of time, for mails were slower in those days than they are now, so he was pretty raw by the time he came to deal with the "rousies."

Their argument, too, had some objectionable features, but none requiring a legal interpretation.

The hours of labour were defined as from daylight till dark.

Saddlestrap pointed out that, as the Barcoo was adjacent to the tropic of Capricorn, daylight began early and dark came late, which meant that the "servant" would be liable to work the sixteen hours or eighteen that the day lasted.

(It was "master" and "servant" in those times, the terms "employer" and "employed" being introduced later.)

It was also stipulated that should the shearing be interrupted "through any cause whatsoever," the "servant" should perform outdoor station work, the nature of which was not specified, but usually included burr-cutting, repairing fences, and destroying prickly pear.

The boss was adamant on some of these points. They had been customary for so long that it seemed hopeless to think of ever getting them altered.

Saddlestrap then tapped him to have beef as well as mutton included on the ration list. Rouseabouts nearly always had to put up with the culls and stags, and a bit of "bull" meat would be welcome as a change, and the request was granted.

When we asked for fresh potatoes instead of the "preserved" spuds (a dietary atrocity continuously supplied to station dining tables), the boss reared up at the bare idea of rouseabouts asking for fresh vegetables. No wonder the country was going to the dogs, he said, but he agreed to wire to Rockhampton for a few tons.

The old chap then chatted him with regard to the objectionable habit of sacking men at a moment's notice.

It nearly always happened that when a man made himself conspicuous by speaking on behalf of the crowd at the roll-call, he would be the first to get the sack. It was one of the many mean ways in which victimisation was practised.

The boss nearly developed St. Vitus's dance when our mouthpiece voiced his objection to any man being "tramped" before he had the chance to earn a few shillings for the track.

He asked that no man should be sacked without a week's notice or a week's pay, or, on the other hand, that rouseabouts should be at liberty to leave at a moment's notice.

The boss's sheep had fifteen months' wool on them, and the season was getting late; the other big sheds would be starting, and perhaps that was why the final draft of the rouseabouts' agreement provided for fourteen days' notice on either side.

Saddlestrap quoted some more scripture and work started, and, as it happened, we had a good run, the only lost time being when a cyclone blew up one night and scattered the roof of the shed, and we had no dry sheep for a day or two.

There was only one sacking match, and it was more comical than otherwise.

Billy Bray, a hard case, who was carting water for the engine from the river to the shed, told us one morning that the boss had sacked him. He did not know why, but thought it might have been because he was wearing a cabbage-tree hat. The real reason was the boss's liver.

When he went for his cheque he mentioned about the fortnight's notice, which the boss had evidently overlooked.

"A fortnight's wages will do me," he said.

At this the big man snorted.

We were there to shear 180,000 sheep, and yet from the fuss he made about paying a fortnight at thirty shillings a week in lieu of notice you'd think they were on the edge of bankruptcy.

"Damned if I'll give you a fortnight's pay," he snapped. "Take a fortnight's notice now, and go back and drive the team again."

"Righto," said the hard case. "But how about the other bloke? Have I got to fight him for the job?"

"What other bloke?"

"Him that you put on in my place. He's away with the team now. The engine must have water, you know, or the men can't shear. What are you going to do? Give him a fortnight, too?"

I do not know if the boss had heard of Jacky Dow, who hired a swagman to swing a gate all day, but he set Billy to something equally silly for a fortnight.

"Walk from the engine to the Barcoo and back, and keep on doing it till your time is up," he said, and Billy did, and offered to do it by the year, or for life. The rouseabouts' cook gave two weeks' notice to get to another shed for a chance of being put in as shearers' cook.

This would not be worth mentioning, only that it led to a happening illustrating the difficulties and drawbacks of early unionism.

The substitute cook, a stranger, but a real ding-donger, sold about sixty tickets in the Central Queensland Labourers' Union, which had just started at Barcaldine.

Months later, when the membership list came out, I noticed that none of the sixty were included. He had defaulted.

We never saw him again, but heard he was drowned at Isisford; that he broke the two-up school at Thargomindah, and that he had got six months for robbing a Chinaman at Bourke.

"A good cook he was," said Saddlestrap, "but a wolf in snake's clothes all the same."

JULIAN STUART in *The Australian Worker*, Sydney,
April 13, 1927.

SPENCE'S STATION

In the old Union days it was a favourite gag with squatters to tell union men that Spence (W. G. Spence, one of the founders of the Australian Shearers' Union.—Ed.) was making a good thing out of them. In New South Wales I've heard them say Spence had a station in Victoria; in Victoria they'd say he had a run in New South Wales. Have known Spence many years, and have travelled Australia from the Territory to the Bight, but could never locate Spence's Station.

Beyond the furthest far-outback, beyond the setting sun,
Beyond the western desert plain, where rivers never run;

Away beyond the border fence, 'neath azure summer skies,
Where droughts and floods are both unknown—there Spence's
Station lies.

He owns five hundred million sheep of Lincoln-Leicester breed,
That's crossed with old Merino strain, true type of squatter's
need;
His stud ram weighs ten thousand pounds, of wool he cuts a ton;
He's three weeks' shearing with the blades for Howe, the Queens-
land gun.

His shed is roofed with beaten gold, brought from the planet
Mars;
From huts to shed the shearers ride in cushioned motorcars.
The drummer shears two hundred sheep and never turns a hair;
No cuss words on the place are used, all work doth start with
prayer.

He got eight million pounds, we've heard, by pinching union
funds,
And purchased houses in the moon and many station runs;
And when he's made his pile they say he'll give the union best,
And live in regal style while we are tramping in the west.

I've toured this land from north to south, from westward to the
east,
In times of flood, in times of drought, of famine and of feast;
I've tramped it when the plains were dry and when the plains
were wet,
But never crossed the boundary fence of Spence's Station yet.

F. J. MURRAY in the Brisbane *Worker*.

THE STORIES THAT ARE WANTED

I received a letter recently (in reference to the resolution
carried at convention about labour records and the compilation
of labour history) in which the writer said: "I, along with others,
have felt that it is essential that the stirring tales of the early fights
and the sacrifices of the pioneer battlers should not be lost. We feel
that their publication would be a great incentive to the younger
members and bring them to a realisation of the great heritage
handed down to them. At convention mention was made of
Spence's book (*Australia's Awakening*—Ed.) but, unfortunately,

that history is but a collection of the dry bones. What is wanted is the full-blooded meaty stories of the personal experiences of the battlers of those times."

These words, written presumably by one of the younger generation, touch on a very interesting phase. If the knowledge of anything done in the past is likely to be of benefit to the people of the future, then an effort should be made to have it retained and made available in the most attractive or appealing form.

There are so many counter-attractions these days that the average youth, though reaping the benefits and enjoying the advantages that grandfather's battling helped to secure for him, has "no time" for the old man, and starts whistling jazz ditties if you try to point out that grandad sometimes did things worth emulating.

Of course, not all are tarred with the one brush. If they were, the letter from which I am quoting would not have been written.

As to Spence's book, it gives labour history from the point of view of the man who was in office most of his time, and sure of three meals a day, and that makes a difference mostly.

It would be well if we could have the experiences of the man who, let us say, sold a horse rather than take a job at low wages or at strike time sold another to keep going; sold his saddle horse and humped his swag before the trouble ended; lived on damper or mutton when he could get it, and on johnny cake and paroo tart when there was nothing better, and sometimes did without any or all of them.

To many a man it was not merely an isolated incident, but seemed as though incorporated in the condition of his continued existence.

Stray sidelights on past happenings are recalled by late events, and the past does not seem so far separated from the present after all.

Thomas Givens, who died recently, was a senator, and also for a time president of the Senate, but I had no knowledge of him in either capacity. It was as Tom Givens, a mine worker at Charters Towers, that I remembered him.

On one occasion W. D. Casey, managing director of the company for which Tom was working was reported to have said something slanderous or derogatory about the underground workers at the mine.

Tom heard it when he came off shift, and bought a horsewhip on his way home, and when he met the manager he publicly horsewhipped him. Most of us would have been satisfied to give him a punch, but the horsewhip was a good idea. In a way it lent tone to the occasion, and kept it from being a common brawl.

Givens was fined for assault and battery, and the fine was derisively paid by a threepenny collection.

The whip, to which was attached a big placard with a suitable inscription, was on view in a glass case in the vestibule of a hotel near the Stock Exchange. Disliking the publicity, Casey asked the publican to take it down, but was told it had a trade value.

When he asked "How much?" he was told it was worth a hundred guineas to the hospital (or the miners' accident fund, I forget which), and business must have resulted, for the whip disappeared from public view next day.

Fitzgerald's sword is worth telling about, too.

Charlie Fitzgerald, a young lawyer of Dalby, held the position of lieutenant in the local Queensland defence force, and when the unit was ordered to "take the field" and go to the front and suppress the insurrectionary shearers at Barcaldine and Clermont, Charlie refused to lead them, whereupon he was told to "return his commission" and hand back his sword.

He did one, but not the other—the sword was raffled, a hundred tickets at a pound each, and the money went to the union defence fund.

Many bushmen would rather that nothing was said about the part they played, being sensitive and afraid that it might look as though they wanted limelight and publicity.

Bushmen those days, too, had a wholehearted contempt for anyone who would show any tendency to "trade" on unionism or make a profit out of his principles.

To them the idea of "capitalising martyrdom" was utterly repugnant, and often they rode on their way, saying nothing, and we were the poorer through their silence.

JULIAN STUART in *The Australian Worker,* July 11, 1928.

A UNION TOWN

He was a tourist, and English don't you know. He was on his way to pay a visit to his brother-in-law, a squatter on the Darling, and stayed over one night in an hotel in Talleytown. It was during the great strike. He said "it was awful, don't you know." In the morning he arose, and while he was fixing his collar he happened to glance out through the window and saw two bodies hanging to the limb of a tree across the road.

About three seconds later he tumbled down the back stairs on top of a Darling "whaler," who rose up, collared him, and made inquiries in language totally unfit for publication.

"Oh, my God!" gasped the tourist, "there's been murder done!"

"What?"

"Murder! Run for the police. Fetch the police. There are two men hanging to a tree in front of the hotel. They've been lynched in the night. Oh, my God! it's awful."

The tourist collapsed into a chair, and the whaler went to look. When he returned he seemed calmer and wore an interested expression.

"Well, have you informed the police?" gasped the new-chum, still trembling, and with a corpse-like face.

"No," said the other sadly.

"Why? Why didn't you tell them?"

"Because it's no use. The unionists hold this town. The poor fellows are past all help now——."

"What—what do you mean?"

"Well, those men were non-unionists; the boys caught them last night and choked 'em off. That's about it."

"Great Scott! Does the law of this country allow men to be murdered in cold blood? . . . My God! It's awful!"

"Well, it seems so," said the whaler, in reply to the first part of the question. Then an idea seemed to strike him.

"By the way," he asked, in a hurried anxious tone, "have you got a ticket? Do you belong to the Union?"

"N-no—I-I don't know anything about it."

"Well, you will soon, if you don't pull your wits together. Are you a jackeroo?"

"A what? I suppose I'm a new-chum, if that's what you mean."

"Well, it amounts to the same thing—a jackeroo is a new-chum, and a new-chum is a jackeroo. Now these poor fellows hanging out there were jackeroos."

"My God! it's awful."

"It will be awfuller if you don't pull yourself together. Now, listen here, I'm a union man, and true to my mates, but I don't like this business. I don't want any more choking off done. I like your looks, and I'll save you if I can——."

"My God! it's awful."

"Don't interrupt me. There's no time to lose. Get your bag and get down to the station before the boys in the union camp are up and on your track. There's a train in twenty minutes. Get your ticket and keep out of sight till she starts; then jump in."

"I will. My——."

"Never mind that. Off with you, and do exactly as I tell you."

"I will."

And he did, and nearly got hauled up for boarding a train while in motion. He didn't visit his uncle; he came back to the city. Whenever he referred to the adventure he said it was awful.

The effigies of two notorious non-unionists are hanging there yet.

HENRY LAWSON.

A WISE STEWARD AND A SILENT WORKER

When Ben Tetley started working in the timber mill in the south-west (of Western Australia—Ed.) he found that only about half of the "jarrah jerkers" were in the Timber Workers' Union. He was a little ginger chap, with wire whiskers and lots of energy, and started to make a noise about it. He "rang the gong," and called a meeting to straighten things out. It was moved, seconded, and carried unanimously "That Mr. Tetley be appointed steward, with full power to act."

Proceedings were about to terminate as though nothing more were necessary, but Tetley made a bit of a speech. "What do you mean by 'full power to act?' " he asked. "There's no backing and filling about me. I don't like working with a man who ain't in the union—so it's him or me for it to leave the job. I can't afford it. I've a wife and kids, and want to knock up a cheque for Christmas, but I'll take a sporting risk. I'll fight any man who refuses to take a ticket. If he beats me I leave. If I beat him he must take the pasteboard, or leave the job. Where do I start? A little fighting or a little writing first?"

They came forward, but with no great alacrity. At the back of the hall some of them gathered together, and there was a lot of whispering and gesticulation going on. He concluded that they were foreigners—Greeks or Italians, who "had not the English."

By and by a tall, well-set-up young fellow came forward. He was good looking, curly dark hair and complexion, like the portraits of Byron in his youth, and wide, soulful eyes that had not left Tetley's face all the while he had been speaking. Viewing him as a prospective opponent, he had to admit that he "looked the goods."

He leant down at Tetley's table, took a small slate from his pocket, and wrote: "I am deaf and dumb, but read your lips. Cannot make a speech like you, but I fight like —— hell. Tell me any men don't join, and I'll chew them up into dog's meat."

Taking up a position behind the steward's chair, his pathetic eyes continued to gaze sorrowfully round the room, nor did he move till tickets had been issued to the last man on the pay-sheet. Evidently they all knew him.

Before they parted he again produced the slate, and wrote: "How do you go in a scrap? Pretty good?"

Tetley grabbed the pencil, and wrote:

"Fight? Me? I could not fight my way out of a paper-bag!"

JULIAN STUART.

(From an old newspaper cutting, unnamed and undated
supplied by Mrs. LYNDALL HADOW.)

BILLY LANE'S DESCRIPTION OF MATESHIP

"Mates! Do you know that's a word I like?" said Ned. "It makes you feel good, just the sound of it. I know a fellow, a shearer, who was witness for a man in a law case once, and the lawyer asked him if he wasn't mates with the chap he was giving evidence for.

" 'No,' says Bill, 'we ain't mates.'

" 'But you've worked together?' says the lawyer.

" 'Oh, yes!' says Bill.

" 'And travelled together?'

" 'Oh, yeas!'

" 'And camped together?'

" 'Oh, yeas!'

" 'Then if you're not mates, what is mates?' says the lawyer, in a bit of a tear.

" 'Well, mister,' says Bill, 'mates is them wot's got one purse. If I go to a shed with Jack an' we're mates an' I earn forty quid and Jack gets sick an' only earns ten or five, or mebbe nothin' at all, we puts the whole lot in one pus, or if it's t'other way about an' Jack earns the forty it don't matter. There's one pus no matter how much each of us earns an' it b'longs just the same to both of us alike. If Jack's got the pus and I want half-a-crown, I says to Jack, says I, "Jack, gimme the pus." An' if Jack wants ten quid or twenty or the whole lot he just says to me, "Bill," says he, "gimme the pus." I don't ask what he's goin' to take, and I don't care. He can take it all if he wants it, 'cos it stands to reason, don't it, mister?' says Bill to the lawyer, 'that a man wouldn't be so dirt mean as to play a low-down trick on his mate. So you see, mister, him an' me warn't mates 'cos we had two pusses an' mates is them wot's got one pus.' "

"John Miller" (William Lane), *The Working Man's Paradise.**

JACK DUNN OF NEVERTIRE

To help a mate in trouble Jack would go through flood and fire.
Great Scott! and don't you know the name of Dunn of Nevertire?
    Big Dunn of Nevertire,
    Long Jack from Nevertire;
He stuck to me through thick and thin,
    Jack Dunn of Nevertire.

Henry Lawson.

THEY WERE MEN

The hottest drought that ever blazed could never parch the souls
    of men;
And they were men in spite of all, and they were straight, and
    they were true;
The hat went round at trouble's call in ninety-one and ninety-two.

Henry Lawson, "Bourke."

"OUR LAST MAN AND OUR LAST SHILLING"

The electoral campaign was in full swing throughout Australia after the prorogation of Parliament on June 27 (1914), and was characterised by the usual features, without any recorded instance of an allusion to the imminence of war till the end of July. On the 31st of that month both the Prime Minister, Mr. Cook, and the leader of the Labor Party, Mr. Fisher, addressed meetings in Victoria. . . . Mr. Fisher's declaration in his speech at Colac . . . contained a phrase which he repeated more than once in later speeches, and which possessed peculiar significance in relation to later developments.

* Born in Ireland, William Lane spent several years in America before migrating to Australia in the mid-eighties. A man of vast energies and a brilliant organiser, he was largely responsible for the building of the Australian Labour Federation in Queensland. He was also responsible for launching the first mass-selling labour paper in Australia—the Brisbane *Worker*. Following the 1890-91 strikes, Lane's hopes of a socialist Australia, based as they were very largely on the teachings of Bellamy, Fourier, and Robert Owen, gave way to disillusionment, and he then gathered together a band of his faithful disciples and set off in 1893 in the *Royal Tar* to found a utopian socialist community in Paraguay. This project of a "New Australia" proved completely abortive.

Turn your eyes to the European situation (said Mr Fisher) and give the kindest feelings towards the mother country at this time. I sincerely hope that international arbitration will avail before Europe is convulsed in the greatest war of any time. All, I am sure, will regret the critical position existing at the present time, and pray that a disastrous war may be averted. But should the worst happen after everything has been done that honour will permit, Australians will stand beside our own to help and defend her to our last man and our last shilling. (Melbourne *Argus*, August 1.)

ERNEST SCOTT in *The Official History of Australia in the War of 1914-1918, Vol. XI.*

POLLIE

> Oh! pollie, we can't use you, dear,
>   To lead us into clover,
> This fight is *ours,* and as for you,
>   Clear out and get run over.*

An I.W.W. slogan.

BUMP ME INTO PARLIAMENT

Air: "Yankee Doodle."

> Come listen, all kind friends of mine,
>   I want to move a motion,
> To make an El Dorado here
>   I've got a bonzer notion.

Chorus:

> Bump me into Parliament,
>   Bounce me any way,
> Bang me into Parliament,
>   On next election day.

> Some very wealthy friends I know
>   Declare I am most clever,
> While some may talk for an hour or so
>   Why, I can talk for ever.

> I know the Arbitration Act,
>   As a sailor knows his riggin's,
> So if you want a small advance,
>   I'll talk to Justice Higgins.

* "Pollie" is a contemptuous abbreviation of politician.

Oh, yes, I am a Labor man
  And believe in revolution;
The quickest way to bring them on
  Is talking constitution.

To keep the cost of living down
  A law I straight would utter,
A hundred loaves for a trey I'd sell,
  With a penny a ton for butter.

I have been asked what I could do
  If e'er the Germans came here,
A regulation I would make
  To say they shan't remain here.

They say that kids are getting scarce,
  I believe there's something in it;
By extra laws I'd incubate
  A million kids a minute.

I've read my library ten times through,
  And wisdom justifies me,
The man who does not vote for me,
  By cripes he crucifies me.

So bump 'em into Parliament,
  Bounce 'em any way,
Bang 'em into Parliament,
  Don't let the Court decay.

BILL CASEY.*

THE TWELVE

During 1916, twelve members of the Industrial Workers of the World were condemned to gaol terms of up to ten years. The main crown witnesses were Scully and Goldstein, two police informers. There was a prolonged agitation for the "Release of the Twelve," which culminated in a Royal Commission presided over by Mr. Justice Ewing, which found that some of the men had been unjustly convicted and others had served enough. They were released.

* The late Bill Casey, of the One Big Union League, Melbourne. This was a popular song during the first world war.

All hail, our martyred heroes,
   Ye men of lion heart;
Ye pay the price of playing
   Emancipators' part.

.   .   .   .

Twelve workingmen in fetters
   For Working-Class ideals!
Ah, everyone with worker's heart,
   Humiliation feels.

.   .   .   .

The gleam of your golden sacrifice,
   Through Iniquity's shadowing gloom,
O'er Labor's restless ocean,
   Is herald of Capital's doom.

When the storm arisen from words ye spake,
   With the might of a tempest's waves,
Will wreck our masters of tyrant make,
   On the rocks of the wrongs of slaves.

W. H. LEVEY in *Direct Action*, December 23, 1916.

THE RELEASE OF THE I.W.W. MEN

Rejoice! you fellow workingmen
   Your comrades are set free,
Who have suffered for these long years
   In want and misery;
Locked up within grim prison walls
   Surely an earthly hell,
The anguish that they have endured
   None but themselves can tell.

Sent there by crawling perjurers
   Who made up a false tale,
Now Scully and the Goldsteins too
   Ought to be sent to jaol;

Q

No one is safe while they're about
  To mix with honest men,
What they have done for greed and gain
  They'd do the same again.

.   .   .   .

Now that they are with us once more
  Let's help them with our might,
To cheer and make them strong again
  The workers' cause to fight;
Success to all who did work hard
  To cause those men's release,
May Judge Ewing live for many years
  In happiness and peace.

P. F. COLLINS in a contemporary broadsheet.

6. REPUBLICANISM AND NATIONALISM

(i) REPUBLICANISM

DR. J. DUNMORE LANG, REPUBLICAN

. . . On the 31st March, 1831, the first steam-boat in Australia was launched; two other steam-boats came into use within a few months. Close upon the steam-boat came Dr. Lang, from Scotland, the first Australian agitator, a Presbyterian O'Connell, who, after professing and printing every shade of political opinions, has recently avowed his preference for a republic, and his hopes that he "shall yet see the British flag trailed in the dust."

> SAMUEL SIDNEY, *The Three Colonies of Australia—New South Wales, Victoria and South Australia; their Pastures, Copper Mines and Gold Fields* (Second edition, 1853).

AGAINST REPUBLICANISM

While we cling
To our great mother we are sons and heirs

To all the heroes in her Abbey laid;

.   .   .   .   .   .

Divide us, and we sink at once to bourgeois,
Received in the society of nations
Just for our wealth, and laughed at secretly
By the proud Governments of ancient blood
Who ever wear their rapiers at their sides
To draw for fancied insults. . . .

.   .   .   .   .   .

Dear land of my adoption, sever not
The right hand from thy parent, nor despoil
Thy mother of her youngest, fairest child!

DOUGLAS B. W. SLADEN, "Quis Separabit?"

REPUBLICANISM AND THE SYDNEY *BULLETIN*

The *Bulletin* favours—

1. A republican form of government.
2. Payment of members.
3. One person, one vote.
4. State revenue derived directly from the land.
5. Complete secularisation of education.
6. Reform of the criminal code and prison system.
7. United Australia and protection against the world.

The *Bulletin* denounces—

1. Religious interference in politics.
2. Foreign titles.
3. The Chinese.*
4. Imperial federation.

Sydney *Bulletin*, August 29, 1891.

A REPUBLICAN CONVERTED

This rhyme refers to Sir George Dibbs, New South Wales politician. It was written by Dowell O'Reilly. "O'Reilly," writes H. V. Evatt in Australian Labour Leader, *"denounced Dibbs's expenditure of £1000 of public money on his trip abroad and the knighthood which marked a conversion from the Premier's early republicanism."*

* See references on page 143.

Ladies to right of him,
Ladies to left of him,
Ladies in front of him,
    Curtsied and wondered.
Charmed with their subtle spell,
Boldly he strode, and well
    He, the Republican—
Up to the Royal Throne:
"Arise, sir, happy one!"
    Noble ten hundred!

Flashed all his sovereigns there,
Flashed as they turned in air,
Spinning through golden hair,
Charming the darlings, while
    All the world wondered!
Plunged in tobacco smoke
With Royalty he spoke—
    The gross Republican
Reeled from that master-stroke
    Shattered and sundered,
Then he came back, but not—
    Not with ten hundred.

DOWELL O'REILLY in the Sydney *Worker*, September 9,
1893.

(ii) AUSTRALIA AND ENGLAND

AUSTRALIA versus ENGLAND—A GOLD DIGGERS' SONG

Air: "Bob and Joan."

No workhouse have we here,
    No poor law coves so cruel,
No bullying overseer,
    No paltry water gruel,
No masters to oppress
    A wretched starving devil,
But here, I rather guess
    We're all upon a level.

When great folks come, they find
    That labour's in the ascendant;
No cringing beggars, mind,
    But all are independent;

Their pride receives a blow,
     Their greatness is a failure;
And to England back they go
     And run down poor Australia.

CHARLES THATCHER, *Thatcher's Colonial Minstrel* (1864).

"AUSTRALIA FOR THE AUSTRALIANS"

"Australia for the Australians" is a cry very often heard. It is a healthy, good and laudable watchword because Australia is always ready to hold out the hand of friendship to honourable men, ready to work as her own sons work.

EDWARD KINGLAKE, *The Australian at Home* (1891).

AUSTRALIA THROUGH ENGLISH EYES

1. "Bare, bald, prosaic."

A township like
All others, with its houses, church, and school—
Bare, bald, prosaic—no quaint wild tower
Nor ancient hall to add poetic touch,
As in the dear old land—no legend old
Adds softening beauty to the Buddawong Peak,
Or near-home ranges with too barbarous names.
But everything is cold, new, new, too new
To foster poesy; and famish'd thought
Looks back with longing to the mountain dream.

"Australie" (MRS. HUBERT HERON), "From the Clyde to
                                            Braidwood."

2. "Scentless and songless."

They are rhymes rudely strung with intent less
     Of sound than of words,
In lands where bright blossoms are scentless,
     And songless bright birds;
Where, with fire and fierce drought on her tresses,
Insatiable Summer oppresses
Sere woodlands and sad wildernesses,
     And faint flocks and herds.

ADAM LINDSAY GORDON, *Bush Ballads and Galloping
                                            Rhymes.*

3. "Weird melancholy."

What is the dominant note of Australian scenery? That which is the dominant note of Edgar Allan Poe's poetry—weird melancholy. A poem like "L'Allegro" could never be written by an Australian. It is too airy, too sweet, too freshly happy. The Australian mountain forests are funereal, secret, stern. Their solitude is desolation. They seem to stifle, in their black gorges, a story of sullen despair. No tender sentiment is nourished in their shade. In other lands the dying year is mourned, the falling leaves drop lightly on his bier. In the Australian forest no leaves fall. The savage winds shout among the rock clefts. From the melancholy gum strips of white bark hang and rustle. The very animal life of these frowning hills is either grotesque or ghostly.

> MARCUS CLARKE, Preface to *Poems of the late Adam Lindsay Gordon* (1880).

4. "No ancient churches, castles, ruins."

There are no ancient churches, castles, ruins—the memorials of generations departed. You need no Baedecker in Australia. From the point of view of literature this means that we can never hope to have a Scott, a Balzac, a Dumas . . . nor a poetry which reflects past glories.

> G. H. COWLING in the Melbourne *Age*, February 16, 1935.

AUSTRALIA THROUGH AUSTRALIAN EYES

1. "Oh! 'tis jolly."

Oh! 'tis jolly to follow the roving herd
  Through the long, long summer day,
And camp at night by some lonely creek
  When dies the golden ray.
Where the jackass laughs in the old gum-tree,
  And our quart-pot tea we sip;
The saddle was our childhood's home,
  Our heritage the whip.

> From "The Stockman," a bush ballad.

2. "Home."

The past has proved that we have no need to depend for our literature on hack writers overseas, whose tales leave us cold in so far as knowledge of the places of which they write is concerned —usually some remote countryside or obscure foreign suburb. Harry (Henry Lawson—Ed.) taught us that we must regard Australia as "home" without any disloyalty to the motherland from which we came—and in Australia, with her mixed types of people, that motherland was not always Great Britain.

BERTHA LAWSON, *My Henry Lawson.*

3. "The bush is never sad."

"A land where dull Despair is king
  O'er scentless flower and songless bird!"
But we have heard the bell-birds ring
  Their silver bells at eventide. . . .

For us the bush is never sad:
  Its myriad voices whisper low,
In tones the bushmen only know,
  Its sympathy and welcome glad.
For us the roving breezes bring
  From many a blossom-tufted tree—
Where wild bees murmur dreamily—
  The honey-laden breath of Spring.

A. B. PATERSON, "Song of the Future."

4. "Worthy to be loved."

It is the duty and should be the pride of every father and mother and teacher of Australian children to intensify the natural love of Australia, and to point out in how many ways Australia is eminently worthy to be loved—both the actual land and the national ideal. Good and evil are mingled everywhere; but there is no land with more beautiful aspects than Australia, no ideal with greater potentialities of human achievement and human happiness. Australia may never be a great country; but it will be the fault of the people, not of the land, if it is not one of the best countries to live in and die in—given that we are free from foreign aggression until we are able to resist foreign aggression. The grotesque English prejudice against things Australian, founded on no better reason than that they are unlike English things, still remains to vitiate the local sense of local beauty; but every year is teaching us wisdom. We are gradually learning that there are no more beautiful trees in the world than Australian gum trees—particularly if seen against the sky, when amber days or purple nights play hide-and-seek among the wayward branches. We have learnt to laugh at the ridiculous and reiterated fiction that our flowers have no scent and our birds no song. Why, the whole bush is scented; and in no land is there a greater wealth of aromatic perfume from tree and shrub and flower, making the daisied meadows of England, as honest Englishman Henry Kingsley avers, tame and suburban by comparison. And if you go up beyond the tropic line, and walk out of your tent at dawn, the air is literally weighed down with the fragrance of a hundred brilliant flowers. What would they not give in England for ten acres of wattle-blossom on Wimbledon Common? and how many nightingales would they exchange for a flight of crimson lories at sunrise—a shower of flaming rubies?

A. G. STEPHENS in the Sydney *Bulletin*, December 12, 1899.

POSTSCRIPT TO TEXAS JACK

P.S.—As poet and as Yankee I will greet you, Texas Jack,
For it isn't no ill-feelin' that is gettin' up my back;
But I won't see this land crowded by each Yank and British cuss
Who takes it in his head to come a-civilisin' us.
Though on your own great continent there's misery in the towns,
An' not a few untitled lords, and kings without their crowns,
I will admit your countrymen is busted big, an' free,
An' great on ekal rites of men and great on liberty:
I will admit your fathers punched the gory tyrant's head—
But then we've got our heroes, too, the diggers that is dead,
The plucky men of Ballarat, who toed the scratch so well,
And broke the nose of Tyranny and made his peepers swell,
For yankin' Lib's gold tresses in the roarin' days gone by,
An' doublin' up his dirty fist to black her bonny eye. . . .

They came to learn us cricket in the days of long ago,
An' Hanlan came from Canada to learn us how to row,
An' "doctors" come from Frisco just to learn us how to skite,
An' pugs from all the lands on earth to learn us how to fight;
An' when they go, as like as not, we find we're taken in,
They've left behind no learnin'—but they've carried off our tin.

HENRY LAWSON, "A Word to Texas Jack."

"BIRTHSTAINS"

On a pleasant day in one of the later years of the nineteenth century an English gentleman who had come to Australia to fill a high administrative post was lunching at a country house in New South Wales. The beautiful view from the dining room windows had been brought to his notice. He called attention to a strip of well-made road showing out against the green of a distant hill. Someone said that this particular stretch of road had once been the scene of a sharp struggle between police and the convicts who were making it.

The great man said "Oh!", raised his eyebrows, and glowered, his expression plainly saying "What imprudence and bad taste to mention the word convict." He immediately changed the conversation and gave someone to understand he had made a dreadful mistake. Someone chuckled. "It was so palpable," says Edward Kinglake, the narrator of this little episode, "that the great man had been warned that he must above all things avoid that subject and consider it taboo in the colonies."

The visitor's embarrassment arose from the widely held view in England that Australians suffered from a sort of guilt complex where their national origins were concerned. Scratch an Australian and you would find a convict. There was talk of "birthstains" which must be cleansed, of "taints" that had to work themselves out.

The subject provided an occasional good jest over the port in London's clubrooms—like the one about the colonial who was told that he came of good stock "which had been selected by the best English judges."

By 1899 Earl Beauchamp, then Governor of New South Wales, was pleased to note that Australia had done much to erase her criminal record:

Your birthstains have you turned to good,
    Forcing strong wills perverse to steadfastness,
The first flush of the tropics in your blood,
    And at your feet success. . . .*

If the local populace was duly impressed by this utterance, there appears to be no evidence of the fact. On the contrary, for most Australians the convict period belonged to the almost forgotten past, to be regarded with curiosity and interest, certainly not with guilt. For some, there was a deep sense of pride in the foundations of nationhood which the convicts had laid. For most, there was the knowledge that but for the stout-hearted efforts of their forefathers, transportation from Her Majesty's English gaols would still be in force at the end of the century.

* See Rudyard Kipling's "Song of the Cities of the Empire".

The eighteen eighties and nineties saw the rise of a strong, aggressive nationalism among the Australian people. We shall see some expressions of it in the following pages. The English might still look on Australians as wild colonials, using them as the butt of many an imperial joke; they might still try through snobbishness, arrogance and reference to "hereditary taints" to instil into the native-born a sense of their inferiority and of their obligations to the British investor. But the Australians had come to see themselves as a people and a nation. The cry, "Australia for the Australians" was a reflection of the widespread desire for national independence. In answering the English jibes, the people always had recourse to the old weapon of laughter. The "cousin from Pall Mall," the "new-chum," were figures of fun who had to prove themselves "good sports and good Australians" before they were accepted with dignity and respect. The pompous and patronising visitor was not welcome.

"Considering all this," wrote Edward Kinglake in 1891, "it will not appear strange that when an Australian newspaper remarks that the son of one of England's greatest novelists has not been successful as a member of a colonial parliament, the taunt returned by an English journal that the descendants of convicts are not likely to appreciate a decent person, raises only a smile at its very ludicrousness."

THE EDITOR

(iii) PRIDE OF NATIONHOOD

AUSTRALIA IN THE EIGHTIES

I see a land of desperate droughts and floods:
I see a land where need keeps spreading round,
And all but giants perish in the stress:
I see a land where more, and more, and more
The demons, earth and wealth, grow bloat and strong.

I see a land that lies a helpless prey
To wealthy cliques and gamblers and their slaves,
The huckster politicians: a poor land
That less and less can make her heart-wish law.

Yea, but I see a land where some few brave
Raise clear eyes to the struggle that must come,
Reaching firm hands to draw the doubters in,

Preaching the gospel: "Drill and drill and drill!"
Yea, but I see a land where best of all
The hope of victory burns strong and bright!

FRANCIS ADAMS, "Australia."

FLING OUT THE FLAG!

As the sky above is fair for all, whoever, wherever he be,
As the blessed stars on all shed their light of hope and of liberty;
So let the earth, this fertile earth, this well-loved southern land,
Be fair to all, be free to all, from strand to shining strand!
Let boy and girl and woman and man in it at least be sure,
That all can earn their daily bread with hearts as proud as pure;
Let man and woman and girl and boy in it for ever be
Heirs to the best this world can give, happy, fearless, free!

Fling out the Flag! let her flap and rise in the rush of the eager air,
With the ring of the wild swan's wings as she soars from the
   swamp and her reedy lair!
Fling out the Flag! and let friend and foe behold, for gain or loss,
The sign of our faith and the fight we fight, the Stars of the
   Southern Cross!
Oh! Blue's the sky that is fair for all, whoever, wherever he be,
And silver's the light that shines on all, for hope and for liberty;
And that's the desire that burns in our hearts, for ever quench-
   less and bright,
And that's the sign of our flawless faith, and the glorious fight we
   fight.

FRANCIS ADAMS, "Fling Out the Flag."

THE DREAM OF FEDERATION

So flows beneath our good and ill
A viewless stream of Common Will,
A gathering force, a present might,
   That from its silent depths of gloom
At Wisdom's voice shall leap to light .
   And hide our barren feuds in bloom.

BRUNTON STEPHENS, "The Dominion of Australia," A
Forecast, 1877.

How long, O Lord, shall this, my country, be
A nation of the dead? How long shall they

Who seek their own and live but for the day,
My country hinder from her destiny?

WILLIAM GAY, "Australia Infelix."

THE NATION IS BORN

From all division let our land be free,
For God has made her one: complete she lies
Within the unbroken circle of the skies. . . .

WILLIAM GAY, "Australian Federation."

Do ye feel the holy fervour of a new born exultation?
For the task the Lord has set us is a trust of noblest pride—
We are named to march unblooded to the winning of a nation,
And to crown her with a glory that may evermore abide.

EDWARD DYSON, "Men of Australia—On the Eve of
Federation."

There's a word in the south, where the winter speeds forward,
That kindles young hearts into jubilant flame;
There's a word where the summer is fleeing to nor'ward
That lights up young eyes with the pride of the name;
There's signal and token, there's welcome bespoken,
There's a star at whose shining the darkness grows pale,
The barriers are broken, the sleepers have woken—
She comes, a fair nation! Australia, hail!

A. G. STEPHENS, "Ave, Australia!"

She is a temple that we are to build:
For her the ages have been long preparing:
She is a prophecy to be fulfilled!

.   .   .   .

She is the scroll on which we are to write
Mythologies our own and epics new. . . .

BERNARD O'DOWD, "The Bush."

And I said to him, "Jack!" and he gripped my hand fast,
"Oh, I hear that our country's a nation at last!"

HENRY LAWSON, "Jack Cornstalk."

THE TOAST OF HONOUR

This great Australia that our fathers won
   In proud defiance of a thousand fates!
This ocean-garden sacred to the sun!
   This land of home! This land where men are mates!
Drink to your native ranges and your plains,
Men with the sunlight singing in your veins!

                BARTLETT ADAMSON, *circa* 1917.

EDITOR'S NOTE

I would appreciate hearing from readers who have comments and criticisms they may want to make about any aspect of this book.

I would also welcome information throwing additional light on the material included, and any Australian ballads, bush yarns, local legends, industrial lore, sayings and popular stories not appearing in this collection.

The importance of preserving our folklore cannot be too strongly stressed. Much of it that is of tremendous value to present and future historians, students, writers, musicians and artists will be lost if it is not soon put on permanent record. If sufficient material is forthcoming, it will be possible to eventually publish another collection—or even a series of volumes—similar to this.

BILL WANNAN

23 Malvern Grove,
Caulfield, Victoria.